BICYCLE

BICYCLE

THE DEFINITIVE
VISUAL HISTORY

DORLING KINDERSLEY

Senior Editor Chauney Dunford

Senior Art Editor Gillian Andrews

Editors Jemima Dunne, Hazel Eriksson, Natasha Kahn,
Georgina Palffey, Marianne Petrou

Designers Stephen Bere, Katie Cavanagh, Phil Gamble

Design Assistance Renata Latipova

US Editors Shannon Beatty, Christine Heilman

Photographers Gerard Brown, Gary Ombler

Picture Research Sarah Smithies

Picture Research Assistant Megan Taylor

DK Picture Library Laura Evans, Romaine Werblow

Jacket Designer Mark Cavanagh

Jacket Editor Claire Gell

Jacket Design Development Manager Sophia MTT

Producer, Pre-Production Nadine King

Producer Luca Bazzoli

Managing Editor Gareth Jones

Managing Art Editor Lee Griffiths

Art Director Karen Self

Publisher Liz Wheeler

Publishing Director Jonathan Metcalf

DK INDIA

Managing Editor Rohan Sinha

Managing Art Editor Sudakshina Basu

Senior Editor Dharini Ganesh

Senior Art Editors Mahua Mandal, Stuti Tiwari

Art Editor Anjali Sachar

Assistant Editors Sneha Sunder Benjamin, Riji Raju

Assistant Art Editors Yashashvi Choudhary, Ansuri Saha,
Sonakshi Singh

DTP Designers Vijay Kandwal, Bimlesh Tiwari

Senior DTP Designers Sachin Singh, Harish Aggarwal

Pre-Production Manager Balwant Singh

Production Manager Pankaj Sharma

Jacket Designer Suhita Dharamjit

Managing Jackets Editor Saloni Singh

Consultants Claire Beaumont, Luke Edwarde-Evans,
Richard Gilbert, John Gill, Tony Hadland,
Hans-Erhard Lessing, Chris Sidwells

US Consultant Joseph O'Brien-Applegate

Published in the United States in 2016 by
DK Publishing, 345 Hudson Street,
New York, New York 10014

16 17 18 19 20 10 9 8 7 6 5 4 3 2 1
001 – 274738 – May/16

A WORLD OF IDEAS:
SEE ALL THERE IS TO KNOW
www.dk.com

Contents

1817–1899: BICYCLE IS BORN

Created out of necessity following a shortage of animal
feed in Europe, the initial craze for the first "running
machines" was later followed by widespread popularity,
as a series of design advances gave rise to the first true
bicycles. This was a time of experimentation, when most
of the features seen on modern bikes were first developed.

1900–1945: COMING OF AGE

While bicycles were once the preserve of the rich, mass
production brought them within reach of the working

BICYCLE

THE DEFINITIVE
VISUAL HISTORY

Penguin Random House

DORLING KINDERSLEY

Senior Editor Chauney Dunford
Senior Art Editor Gillian Andrews
Editors Jemima Dunne, Hazel Eriksson, Natasha Kahn,
Georgina Palffey, Marianne Petrou
Designers Stephen Bere, Katie Cavanagh, Phil Gamble
Design Assistance Renata Latipova
US Editors Shannon Beatty, Christine Heilman
Photographers Gerard Brown, Gary Ombler
Picture Research Sarah Smithies
Picture Research Assistant Megan Taylor
DK Picture Library Laura Evans, Romaine Werblow
Jacket Designer Mark Cavanagh
Jacket Editor Claire Gell
Jacket Design Development Manager Sophia MTT
Producer, Pre-Production Nadine King
Producer Luca Bazzoli
Managing Editor Gareth Jones
Managing Art Editor Lee Griffiths
Art Director Karen Self
Publisher Liz Wheeler
Publishing Director Jonathan Metcalf

DK INDIA

Managing Editor Rohan Sinha
Managing Art Editor Sudakshina Basu
Senior Editor Dharini Ganesh
Senior Art Editors Mahua Mandal, Stuti Tiwari
Art Editor Anjali Sachar
Assistant Editors Sneha Sunder Benjamin, Riji Raju
Assistant Art Editors Yashashvi Choudhary, Ansuri Saha,
Sonakshi Singh
DTP Designers Vijay Kandwal, Bimlesh Tiwari
Senior DTP Designers Sachin Singh, Harish Aggarwal
Pre-Production Manager Balwant Singh
Production Manager Pankaj Sharma
Jacket Designer Suhita Dharamjit
Managing Jackets Editor Saloni Singh

Consultants Claire Beaumont, Luke Edwarde-Evans,
Richard Gilbert, John Gill, Tony Hadland,
Hans-Erhard Lessing, Chris Sidwells
US Consultant Joseph O'Brien-Applegate

Published in the United States in 2016 by
DK Publishing, 345 Hudson Street,
New York, New York 10014

16 17 18 19 20 10 9 8 7 6 5 4 3 2 1
001 – 274738 – May/16

Published in Great Britain by
Dorling Kindersley Limited.

A catalog record for this book is available from the Library of Congress.
ISBN: 978-1-4654-4393-9

DK books are available at special discounts when purchased in bulk for sales promotions,
premiums, fundraising, or educational use. For details, contact DK Publishing Special Markets,
345 Hudson Street, New York, New York 10014 or specialsales@dk.com

Printed and bound in China

A WORLD OF IDEAS:
SEE ALL THERE IS TO KNOW
www.dk.com

Contents

Introduction: The Bicycle Revolution   **8**

1817-1899: BICYCLE IS BORN

Created out of necessity following a shortage of animal
feed in Europe, the initial craze for the first "running
machines" was later followed by widespread popularity,
as a series of design advances gave rise to the first true
bicycles. This was a time of experimentation, when most
of the features seen on modern bikes were first developed.

1900-1945: COMING OF AGE

While bicycles were once the preserve of the rich, mass
production brought them within reach of the working

classes, for whom they became an essential part of life. Bicycles gave the freedom to travel for work and pleasure, bringing greater independence and, eventually, equality. Design advances saw bicycles becoming lighter and faster, as well as safer and more comfortable to ride.

1946–1959: THE GOLDEN AGE

This was a challenging era for the bicycle industry, as postwar prosperity and a mood for change among the public caused a decline in bicycle sales, while those of automobiles rose. Bicycle racing, however, increased in popularity, and many of the first cycling stars came to prominence, becoming household names.

THE 1960s: CYCLING GOES POP

After a period of decline, the 1960s brought a revival in bicycle sales, as manufacturers, most notably Schwinn in the US, targeted the youth market with radical new bike designs. The adult bicycle market also improved with the introduction of small-wheeled bikes, which were well-designed, easy to ride, and perfect for urban cycling.

THE 1970s: NEW WAVES

Where the 1960s brought exciting new bicycle designs that inspired a new generation of cyclists, this decade saw the rise of entirely new cycling disciplines. Road racing remained hugely popular, especially in Europe, but in the US, more adventurous bicycle sports were emerging—BMX and mountain biking—to take the world by storm.

THE 1980s: BICYCLE EVOLUTION

As bicycle racing became ever more professional, so the 1980s saw a drive to make bikes lighter, faster, and more aerodynamic, with frames made from aluminum, magnesium alloy, and carbon fiber. This was also a defining era in cycling beyond the race track, as mountain biking, in particular, became hugely popular. Their designs evolved rapidly, and there were soon models with front and rear suspension, and complex gears. In contrast, BMX bikes remained true to the original design—simple and robust.

THE 1990s: GOING GLOBAL

Increasing concerns about air pollution and global warming saw the rise of campaign groups advocating the bicycle as a sustainable alternative to the automobile. Commuting by bicycle became common in many cities.

AFTER 2000: BICYCLES FOR ALL

Bicycle designs, components, and materials continue to advance, with hydraulic braking, electronic gear-shifting, and battery-assisted propulsion becoming available. Cycling has become an integral part of urban living once more, and many cities now offer bicycle rentals.

BICYCLE COMPONENTS

This chapter explains the basics of bicycle engineering, detailing how important components function.

The Bicycle Revolution

Nowadays, children can learn to ride a bicycle in no time thanks to a new invention—the "balance bike." They no longer need to resort to the unnatural equilibrium of stabilizers to avoid overbalancing. Now anyone can discover the carefree joys of balancing on two wheels immediately.

But how many people realize that the balance bike is actually 200 years old? First built for adults in 1817, and called a draisine, after its inventor, or *Laufmaschine* (running machine), it was seen as a possible alternative to traveling by horse following the eruption of Mount Tambora, Indonesia, which led to the so-called "year without a summer", and a shortage of animal feed.

The inventor was aware that people were reluctant to take both feet off firm ground, which restricted possibilities for propulsion. The biggest factor limiting the popularity of this new man–machine–road system was potential rider anxiety. It took 50 years for people to feel safe enough to put both feet on pedals, in 1864, eased by the roller-skating boom started on American rinks. Once mastered, the bicycle became the freedom machine for the young at heart. Turn-of-the-20th-century memoirs are full of happy reminiscences of increased opportunities for travel and encounters with the opposite sex. Young couples quickly learned to evade their chaperones by taking to the bicycle. And, once married, they could use a tandem for their honeymoon.

Meanwhile, in the early 20th century, French cycle touring clubs invented a system of *"diagonales"*—routes crisscrossing the whole of France—which they even rode at night. Pioneering round-the-world cyclists increased the distances traveled, often passing through dangerous and remote areas. Indeed, the first circumnavigation of the globe as far as possible on dry land was achieved on a bike. Today, transcontinental cycling has become a form of mass tourism, undertaken by increasing numbers of riders. Records for the fastest journey following specific routes are broken repeatedly.

On a more practical level, as bicycles became more affordable from the late 1890s onward, factory and office workers used them to reach better housing in the suburbs. The bike also became a means to deliver goods, mail, and telegrams faster. In cities and suburbs, doctors, midwives, and clergy used bikes as a quicker and more convenient way to reach the people they served. Moreover, firefighters, paramedics, the police, and the military all took advantage of the speedy bicycle. All the special-purpose motor vehicles of today had bicycle forerunners; the late Victorian equivalent of the automobile was a bicycle. Gradually, these precursors are returning to today's town and cities in updated forms: the messenger bike, the police bike, and the pedicab.

In the cycling boom of the 1890s, particularly in the US, bicycle sales provided rich pickings for businessmen involved in the manufacture and sale of bicycles and accessories. This was disastrous for competing transportation service sectors. Businesses concerned with the supply and care of horses, such as livery stables and feed providers, were also hit hard. In 1896, such businesses lost an estimated $112 million in New York alone. In rich households, the demand for grooms and other horse-care staff was much reduced, too.

Apparently unrelated businesses were affected as well. Young married couples who might once have scrimped and saved for a piano now bought two bicycles instead for the same price.

And when it came to an extravagant birthday or Christmas gift, the bicycle put gold pocket-watches out of fashion: cyclists now wanted wristwatches, which were easier to read while cycling.

Cycling even impacted smoking habits: Americans smoked a million fewer cigars each day, because they could not easily smoke while riding a bike. Cycling also led to people reading fewer books and newspapers, and consuming less alcohol: instead of sitting around, they were out riding their bikes. Even theaters and music halls suffered lower attendance, which had the domino effect of barbers losing the once-obligatory shave before the theater visit.

Hat-making, custom tailoring, and shoemaking also declined considerably. Cyclists used cheap "off-the-rack" club uniforms and bought inexpensive beach shoes, thus creating the ready-made clothing industry. And, for a short while, until step-through frames became commonplace for women's bicycles, women wore the puffy trousers pioneered earlier by Amelia Bloomer's "rational dress" so giving female emancipation a decisive push. Corsets were supplanted, too, by "emancipation garments" such as the newly invented bra. Meanwhile, men adopted the lightweight, woolen clothing and underwear promoted by the German lifestyle reformer Dr. Gustav Jaeger. The Irish author and playwright George Bernard Shaw, an avid cyclist, was an early adopter of Jaeger's so-called "normal clothing." The Jaeger company still exists as a fashion label in the UK today.

After the sewing machine, the bicycle was only the second complex machine to enter private households. It taught vast numbers of laypeople about technology and how to keep it going: tire repair and replacement, tinkering with lights, and repairing technical mishaps, such as broken spokes or worn brake pads. The bicycle served as an interactive test rig for vehicle physics that mechanical engineers could use to assess the performance of equipment, a function it still fulfills in some countries. An early example was the pneumatic tire, which bicycle-makers reinvented after coachmen failed to appreciate its potential decades earlier.

Bicycle technology—long sneered at by the technocrats of the dominant steam power—became the lightweight, high-tech engineering sensation of the late 19th century. Small wonder that it paved the way for the automobile and the airplane. Lightweight steel tubing, brazing, and welding techniques; pressed steel technology; and variable gearing were all given a mighty boost by the evolution of the bicycle. It was no coincidence that so many car manufacturers had their roots in cycle manufacture, nor that the Wright brothers—who built and flew the first airplane—were bicycle mechanics.

The bicycle also had a major impact on road improvement in the US. As the eminent automobile historian James J. Flink said: "No preceding technological innovation—not even the internal combustion engine—was as important to the development of the automobile as the bicycle."

TONY HADLAND & HANS-ERHARD LESSING

BICYCLE HISTORIANS

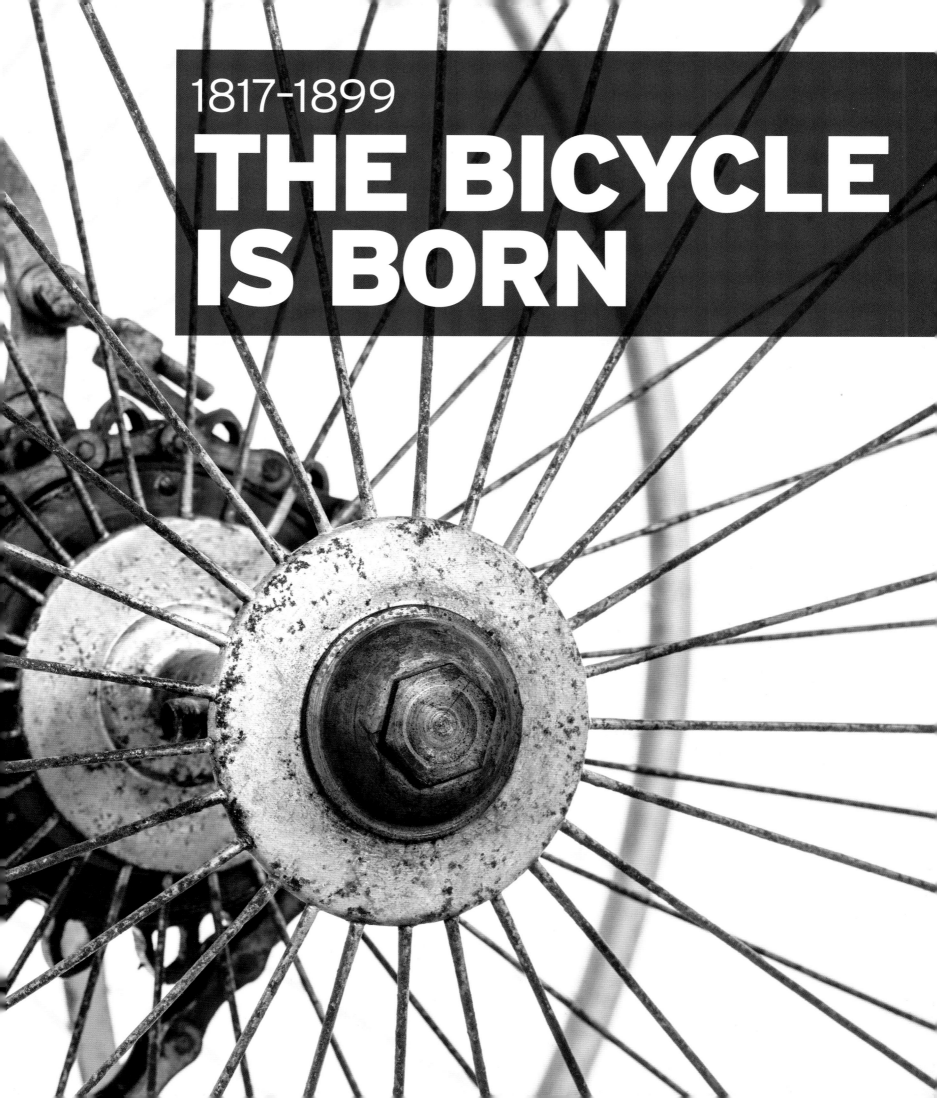

1817–1899
THE BICYCLE IS BORN

THE BICYCLE IS BORN

Like many of the world's greatest inventions, the machine that gave rise to what we now know as the bicycle was born of necessity. A string of poor harvests in Europe from 1812 led a German civil servant to develop a human-powered form of transportation to counter the reliance on horses, which were in short supply due to a scarcity of animal feed. Karl von Drais christened his 1817 invention the *Laufmaschine* ("running machine"), after the swift walking movement required of the rider in order to propel it forward.

Although his design lacked pedals, Drais' breakthrough was the realization that forward motion and balance could be maintained on just two wheels, an idea that he attributed to watching ice skaters. The *Laufmaschine*—also called the draisine, velocipede, or dandy horse—quickly caught on, sparking a craze across Europe. By the 1820s, however, it had died out because of safety concerns.

The idea was revived in the 1860s, when pedal cranks were added to the front wheel of a velocipede in Paris. The inventor of this revolutionary improvement is not known—several claims were made in subsequent decades, none of which could be proven beyond doubt—but the first manufacturer to produce such machines on an organized scale was Pierre Michaux, in 1867. Like von Drais' *Laufmaschine* before it, the pedal velocipede—soon nicknamed the "boneshaker" after its jarring ride—was instantly popular. For the first time, people could propel themselves while balancing on two wheels, with their feet off the ground. The bicycle was born.

△ **Karl von Drais (1789–1851)** was a prolific inventor. His works included a stenograph and a fuel-saving stove, as well as the *Laufmaschine*.

"On your **velocipede!"** That is the rallying cry **loudly repeated** by a few intrepid Parisians, **fanatics** of this new means of **locomotion ...**"

LE SPORT, 1867

◁ **English cycles are mocked in this lithograph**, published by French manufacturer Dombret & Jussy, c.1880–1900.

Key Events

▷ **1817** After first designing a human-propelled four-wheeled carriage, Karl von Drais demonstrates his two-wheeled *Laufmaschine*.

△ **Rise and fall**
Drais' design is copied throughout Europe, but falls in popularity by the 1820s, as many countries impose bans on riding them on sidewalks.

▷ **1830s** Tricycles and quadricycles become popular because of improved safety for the rider.

▷ **1866** Pierre Lallement's 12-mile (19-km) ride to New Haven, CT, is the first record of a pedal velocipede in use outside Europe.

▷ **1868** The first velocipede race is held at the Parc de Saint-Cloud in Paris. Englishman James Moore wins the three-quarter-mile (1,200-m) race.

▷ **1869** Paris-based engineer Eugène Meyer invents tensioned-wire-spoked wheels, and develops the high-wheeler, which has a larger front wheel to enable higher speeds.

▷ **1880** The high-wheeler—later known as the "ordinary" or "penny-farthing"—reaches its zenith with wheels of up to 5 ft (1.5 m) in diameter.

▷ **1885** John Kemp Starley introduces the Rover Safety Bicycle, the world's first commercially successful rear-wheeled, chain-driven bicycle.

▷ **1888** Scottish veterinary surgeon John Boyd Dunlop invents pneumatic bicycle tires, vastly improving cycling efficiency and comfort.

Early Bicycles

The first human-powered, two-wheeled device was the *Laufmaschine*. Invented and patented in 1817 in Germany by Karl Drais, it combined the three main principles of the bicycle, namely, methods of propulsion, steering, and balance. The rider progressed by pushing with their feet while steering with the handlebar to maintain balance. The next development came in the 1860s, when Parisian firm Michaux modified the *Laufmaschine*. By attaching cranks and pedals to the front wheel, Michaux enabled the rider to propel the bicycle with their feet clear of the ground. These bicycles were known as velocipedes.

▽ *Laufmaschine* 1817

Origin	Germany
Frame	Wood
Gears	Single speed
Wheels	Front 24 in (60 cm), Rear 30 in (75 cm)

This was the first commercially successful bicycle, and several thousand of them were built throughout Europe. The *Laufmaschine* was commonly known as the hobby horse or dandy horse. In 1817, Karl Drais traveled 8 miles (13 km) on it in less than an hour.

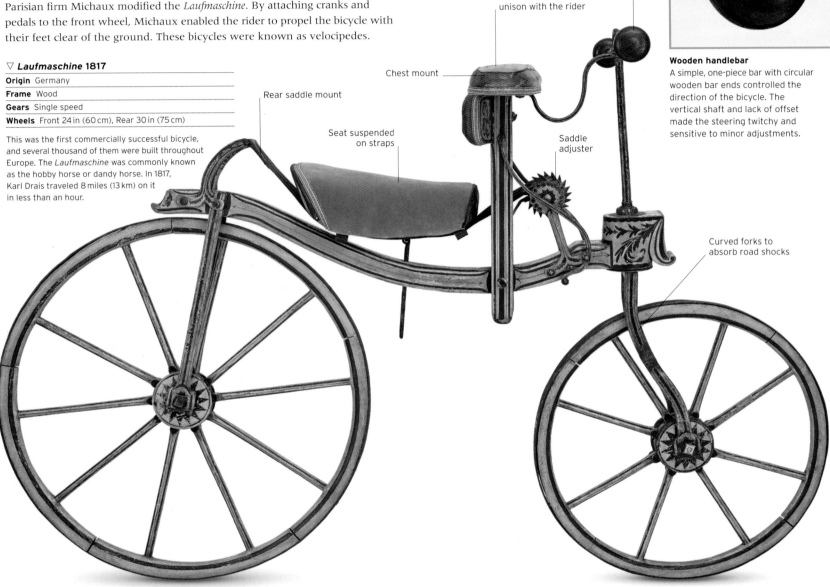

Armrest moves in unison with the rider

Chest mount

Rear saddle mount

Seat suspended on straps

Saddle adjuster

Wooden handlebar
A simple, one-piece bar with circular wooden bar ends controlled the direction of the bicycle. The vertical shaft and lack of offset made the steering twitchy and sensitive to minor adjustments.

Curved forks to absorb road shocks

Rear saddle mount
The saddle was suspended on leather straps to provide a crude type of suspension. It was mounted on two anchor points, one at the front of the frame and another at the rear.

Chest mount
Stuffed with horse hair, the upholstered chest mount provided a padded area of resistance against which the rider could push when scooting. This was necessary to accelerate the bicycle.

Saddle adjuster
Winding the ratchet increased the tension of the leather straps that supported the saddle; turning the ratchet reduced sag. The heavier the rider, the more tension required.

Front frame detail
A carved and painted wooden box was used to house the wooden mechanism that allowed the handlebar to turn the front wheel. Hiding these areas made for a more elegant-looking bicycle.

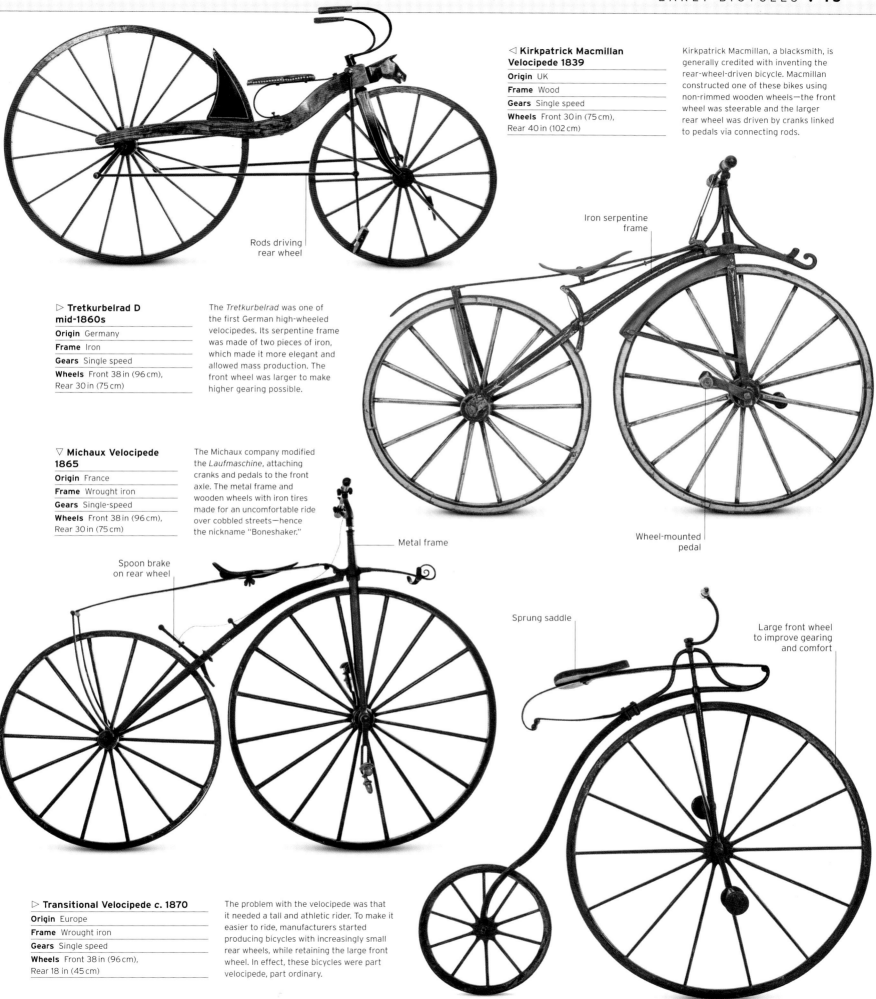

◁ **Kirkpatrick Macmillan Velocipede 1839**

Origin UK

Frame Wood

Gears Single speed

Wheels Front 30 in (75 cm), Rear 40 in (102 cm)

Kirkpatrick Macmillan, a blacksmith, is generally credited with inventing the rear-wheel-driven bicycle. Macmillan constructed one of these bikes using non-rimmed wooden wheels—the front wheel was steerable and the larger rear wheel was driven by cranks linked to pedals via connecting rods.

Rods driving rear wheel

Iron serpentine frame

▷ **Tretkurbelrad D mid-1860s**

Origin Germany

Frame Iron

Gears Single speed

Wheels Front 38 in (96 cm), Rear 30 in (75 cm)

The *Tretkurbelrad* was one of the first German high-wheeled velocipedes. Its serpentine frame was made of two pieces of iron, which made it more elegant and allowed mass production. The front wheel was larger to make higher gearing possible.

▽ **Michaux Velocipede 1865**

Origin France

Frame Wrought iron

Gears Single-speed

Wheels Front 38 in (96 cm), Rear 30 in (75 cm)

The Michaux company modified the *Laufmaschine*, attaching cranks and pedals to the front axle. The metal frame and wooden wheels with iron tires made for an uncomfortable ride over cobbled streets—hence the nickname "Boneshaker."

Wheel-mounted pedal

Metal frame

Spoon brake on rear wheel

Sprung saddle

Large front wheel to improve gearing and comfort

▷ **Transitional Velocipede c. 1870**

Origin Europe

Frame Wrought iron

Gears Single speed

Wheels Front 38 in (96 cm), Rear 18 in (45 cm)

The problem with the velocipede was that it needed a tall and athletic rider. To make it easier to ride, manufacturers started producing bicycles with increasingly small rear wheels, while retaining the large front wheel. In effect, these bicycles were part velocipede, part ordinary.

Racing at the Bois de Boulogne, the popular Paris velocipede venue, c. 1869

Great Manufacturers
Michaux

Although the jury is still out on whether Pierre Michaux invented the machine his name became synonymous with, he was one of the first to produce velocipedes on an organized scale. Behind the scenes was a cast of characters—including the brains behind the venture, the Olivier brothers—whose roles were just as pivotal.

THE EMERGENCE OF the pedal-crank velocipede in 1860s Paris was one step in an evolutionary line that stretched back to Karl Drais' *Laufmaschine* or draisine of 1817. It is regarded as a key moment in the history of the bicycle, and blacksmith Pierre Michaux is closely associated with this phase. The draisine had to be propelled by scooting along in a running motion, which required large strides and wore out the rider's boots. The technological advance that ensured the velocipede caught on was the addition of cranks and pedals, which meant the rider could drive the

Michaux & Cie head badge
Second-generation velocipedes bore the Michaux name (September 1868-April 1869).

front wheel on the flat and uphill. While velocipedes with three or four wheels, sometimes driven by hand- or foot-driven cranks, had developed over the intervening decades, none had achieved widespread acceptance.

Born in Bar-le-Duc in northeastern France in 1813, Michaux moved to Paris at the age of 41 following the failure of an earlier business. He worked for a carriage-maker before setting up his own workshop in 1858 at cité Godot-de-Mauroy, off the Champs-Élysées.

As a blacksmith, Michaux had expertise in *fonte malleable* (malleable cast iron), which seemed to be a cost-effective process for making the frames. He had the tools and skills to shape the other metal parts—forks, sprung saddle, and handlebars—that together made up the "boneshaker" bicycle. The velocipede's wheels, bearings, and brakes were all influenced by parts on the horse-drawn carriages of the day.

Michaux received the backing of a wealthy industrialist family, the Oliviers. René and Aimé Olivier—both engineering students at the École Centrale in Paris—had been captivated by the idea of the velocipede and in 1863 Aimé sketched a design for a pedal-less velocipede in a notebook. A drawing of a design with toe rests was also

found in an 1864 notebook entry of their father, Jules, who owned a series of chemical works.

Michaux was not the first potential manufacturer to have dealings with the Olivier brothers. Charles Sargent, a Paris coach-maker, had built a

Joseph Roux period painting from 1869
Course de vélocipèdes, by Joseph Roux, is one of the earliest known contemporary depictions of a velocipede race. The pictured scene took place in the town of Gray, in southeastern France, near Dijon.

First-generation Michaux 1868

Second-generation Michaux 1868

Wood-wheeled Compagnie Parisienne 1869

Wire-wheeled Compagnie Parisienne 1870

1850s and 1860s A trend for roller-skating hits Europe and the US, proving that balance can be maintained while moving on wheels.

1853 Haussmann's modernization of Paris creates smooth street surfaces that later make velocipedes easier to ride.

1865 The Oliviers test velocipedes made of cast iron instead of wrought iron.

1866 René Olivier works with Pierre Michaux during the first half of the year, making malleable cast-iron velocipedes.

1867 The first-generation Michaux velocipede, with its serpentine frame, is released.

1867 The velocipede is so popular that by the end of the year, up to 150 independent manufacturers are producing them in France.

1868 The term "bicycle" is first used in France, the US, and UK to describe a two-wheeled pedal velocipede, replacing the cumbersome *vélocipède a pédales* (pedal velocipede).

1868 The second-generation Michaux velocipede features patented improvements by the Oliviers and Georges de la Bouglise—a cord-operated brake, adjustable cranks with self-righting pedals, and wheels that have self-lubricating axles.

1868 Michaux velocipedes win a royal seal of approval from the 12-year-old Prince Imperial, Louis-Napoléon.

1869 In April, the Oliviers sever the link with Pierre Michaux in a court case.

1869 René Olivier forms Compagnie Parisienne, and organizes the popular Paris–Rouen road race in September. Monthly sales peak at 300.

1874 Compagnie Parisienne is declared bankrupt, with debts of more than 1 million francs.

1890s Fueled by nationalism, rival German and French claims emerge over the invention of the bicycle. The French case argues that Pierre Michaux and his son were "fathers" of the bicycle.

prototype velocipede for them in 1864, while Pierre Lallement, who claimed to have built a velocipede in 1863, is also thought to have worked with them. However, it was Michaux who built the first pedal velocipedes for the Oliviers.

In spite of the financing and much of the intellectual input deriving from the Oliviers and their talented engineer friend Georges de la Bouglise, it was Michaux's name that appeared on all the velocipedes they built.

While the identity of the individual who first fixed pedals and cranks to a two-wheeled velocipede has never been proven, pedal velocipedes were seen in Paris as early as 1864.

Lallement emigrated to the US in 1865, taking a number of velocipede parts with him. That same year, the Olivier brothers cycled with de la Bouglise from Paris to Lyon— a distance of 300 miles (482 km). Meanwhile, a young Englishman who lived near the Michaux workshop, James Moore, purchased one of Michaux's wooden-framed velocipedes. He would later win one of the first velocipede races.

A year later, news of pedal velocipedes began to be reported in the newspapers. Chinese officials

"The amusement of **golden youth** and the dream of **employees**."

LA VIE PARISIENNE, 1868, DESCRIBING THE MICHAUX VELOCIPEDE

touring Western Europe in 1866 described draisines and velocipede-like vehicles, which riders "propelled by foot pedaling … they dash along like galloping horses" on the streets of Paris. In April that year, French newspaper *Le Journal de l'Ain* described three young men riding cranked velocipedes. In November, Lallement filed the first known patent for a velocipede, submitting to the US authorities a design that was virtually identical to Michaux's.

Serious production of Michaux's velocipedes began in 1867. His workforce grew from four, including himself and his son Ernest, to around 15. The first-generation velocipede of that year featured a serpentine, malleable cast-iron frame to which a leather saddle was mounted via an elongated spring; this provided suspension to offset the jolts of the road. The wheels had wooden spokes and iron "tires," the front wheel being slightly larger—around 36 in (91 cm) in diameter—than the rear. Braking was achieved by pedaling backward or

twisting the handlebars to activate a leather strap, which pushed a brake block against the rear wheel. By 1868, Michaux had grown to 60 employees. With velocipede-mania taking off, existing carriage-makers jumped on the bandwagon.

Suspicious of Michaux's ability to run the business at a profit, René Olivier instigated a partnership agreement, forming Michaux Cie in May 1868. Michaux was put in charge of running the workforce and production in Paris, and the Oliviers handled purchasing, publicity, and accounts from Lyon.

Production of a second-generation velocipede that featured a series of patented improvements from the Olivier brothers and de la Bouglise began that same summer. The new frame was made from stronger forged iron rather than the malleable cast iron of Michaux's design, and was shaped in a single diagonal beam that terminated in forks for the rear wheel, replacing the weaker serpentine frame. The riding position was raised so that the rider's

René Olivier
(1843–1875)

A new craze
Left is a late-19th-century book showing the social aspect of Michaux velocipedes, while on the right is a *c.* 1869 sketch for a Compagnie Parisienne poster.

feet were off the ground, a trend that would culminate in the high-wheeler "penny farthing" design.

Despite the popularity of the new velocipede, all was not well at Michaux Cie. A rift between the Oliviers and Michaux, who had helped himself to cash from the business, led to liquidation of the company in April 1869, although Michaux continued to trade under his own name until the end of the year.

The Oliviers founded Compagnie Parisienne, "Formerly House of Michaux," in April 1869, investing heavily in the company, refitting the workshops, and adding new designs, such as wire-spoked wheels. The outbreak of the Franco-Prussian War in 1870, the wane of the velocipede craze in 1872, and poor management meant that just five years later, the company folded. The Michaux brand, along with the contribution of the Oliviers, was consigned to history.

High-Wheelers

The 1870s saw several advances in metallurgy, including hollow frame tubes and wire-spoked wheels. Together with the ever-increasing diameter of front drive wheels—which allowed both a smoother ride and more ground covered with each revolution of the pedals—this led to the introduction of the high-wheeled ordinary bicycle or penny-farthing. It was considered a dangerous machine since the rider could be thrown off head-first in the event of a fall. However, it was simpler, lighter, and faster than the velocipedes of the time, and although it cost the equivalent of several weeks' wages, it was very durable. The inspiration for high-wheelers was the huge drive wheel of Crampton locomotives. Paris-based mechanic Eugène Meyer patented the suspension wheel used in high-wheelers, using radial wire spokes. Coventry's James Starley improved on this with tangential spokes, which are still the norm today.

▷ **Ordinary Bicycle** *c.* **1870s**

Origin	Unknown
Frame	Steel
Gears	Single speed
Wheels	Front 58 in (147 cm), Rear 18 in (45 cm)

A typical mass-produced ordinary, this bicycle featured a large front wheel that could easily roll over the unpaved roads of the day. The hollow-tubed frame followed the curve of the front wheel, which held the pivoting fork. A mounting peg was fitted above the rear wheel.

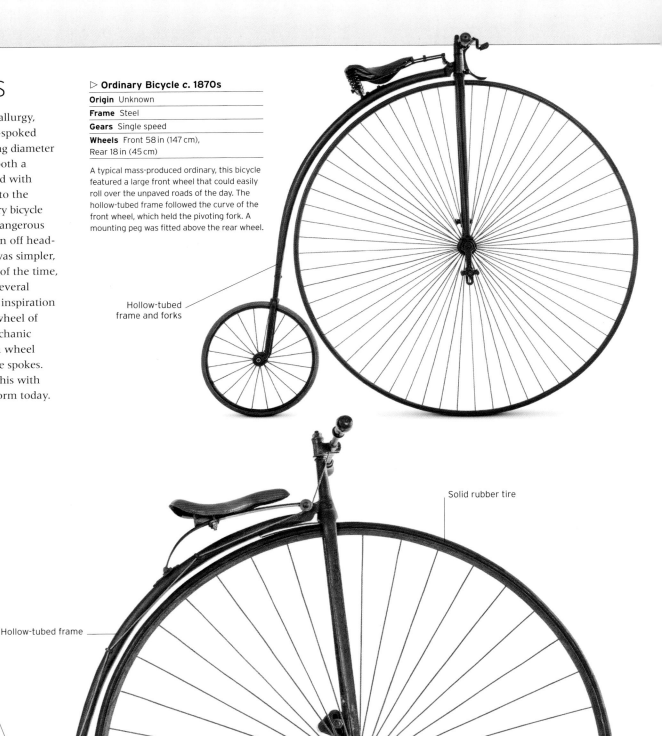

Hollow-tubed frame and forks

Solid rubber tire

▷ **Ordinary Bicycle** *c.* **1870**

Origin	UK
Frame	Steel
Gears	Single speed
Wheels	Front 50 in (127 cm), Rear 18 in (45 cm)

This penny-farthing was manufactured by Coventry Machinists, the largest of 200 cycle-makers in Coventry, UK. Originally sewing-machine makers, they were renowned for high-quality workmanship. Many individuals leading the development of bicycles worked there, including English inventor James Starley.

Rear brake mechanism
This cord-operated spoon brake was reminiscent of cranked Parisian velocipedes. To avoid skidding when braking, riders had to shift their weight onto the rear wheel.

Hollow-tubed frame

Wire-spoked wheel

Large front wheel

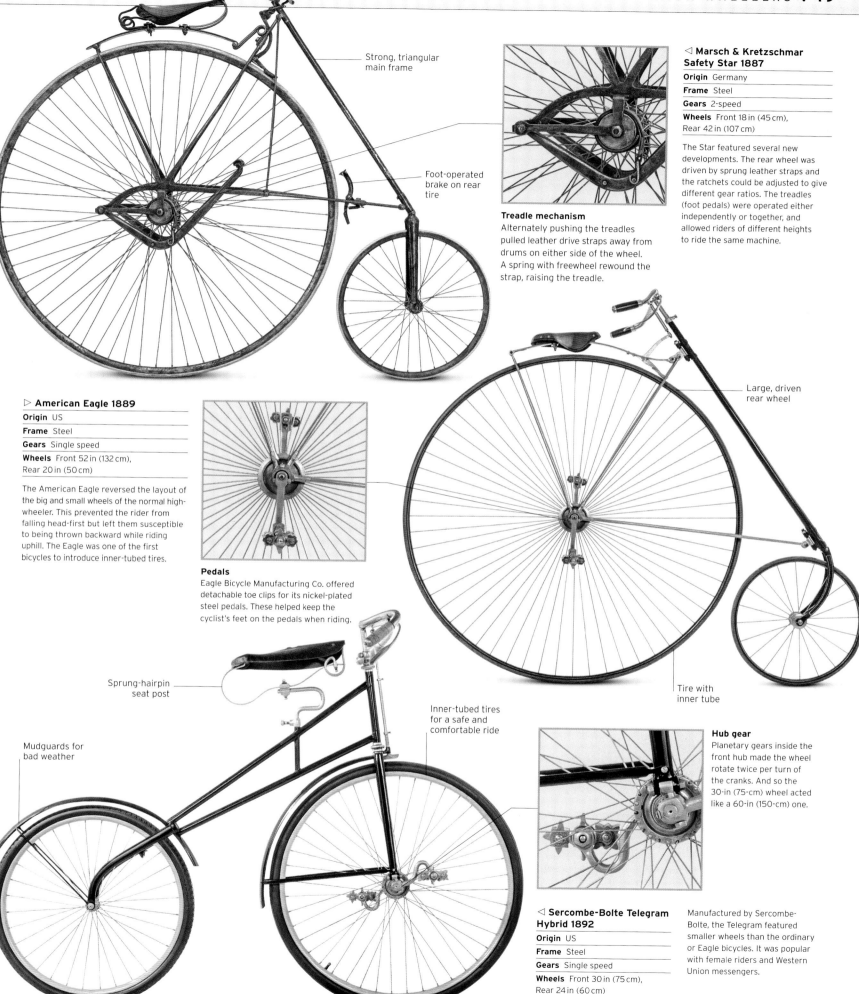

Strong, triangular main frame

Foot-operated brake on rear tire

◁ Marsch & Kretzschmar Safety Star 1887

Origin Germany

Frame Steel

Gears 2-speed

Wheels Front 18 in (45 cm), Rear 42 in (107 cm)

The Star featured several new developments. The rear wheel was driven by sprung leather straps and the ratchets could be adjusted to give different gear ratios. The treadles (foot pedals) were operated either independently or together, and allowed riders of different heights to ride the same machine.

Treadle mechanism
Alternately pushing the treadles pulled leather drive straps away from drums on either side of the wheel. A spring with freewheel rewound the strap, raising the treadle.

▷ American Eagle 1889

Origin US

Frame Steel

Gears Single speed

Wheels Front 52 in (132 cm), Rear 20 in (50 cm)

The American Eagle reversed the layout of the big and small wheels of the normal high-wheeler. This prevented the rider from falling head-first but left them susceptible to being thrown backward while riding uphill. The Eagle was one of the first bicycles to introduce inner-tubed tires.

Pedals
Eagle Bicycle Manufacturing Co. offered detachable toe clips for its nickel-plated steel pedals. These helped keep the cyclist's feet on the pedals when riding.

Large, driven rear wheel

Tire with inner tube

Sprung-hairpin seat post

Inner-tubed tires for a safe and comfortable ride

Hub gear
Planetary gears inside the front hub made the wheel rotate twice per turn of the cranks. And so the 30-in (75-cm) wheel acted like a 60-in (150-cm) one.

Mudguards for bad weather

◁ Sercombe-Bolte Telegram Hybrid 1892

Origin US

Frame Steel

Gears Single speed

Wheels Front 30 in (75 cm), Rear 24 in (60 cm)

Manufactured by Sercombe-Bolte, the Telegram featured smaller wheels than the ordinary or Eagle bicycles. It was popular with female riders and Western Union messengers.

Starley Royal Salvo

A sedate older cousin to the more daring, upstart high-wheeler, the Starley Royal Salvo represented a refined form of cycling for leisurely, genteel riding. The stability and comfort of tricycles eliminated the risk of falling inherent in riding high-wheelers and boneshakers. The Salvo was the most advanced tricycle of its day when it debuted in 1877, and featured several innovations still central to bicycle technology today.

ONE OF THE PIONEERS OF THE TRICYCLE was Briton James Starley, an irrepressible and generous-spirited inventor who progressed from fixing and improving sewing machines to modifying Michaux-style boneshakers. This led to the creation of early high-wheelers, one of which he adapted to allow a female rider to sit adjacent to the front wheel, rather than astride it. The new machine was highly unstable, and so a third wheel was added, resulting in Starley's first tricycle.

One of Starley's later tricycles, the 1877 Salvo—dubbed "Royal" after Queen Victoria purchased two of them in 1881—was ground-breaking in its technology. The first tricycle to be equipped with pedals and a chain, it also boasted a differential drive—an arrangement of interlocking cogs on the axle that allowed the left and right wheels to rotate independently, which improved cornering.

The Salvo was successful in the UK, where tricycle manufacturing was at its cutting edge. The trend then caught on in the US, and exports to Europe, Asia, and Australia followed. Since Starley freely offered his ideas for use by other engineers, the Salvo also played an important role in advancing the technology used in bicycles, tricycles, and even automobiles—differential gears and chain drives were integral to the first cars.

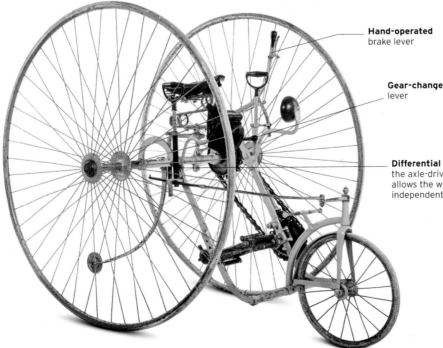

Hand-operated brake lever

Gear-change lever

Differential gear, located in the axle-drive mechanism, allows the wheels to turn independently

Rear balance wheel to prevent the machine from tipping over backward

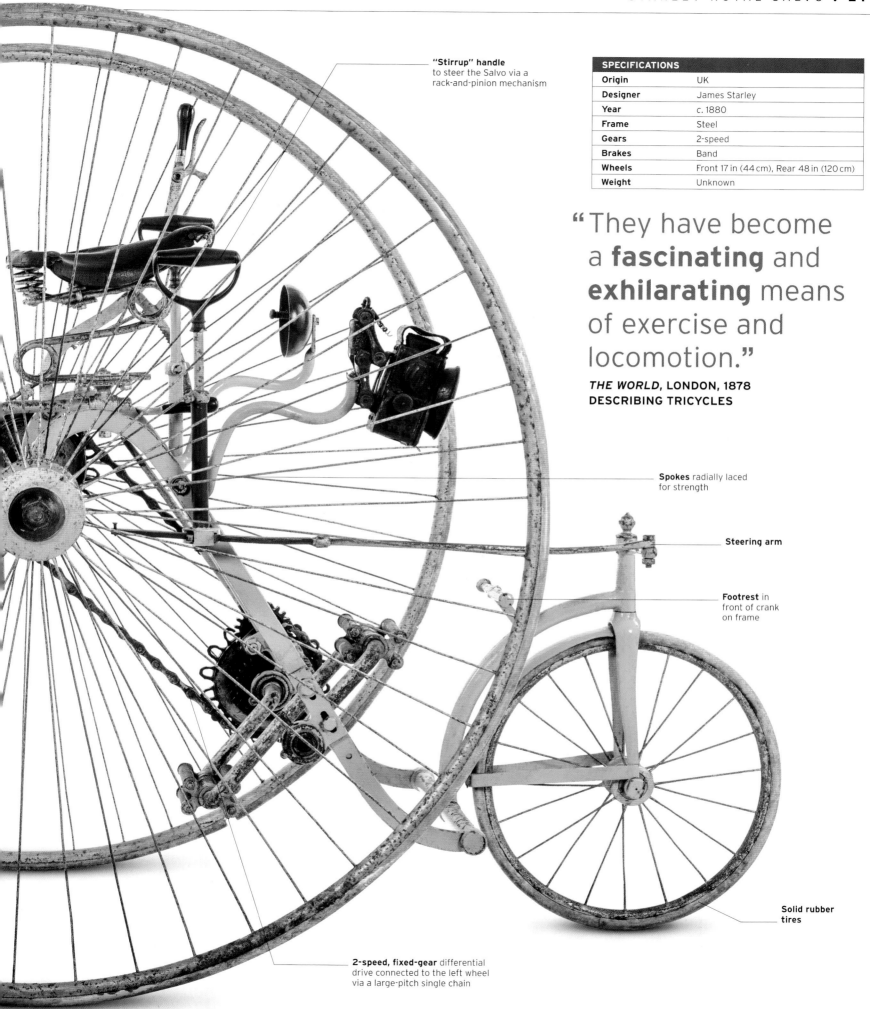

"Stirrup" handle
to steer the Salvo via a
rack-and-pinion mechanism

SPECIFICATIONS	
Origin	UK
Designer	James Starley
Year	c. 1880
Frame	Steel
Gears	2-speed
Brakes	Band
Wheels	Front 17 in (44 cm), Rear 48 in (120 cm)
Weight	Unknown

" They have become
a **fascinating** and
exhilarating means
of exercise and
locomotion."

THE WORLD, LONDON, 1878
DESCRIBING TRICYCLES

Spokes radially laced
for strength

Steering arm

Footrest in
front of crank
on frame

Solid rubber
tires

2-speed, fixed-gear differential
drive connected to the left wheel
via a large-pitch single chain

THE COMPONENTS

While the Salvo appealed to a growing number of curious admirers of the bicycle who were looking for a less risky form of enjoyment, its success was also due to its advanced features and high-quality construction. With a lever-operated brake, front-wheel steering, cranks and pedals, radially laced wheels, and even a light, the Salvo was at the cutting edge of tricycle technology.

1. Brooks leather saddle on double-hairpin-sprung mount **2.** Rear balance "wheel" **3.** Hub and spokes, rear drive wheel **4.** Transmission comprising large-pitch chain, hub-mounted cog with band-type brake, and 2-speed fixed gear operated by a hand lever **5.** Pedal with four rubber-surfaced shafts **6.** Left-hand stirrup handle for steering **7.** Brake lever **8.** Bell with rear-facing "clapper" **9.** Carbide lamp emitting white and red light

Great Races
Paris–Roubaix 1896

The most prized one-day race in cycling is famous for the fact that, since its inception, the riders have cycled largely on roads paved with cobblestones. Since 1977 the winner has even received a cobblestone as part of the prize.

A poster advertising the 1896 Paris–Roubaix race

ALMOST EVERY PROFESSIONAL CYCLIST would love to win the Paris–Roubaix, but few can handle its challenging nature. A cobblestone surface is demanding for any cyclist, and so this race is one that requires strong, fearless, and skilled racers. In 1896, most of the roads of northern France were surfaced with cobbles; today, the race organizers have to search for cobbled roads.

Roubaix is in the French *département* of Nord (part of Nord Pas de Calais), on the Belgian border. This was once the industrial heartland of France, full of coal mines, steel mills, and textile factories. Cobblestones were the perfect surface for horse-drawn carts and, later on, heavily laden trucks. The mines, factories, and mills employed large numbers of workers and, although the work was hard, this new working class had some leisure time and enjoyed watching cycle racing. To cater to this enthusiasm, two textile manufacturers, Théodore Vienne and Maurice Perez, built a velodrome in the town, on Rue Verte. It opened in 1895, and legendary American sprinter Major Taylor made one of his first European appearances at an early track event at the velodrome.

Vienne and Perez needed publicity to help promote their ambitious program of events in the velodrome. They thought that staging the finish of a big road race from Paris would grab attention. With the help of the major French cycling newspaper, *Le Vélo*, these two industrialists conceived the first Paris–Roubaix in 1896.

THE VERY FIRST EVENT
The first race was 174 miles (280 km) long. It started outside the offices of *Le Vélo* in Paris and traveled north, through the *région* of Picardie to Amiens, then Doullens, where it

Champion cyclist Maurice Garin
Third in the first Paris–Roubaix, Garin won it in 1897 and 1898. He also won the first-ever Tour de France in 1903.

veered northeast to Arras, and then north again to Roubaix. Unfortunately, half of those who had entered the race did not even start. Most of them had never seen the roads of northern France, and tales of how bad they were put them off. It was raining on race day, too.

Soon after the start, the field split up. Professional pacers riding tandems paced the top competitors to maintain a good speed. Exposed, rolling roads in Picardie were the first obstacle. Not only were roads cobbled for most of the way, but the surfaces also worsened the farther north the riders went.

In the end, Josef Fischer of Germany won in a time of 9 hours and 17 minutes, having ridden at an average speed of 18.7 mph (30.2 km/h). He entered the velodrome some 25 minutes ahead of the next rider, Charles Meyer of Denmark. However, when Fischer entered the stadium, the crowd, who had been enjoying some track racing and were informed of the progress

of the Paris–Roubaix riders by telegram dispatches, were strangely muted. They were shocked by his appearance; he was covered in coal dust and mud from the roads, and dried blood because of several crashes along the route. Only two more riders finished within an hour of Fischer. They were Frenchman Maurice Garin, who would go on to win the first-ever Tour de France seven years later, and a Welsh rider, Arthur Linton. It was 119 years before another German, John Degenkolb, won the race, in 2015.

Competitors at the start of the first Paris–Roubaix
Held on Sunday April 19, 1896, the race had originally been scheduled for Easter day, two weeks earlier, but protests on religious grounds forced its postponement. In subsequent years it was held at Easter and for a while became known as La Pascale, or the Easter race.

Challenging surfaces on the "Hell of the North"
Belgian rider Jürgen Roelandts tackles a tricky corner in the 2015 Paris-Roubaix. The cobbled sections are rated from one to five stars according to severity, and are also legally protected and maintained by enthusiasts known as *Les Amis de Paris-Roubaix*.

KEY FACTS

RESULTS
First: Josef Fischer, Germany
Second: Charles Meyer, Denmark
Third: Maurice Garin, France

THE COURSE
This map shows a recent Paris-Roubaix race. The 1896 race followed main roads, which were all cobbled, but as time passed these roads were improved and resurfaced. Paris-Roubaix was in danger of losing what made it unique—and gave it the nickname *l'enfer du Nord* ("the Hell of the North"): the cobbled surfaces. And so in 1968, although the race still ran from Paris to Roubaix, the course was changed and the route redirected onto cobbled back lanes, known as the cobbled sectors of the race. They start after Saint-Quentin in the Aisne *département*, and are linked in zigzag fashion by smooth roads.

The modern race
The race now starts 50 miles (80 km) north of Paris in Compiègne. The riders hit the first of 27 cobbled sections after the first 62 miles (100 km).

> **"You must be strong** to ride so far over cobblestones, **and I am strong**, I know that about myself."
>
> JOSEF FISCHER, RACE WINNER, 1896

Early Tricycles

For those who were afraid to ride a bicycle, or physically incapable of doing so, there was the three-wheeler. Tricycles started appearing very after the draisine in France, the UK, and the US, and some had mechanical drive systems. In the 1840s and 1850s, carriage-makers produced tricycles in small numbers, mainly as invalid carriages or toys. But with the arrival of the pedal-propelled bicycle, from the mid-1860s onward, came a surge of tricycle development. For a while it was unclear whether the bicycle or the tricycle would become the dominant form of personal transportation.

Steering lever turns backrest as well

Steering lever

Hand-operated brake

Adjustable platform for driver's feet

▷ **Boardwalk Tricycle c. 1880**

Origin	Unknown
Frame	Steel
Gears	Single speed
Wheels	Front 27 in (68 cm), Rear 17 in (44 cm)

Three-wheelers such as this were available to rent on boardwalks. The hand chain drive was easily mastered and speed was not important. The driver steered by pulling the lever on the left side.

Alternative Designs

In the 1890s, competitive cycling governing bodies had not yet standardized the racing bicycle. Thus, designers got creative: for example, by combining features of the high-wheeler and the back-to-front Star bicycle to avoid headers and tipping backward. This creativity dwindled as the diamond-framed safety bicycle became the standard.

Handlebar steers front and rear wheels

Jointed flexible frame

Band brake controlled by rider's foot

◁ **Unknown Manufacturer c. 1880**

Origin	US
Frame	Wood and steel
Gears	Single speed
Wheels	Front and rear 13 in (33 cm), Middle 29 in (74 cm)

This machine could be called "The Unknown" as there is very little information available about it. The larger central wheel aligns with the front and back wheels when a rider is sitting on the bicycle.

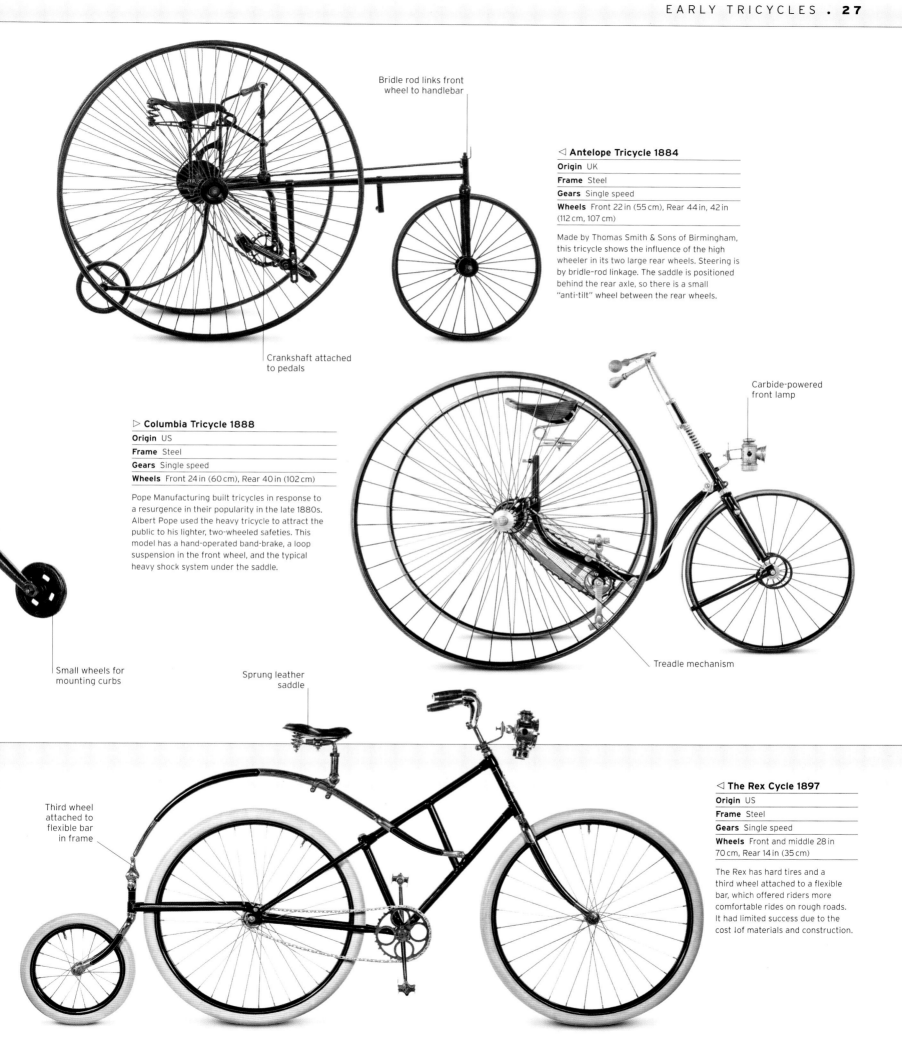

Bridle rod links front wheel to handlebar

◁ **Antelope Tricycle 1884**

Origin UK

Frame Steel

Gears Single speed

Wheels Front 22 in (55 cm), Rear 44 in, 42 in (112 cm, 107 cm)

Made by Thomas Smith & Sons of Birmingham, this tricycle shows the influence of the high wheeler in its two large rear wheels. Steering is by bridle-rod linkage. The saddle is positioned behind the rear axle, so there is a small "anti-tilt" wheel between the rear wheels.

Crankshaft attached to pedals

Carbide-powered front lamp

▷ **Columbia Tricycle 1888**

Origin US

Frame Steel

Gears Single speed

Wheels Front 24 in (60 cm), Rear 40 in (102 cm)

Pope Manufacturing built tricycles in response to a resurgence in their popularity in the late 1880s. Albert Pope used the heavy tricycle to attract the public to his lighter, two-wheeled safeties. This model has a hand-operated band-brake, a loop suspension in the front wheel, and the typical heavy shock system under the saddle.

Treadle mechanism

Small wheels for mounting curbs

Sprung leather saddle

Third wheel attached to flexible bar in frame

◁ **The Rex Cycle 1897**

Origin US

Frame Steel

Gears Single speed

Wheels Front and middle 28 in 70 cm, Rear 14 in (35 cm)

The Rex has hard tires and a third wheel attached to a flexible bar, which offered riders more comfortable rides on rough roads. It had limited success due to the cost lof materials and construction.

Safety Bicycles

The dangers of the high-wheeled bicycle led to the rise of the new "safety" bicycle—so named because the rider sat closer to the ground and farther behind the front wheel, and so was less likely to fall head first over the handlebars. Two key developments made this possible. The first was the arrival of the chain drive, which meant a gear ratio could be chosen independently of the wheel size. The second was the invention of the pneumatic tire, so the smaller wheels could provide a more comfortable ride. In 1885, British inventor John Kemp Starley used these new innovations on the Rover Safety Bicycle, By 1893, high-wheelers were no longer mass-produced.

▷ **Française d'Armes et Cycles Hirondelle "Superbe" 1890**

Origin France
Frame Steel
Gears Single speed
Wheels Front 26 in (65 cm), Rear 30 in 75 cm)

An unusual safety cycle, the Hirondelle Superbe featured a sprung frame made from a single tube. It had a small front wheel and a large rear drive wheel, radial spokes, shock-absorbing spiral handlebars, and an adjustable sprung saddle.

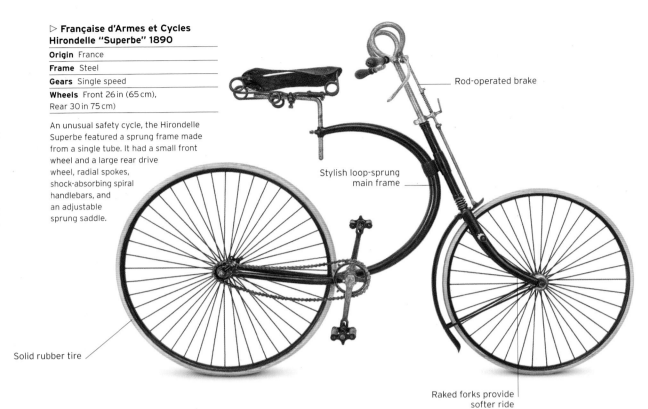

Rod-operated brake

Stylish loop-sprung main frame

Solid rubber tire

Raked forks provide softer ride

▽ **Swift Sprung Safety 1888**

Origin UK
Frame Steel
Gears Single speed
Wheels 30 in (75 cm)

This Swift had a sprung saddle and leading-link front-fork suspension, which gave the cyclist a more comfortable ride than a rigid safety machine. It was a practical bicycle, with small wheels and a chain drive, and it was easier to mount than the ordinary.

Adjustable-height sprung saddle

Front suspension
A pivoting link joins the front fork to the axle, allowing vertical movement and softening bumps for the rider.

Large-pitch chain drive to rear wheel

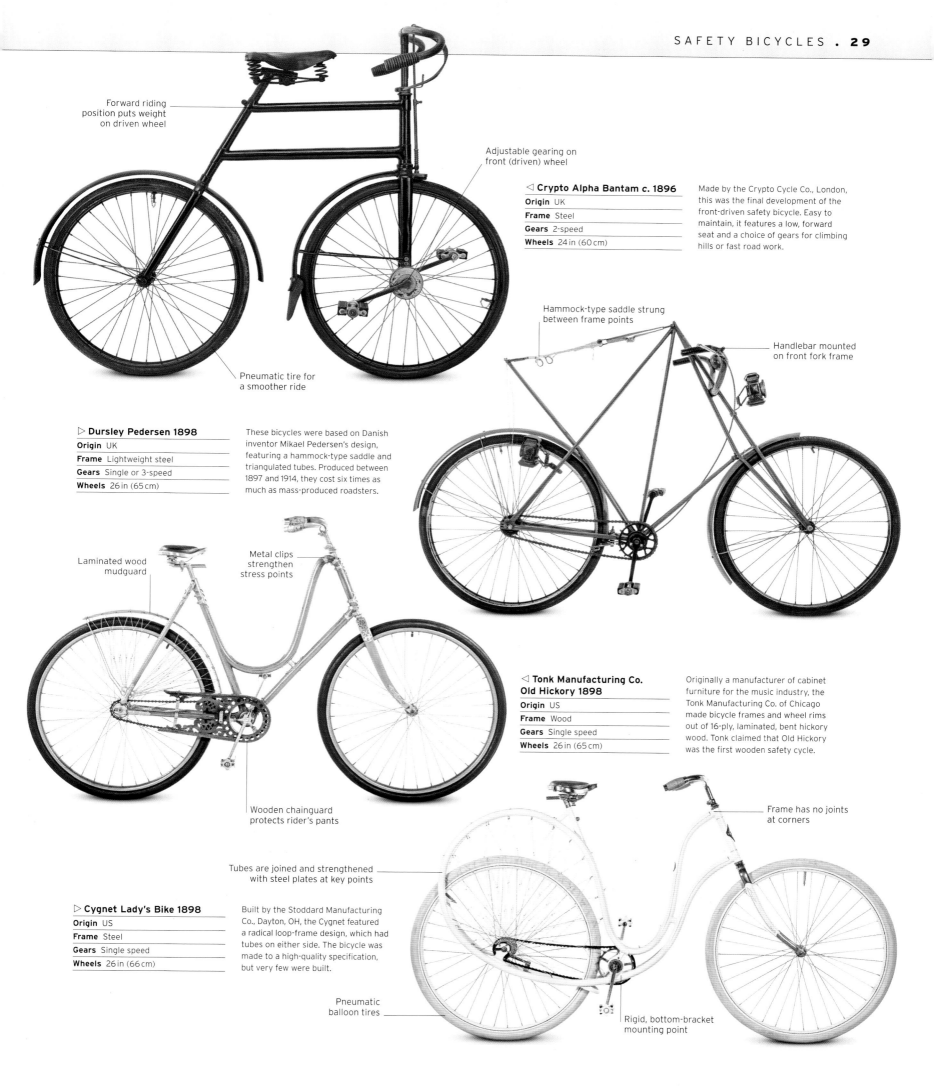

Forward riding position puts weight on driven wheel

Adjustable gearing on front (driven) wheel

◁ **Crypto Alpha Bantam** *c.* **1896**

Origin	UK
Frame	Steel
Gears	2-speed
Wheels	24 in (60 cm)

Made by the Crypto Cycle Co., London, this was the final development of the front-driven safety bicycle. Easy to maintain, it features a low, forward seat and a choice of gears for climbing hills or fast road work.

Pneumatic tire for a smoother ride

Hammock-type saddle strung between frame points

Handlebar mounted on front fork frame

▷ **Dursley Pedersen 1898**

Origin	UK
Frame	Lightweight steel
Gears	Single or 3-speed
Wheels	26 in (65 cm)

These bicycles were based on Danish inventor Mikael Pedersen's design, featuring a hammock-type saddle and triangulated tubes. Produced between 1897 and 1914, they cost six times as much as mass-produced roadsters.

Laminated wood mudguard

Metal clips strengthen stress points

◁ **Tonk Manufacturing Co. Old Hickory 1898**

Origin	US
Frame	Wood
Gears	Single speed
Wheels	26 in (65 cm)

Originally a manufacturer of cabinet furniture for the music industry, the Tonk Manufacturing Co. of Chicago made bicycle frames and wheel rims out of 16-ply, laminated, bent hickory wood. Tonk claimed that Old Hickory was the first wooden safety cycle.

Wooden chainguard protects rider's pants

Frame has no joints at corners

Tubes are joined and strengthened with steel plates at key points

▷ **Cygnet Lady's Bike 1898**

Origin	US
Frame	Steel
Gears	Single speed
Wheels	26 in (66 cm)

Built by the Stoddard Manufacturing Co., Dayton, OH, the Cygnet featured a radical loop-frame design, which had tubes on either side. The bicycle was made to a high-quality specification, but very few were built.

Pneumatic balloon tires

Rigid, bottom-bracket mounting point

Columbia Military Bicycle

Several armies were experimenting with bicycles by the time the safety bicycle evolved. The earliest American formal military bicycle unit was the First Signal Corps of the Connecticut National Guard, formed in 1891. It was equipped with the Columbia Military bicycle, a solid-tired, diamond-frame safety bike with front suspension and numerous attachments for carrying military equipment, including a rifle and bayonet. The owner of the Columbia Bicycle Company, Civil War veteran Colonel Albert Pope, promoted military use of bicycles.

IN 1817, GERMAN INVENTOR KARL DRAIS SUGGESTED the use of his draisine—the first bike—by military messengers; 20 years later, a lecturer at the UK's Royal Military Academy postulated the use of draisines by infantry. By 1875, the Italian army was using bicycle messengers. Formal military cycling sections were established in the UK and Spain in 1887. Authorities had to decide the appropriate specification for a military bicycle: the tried-and-trusted ordinary (nicknamed "penny farthing") or the new safety bicycle? They also needed to look into the most advantageous military role for bicycles.

A British military committee decided that the best use was as a convenient replacement for the horse, for rapidly moving infantry and their equipment long distances. After considering designs by more than 50 bicycle-makers, the committee opted for the safety bicycle because it was more compact, lighter, faster, and easier to handle. American military leaders came to similar conclusions.

The Columbia Military model of 1890 was an ideal choice. The bike boasted attachments for carrying every piece of equipment an infantryman might need. It had solid tires rather than the new, unproven, and fragile pneumatics, and, to give a comfortable ride over rough terrain, it had front suspension and a well-sprung saddle.

Leather saddle mounted on a flexible gooseneck seat post and coil springs

Leather pannier and bugle strapped to rear mudguard

Bayonet case strapped to seat stay

SPECIFICATIONS	
Origin	US
Designer	Albert Pope
Year	1890
Frame	Steel
Gears	Single speed
Wheels	Front 30 in (75 cm), Rear 28 in (70 cm)
Weight	Approx. 50 lb (23 kg) plus equipment

Handlebar rack for a soldier's greatcoat

"A bullet hitting a cycle **'only requires the gunsmith's aid'**, but a horse 'cannot be carried to the repair shop'."

JIM FITZPATRICK, QUOTING CONTEMPORARY WRITERS IN *THE BICYCLE IN WARTIME* **(1998)**

Rifle fixed to TT with clip

Lamp with its own suspension system

Leading-link coil-spring suspension to compensate for the hard ride of the thin, solid rubber tires

Ammunition box

Small chainring provides low gear suitable for rough terrain

THE COMPONENTS

These reflect contemporary state-of-the-art cycle technology, adapted to the specific needs of the army. For example, a decision was made not to adopt the newly available pneumatic tires, which were easily punctured and difficult to repair. Instead, solid tires were used, but comfort was provided by lightweight front suspension and a saddle with sophisticated, two-stage springing.

1. Leather saddle with coil-sprung chassis on flexible gooseneck seat post **2.** Pannier and bayonet case **3.** Block chain, with alternate solid links **4.** Leading-link front suspension with coil springs **5.** Flat pedal with ball bearings and rubber blocks for good grip on army boots **6.** Ammunition case containing 60 rifle cartridges **7.** Brake lever and rod linkage to rear spoon brake **8.** Acetylene lamp on sprung bracket

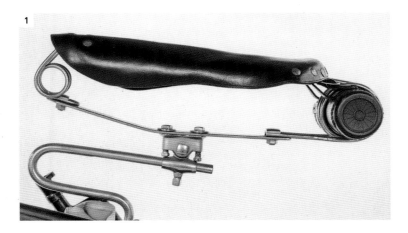

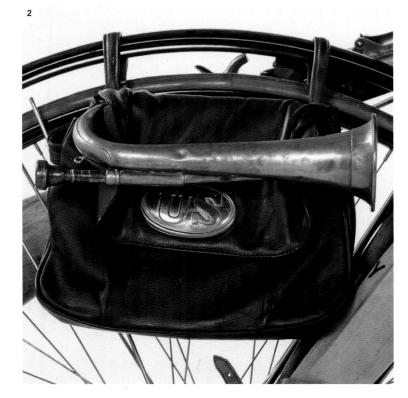

Early Racers

The combination of safety bicycles with pneumatic tires and geared drive by chainrings allowed professional cycle racing to develop rapidly during the 1890s. Races took place on banked tracks known as velodromes and attracted large numbers of spectators. In continental Europe, racing on public roads between cities became very popular (although it was not allowed in the UK). The frames of racing cycles were made of lightweight steel tubing joined by cast lugs, and the wheel rims were made of wood. Sloping frame angles, a high bottom bracket, and a long wheelbase improved performance and stability at high speeds. Drop handlebars helped the rider sit lower down, minimizing wind resistance.

Rear-mounted saddle puts rider's weight on driven wheel

Wheel axle supported on ball bearing to minimize friction

Pneumatic tires on wooden rims

△ Victor Flyer Racer 1895

Origin	US
Frame	Steel
Gears	Single speed
Wheels	28 in (70 cm)

The Victor Flyer model was built by Overman Cycles for track and road racing. It was equipped with pneumatic tires and had a long wheelbase to ensure stability at high speeds. The bicycle weighed 23 lb (10 kg).

▽ Howe Path Racer 1894

Origin	UK
Frame	Steel
Gears	Single speed
Wheels	28 in (70 cm)

This racer featured an unorthodox safety frame with a sloping top tube and track ends at the rear axle mounting. In order to reduce overall weight, the bicycle did not have mudguards and had only a front brake, which applied pressure to the tire.

Toolkit
With the birth of pneumatic tires, punctures were a new hazard, so carrying tools to fix them was a wise choice.

Drop handlebars for riding comfort

Stopping short
This model featured spoon brakes that pressed directly on the front tire. They were ineffective on wet road surfaces and wore out the tires.

Track ends allow quick wheel changes and easier tire repair

Sloping top tube allows for a higher riding position

Tube provides extra frame bracing

◁ **Iver Johnson Truss Frame 1896**

Origin US

Frame Steel

Gears Single speed

Wheels 28 in (70 cm)

This bicycle had an unusual frame design. There was an extra tube connected to the seat tube, as well as top and down tubes. All of this strengthened the frame, which helped efficiency, and gave the rider more precise steering.

Long crank improves leverage

Saddle adjustable for height and lateral position

Lightweight, rigid steel tubular frame

▷ **Zimmy Pneumatic Safety 1896**

Origin UK

Frame Steel

Gears Single speed

Wheels 28 in (70 cm)

Developed by the Nimrod Cycle Co., Bristol, this model was built for, and named after, the renowned American racing cyclist A.A. Zimmerman. The bicycle weighed just 20 lb (9 kg) and was popular with racers around the world.

Track ends on rear axle

Steeply sloped top tube minimizes wind resistance

Rod-operated stirrup brakes at front and rear

Hand pump mounting point

◁ **Senior Wrangler Scorcher 1896**

Origin UK

Frame Steel

Gears Single speed

Wheels 28 in (70 cm)

Aimed specifically at road racing, this radical design allowed the rider to lean low over the front wheel, reducing wind resistance. This machine had a long wheelbase and was one of the first racers with brakes on both wheels.

Features Adler's patented drop handlebars

Saddle has cutaway sides

▷ **Adler Road Racer Model No. 41 1897**

Origin Germany

Frame Steel

Gears Single speed

Wheels 28 in (70 cm)

Marketed by Adler as their road-racing model, this bicycle featured pneumatic tires on wooden rims and a slim but rigid leather saddle. Weighing only 23 lb (10 kg), the Adler No. 41 was another lightweight bicycle.

Skip-tooth chainring

The First Tandems

The idea of two riders sharing a two-wheeler dates back to Karl von Drais' early designs. Thereafter, tandems have been found in every stage of cycle development and in almost all forms of bicycles and tricycles. The normal arrangement today is one rider behind the other—the front person, or "pilot," steers the bicycle, and the rear rider is the "stoker"—but in the 1890s, women sat up front while men pedaled, braked, and steered from the back. Either way, the bicycle is powered by two riders, but has the frontal area of one, giving it a distinct aerodynamic advantage. Occasionally, a side-by-side "sociable" configuration has been used. A tandem also enables a vision-impaired rider to enjoy cycling as a stoker with a sighted pilot.

SCHWINN BICYCLES

In 1895 Arnold Schwinn & Company was founded in Chicago by two German immigrants—bike-builder Ignaz Schwinn from the Adler works, and successful meat-packer Adolph Arnold. Over the years, a dedicated dealer network enabled the Schwinn brand to achieve the status of an American household name—until its bankruptcy in 1992.

A tandem for three Mr. Schwinn sat at the rear of the tandem, with his wife at the front, and their son Frank was between them in his own special safety seat.

Man's high-up seat at the rear

Woman's seat at the front

Brake is applied to rear wheel

△ Olympic Tandem Tricycle 1895

Origin	UK
Frame	Steel
Gears	Single speed
Wheels	26 in (65 cm)

Frank H. Parkyn started making Olympic cycles in Wolverhampton in the 1880s. At the time this pneumatic-tired tandem was built, it was unacceptable for a woman to sit behind a man. She was in front, while he sat behind, steering.

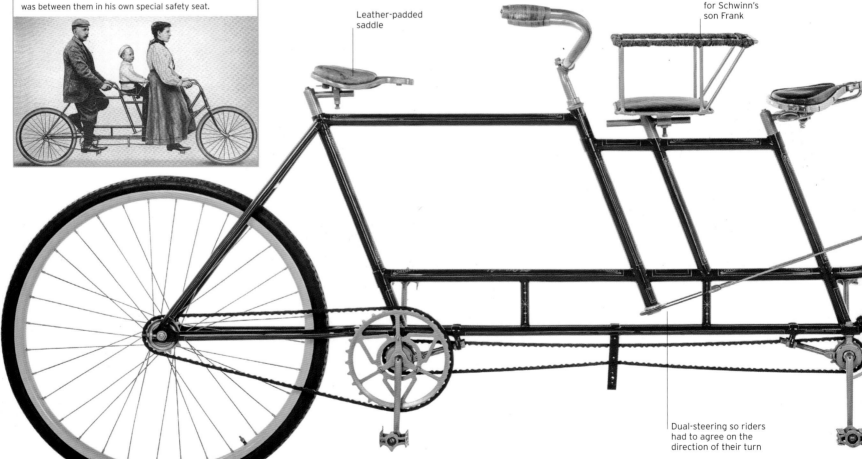

Leather-padded saddle

Central seat for Schwinn's son Frank

Dual-steering so riders had to agree on the direction of their turn

△ Schwinn Family Tandem 1897

Origin	US
Frame	Steel
Gears	Single speed
Wheels	28 in (71 cm)

This tandem is so named because it was made specifically for the company's founder Ignaz Schwinn and his wife. With the financial backing of fellow German Adolf Arnold, Ignaz had founded Arnold, Schwinn & Company in 1895 in Chicago.

Armed with a rifle and two pistols

Rod brake is applied to front wheel

Dual-steering mechanism

◁ **Columbia Military Tandem 1896**

Origin	US
Frame	Nickel steel
Gears	Single speed
Wheels	27 in (69 cm)

Colonel Albert Pope, founder of Columbia, first built bicycles after being passed by high-wheel riders when out on his horse. This tandem was used for reconnaissance as well as carrying people and supplies.

▽ **Adler Bicycle Works AG Triplet 1897**

Origin	Germany
Frame	Steel
Gears	Single speed
Wheels	28 in (71 cm)

This three-rider bicycle was used as a pacer in velodromes. It freed the racer behind it from air resistance, so he could ride faster over longer distances. Heinrich Kleyer founded Adler-Fahrrad-Werke in 1880.

Twin tubes strengthen frame

Cork handlebar

Wooden-rimmed wheels

Equipped with extra-strong chain

Sociable seats side-by-side

Central seat post for use by single rider

Pedals arranged so bicycle could be ridden by one rider

▷ **Punnett Companion Tandem 1897**

Origin	US
Frame	Steel
Gears	Single speed
Wheels	27 in (69 cm)

The Punnett tandem sold for around $100, but was never a commercial success. The company claimed it was easy to ride, steer, mount, and propel. It could be used by one or two riders, but everyone who looked at it thought that weight would be an issue.

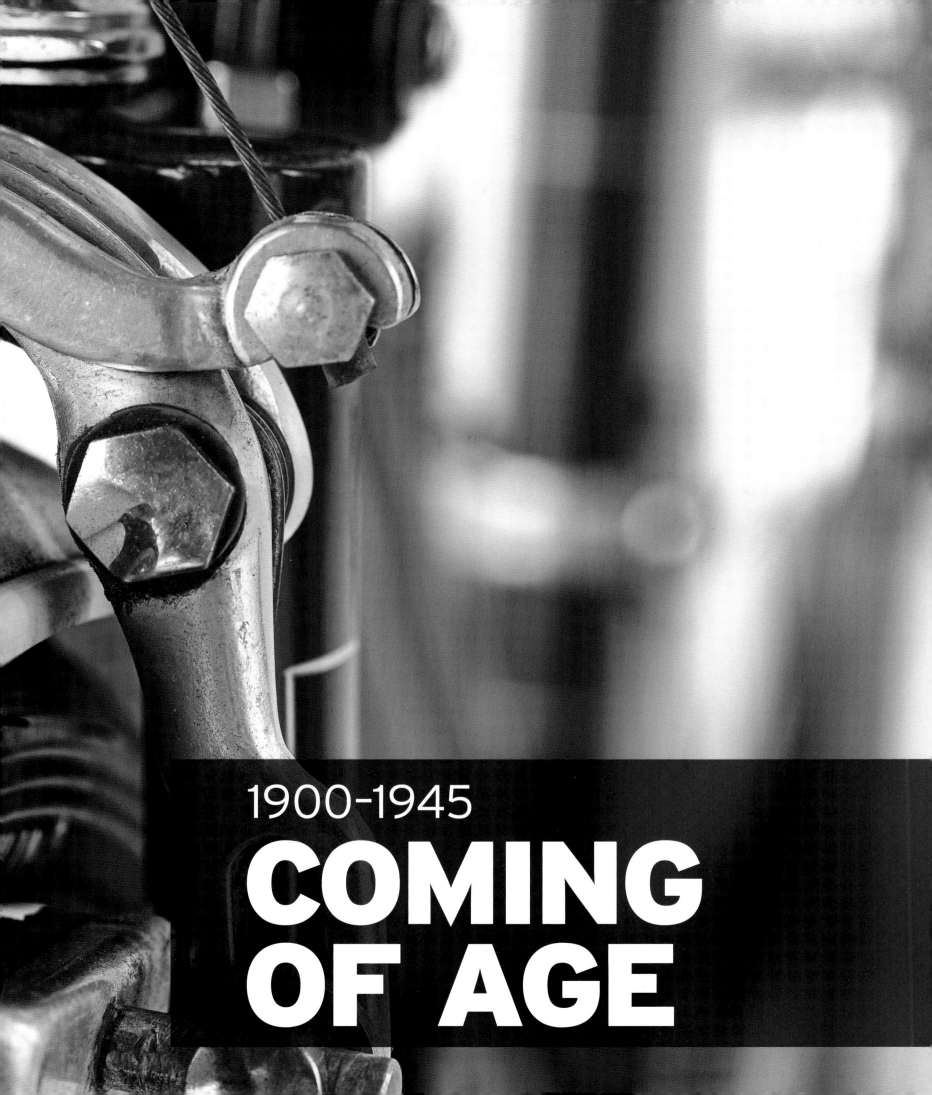

1900-1945
COMING OF AGE

STURMEY·ARCHER
2 SPEED GEAR

THE GEAR THAT MAKES CYCLING EASY

WE FIT IT HERE

COMING OF AGE

△ **A machine for workers**
Bicycles became essential for many businesses, especially those involved in communication, with models designed specifically for the purpose (see pp.62-63).

As the 20th century dawned, bicycle use underwent a demographic revolution. The bicycle's boom and bust of the late 19th century had been fueled by its popularity among the middle classes of Europe and the US, who had the money and leisure time to enjoy the craze of the day. But as cycling began to go out of fashion—challenged by other new forms of personal transportation, including the automobile—the bicycle found popularity as a working-class machine.

Falling costs, partly due to the spread of mass production and new manufacturing techniques, meant that bicycles became more affordable for working men and women. The social effects were soon noted: while the bicycle had brought new freedoms for women in the 1890s and contributed to the female emancipation movement, in the new century the increased mobility it afforded was a factor in the social changes occurring in many countries. Workers could travel under their own steam in their leisure time, meaning that relational webs—including marriages—could stretch farther beyond the immediate locality.

Technologically, innovation was rife. Gears that could be changed at the push of a lever were available in the early 1900s, while frames became stronger and lighter with the use of steel alloys engineered by the aircraft industry in the 1930s. Bicycles found uses beyond recreation and personal transportation, such as for postal deliveries, police patrols, military purposes, and even—in the form of two connected tandems—as ambulances. No longer a prestige item reserved for the elite, the bicycle had fully entered the mainstream.

"Few articles **ever used** by man have **created so great** a revolution in social conditions as **the bicycle**."

US CENSUS REPORT, 1900

Key Events

▷ **1900s** Cycling becomes more comfortable thanks to the invention of the freewheel, allowing the rider to stop pedaling while coasting downhill, and to brake reliably at the bottom.

▷ **1901** The US-designed Sofa Bicycle, one of the earliest recumbent designs, is promoted in Europe.

▷ **1902** The world's first 3-speed hub gear is released by Sturmey-Archer, providing reliable gear-changing at the push of a lever.

▷ **1903** The Tour de France is held for the first time. Bicycle racing moves toward road racing, away from its historical base of track cycling.

▷ **1914-18** Bicycles—including folding designs for scouting—are used on both sides in World War I.

▷ **1930s** Despite the rising popularity of tandems and touring, bicycle use falls in many countries, especially the US, as lobbying from the auto industry ensures the dominance of the car.

▷ **1933** Manufacturer Schwinn introduces the balloon-tired Streamline Aerocycle for the only sector to enjoy healthy sales in the US—the children's market.

▷ **1939-45** Bicycle use increases around the world because of gasoline shortages during World War II.

△ **Made for the family**
Tandems became particularly popular in the interwar period, which coincided with rising living standards and increased leisure time for many working families.

◁ **A poster produced by manufacturer Sturmey-Archer in 1902** advertised its innovative new gear hub mechanism.

Pre-1930s Racers

At the turn of the 20th century, Europe's enthusiasm for competitive cycling soared. The advent of the Tour de France in 1903 and the Giro d'Italia in 1909 gave people something to watch, and bicycle manufacturers a stage on which to promote their products. Bicycles at this time were constructed of heavy varnished steel, and in some races, riders were expected to propel these weighty machines over more than 250 miles (400 km) in a single day. Early models often lacked a rear brake, and cyclists would control their speed by pushing the pedals backward. Most bikes were made to be used with single fixed gears. To change gear, therefore, riders had to pull over and turn their drive wheel around, or fit a different cog, when they approached hills or tough terrain.

▷ **Dayton 1904**

Origin	UK
Frame	Steel
Gears	Single speed
Wheels	28 in (70 cm)

Wooden rims, as seen on this model, were a norm for racing bicycles as organizers feared that the frictional heat of braking during descents would melt the glue that held the tires. Dayton prided itself on its lightweight creations, often boasting about using an amalgam of materials to construct its frames.

Brooks leather saddle

Steel spokes in a two-cross pattern

Early seat post made of steel

Frame bag containing wrenches

Early form of two-speed rear derailleur

◁ **Terrot 1904**

Origin	France
Frame	Steel
Gears	2-speed
Wheels	28 in (70 cm)

French manufacturer Charles Terrot made motorcycles and bicycles until 1958. Many of his bicycles featured the same designs and steel tubing as his basic motorcycles. The 1904 model offered two gears—the first could be selected by pedaling forward, while an easier mode could be chosen by pedaling backward.

▷ **Gloria Rennrad Exportmodell 1920**

Origin	Italy
Frame	Lugged steel
Gears	Single speed
Wheels	28 in (70 cm)

After World War I, bicycle technology advanced and the average speed at races increased. Like many high-end manufacturers, Gloria used hand-cut lugs to join tubes, picking out the pattern in contrasting blue. This bike featured comfortable rubber grips, a mount to attach a pump, and front and rear brakes.

Side pull of rear caliper brake

Rear brake cable

Cotton canvas tire glued to wooden rim

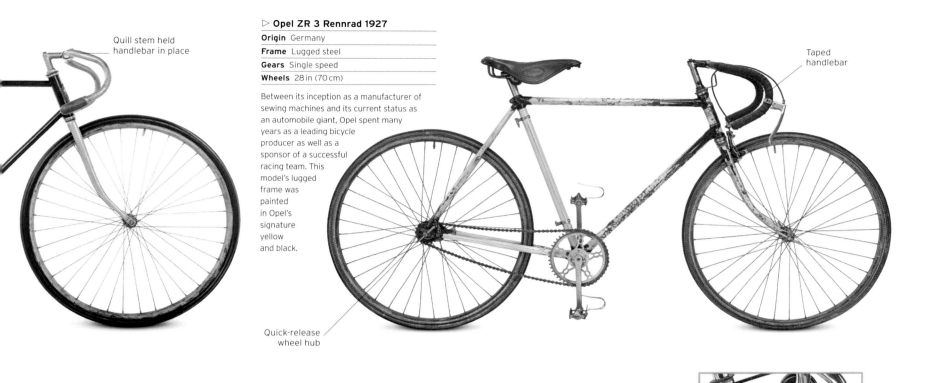

Quill stem held
handlebar in place

▷ **Opel ZR 3 Rennrad 1927**

Origin	Germany
Frame	Lugged steel
Gears	Single speed
Wheels	28 in (70 cm)

Between its inception as a manufacturer of sewing machines and its current status as an automobile giant, Opel spent many years as a leading bicycle producer as well as a sponsor of a successful racing team. This model's lugged frame was painted in Opel's signature yellow and black.

Taped
handlebar

Quick-release
wheel hub

Leather toolbag
strapped to saddle

▽ **Tom Lunn Gamage 1928**

Origin	UK
Frame	Steel
Gears	Single speed
Wheels	28 in (70 cm)

London department store Gamages began producing basic racing bicycles as the popularity of cycling boomed. This model featured a forward-facing dropout at the rear wheel, which allowed easy wheel replacement in the event of a flat.

Quill road pedal
with metal toe clips

Low-slung handlebars
Drop handlebars with a long forward throw helped the rider adopt a lower position to help generate more power when sprinting.

Post-1930s Racers

By the 1930s, most racing bicycles featured drop handlebars, as well as front and rear brakes. Component manufacturers, such as Campagnolo (see *pp46–47*), were beginning to refine the multi-gear mechanism that would later become known as a rear derailleur. Colorful paint finishes, chrome detailing, and elaborately designed frame lugs helped manufacturers differentiate their bicycles from the competition. Pump mounts featured as standard, and in 1937 the Tour de France organizers allowed the use of more durable gears and metal rims.

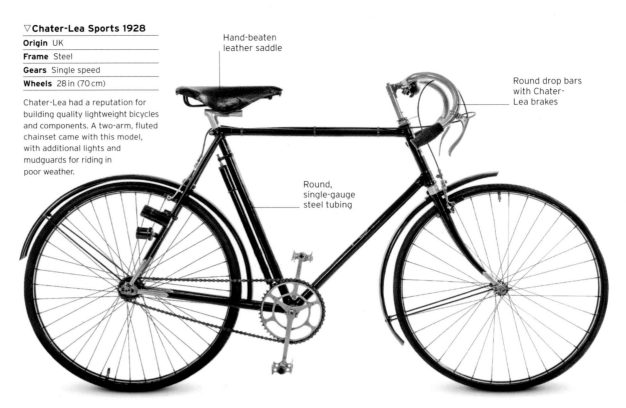

▽ **Chater-Lea Sports 1928**

Origin UK

Frame Steel

Gears Single speed

Wheels 28 in (70 cm)

Chater-Lea had a reputation for building quality lightweight bicycles and components. A two-arm, fluted chainset came with this model, with additional lights and mudguards for riding in poor weather.

Hand-beaten leather saddle

Round drop bars with Chater-Lea brakes

Round, single-gauge steel tubing

Rod gears
A precursor to derailleur gears, this bike featured rods that lift the chain onto the cogs in the rear hub.

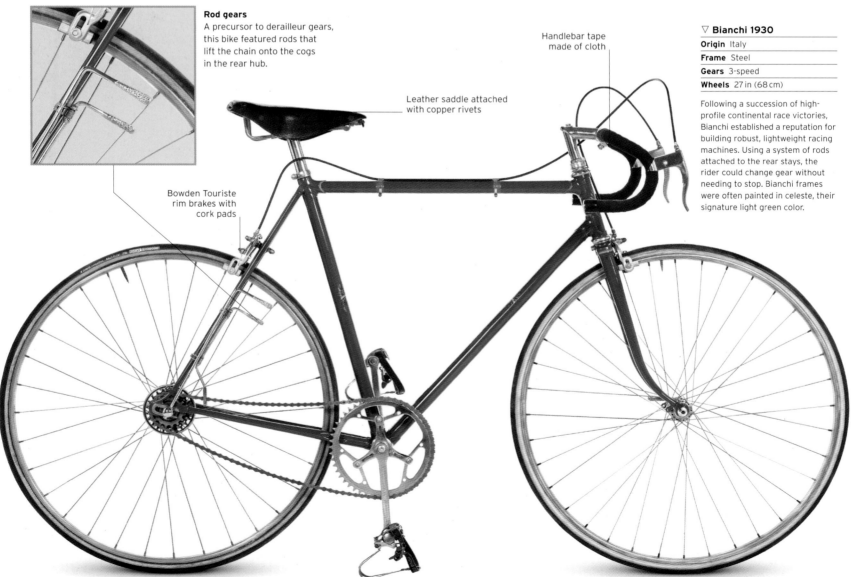

Handlebar tape made of cloth

Leather saddle attached with copper rivets

Bowden Touriste rim brakes with cork pads

▽ **Bianchi 1930**

Origin Italy

Frame Steel

Gears 3-speed

Wheels 27 in (68 cm)

Following a succession of high-profile continental race victories, Bianchi established a reputation for building robust, lightweight racing machines. Using a system of rods attached to the rear stays, the rider could change gear without needing to stop. Bianchi frames were often painted in celeste, their signature light green color.

Wooden bicycle rims
with glued tubular tires

Frame-mounted
bicycle pump

Steel pedals
with leather
toe straps

◁ **CF Davey 1932**

Origin	UK
Frame	Steel
Gears	Single speed
Wheels	27 in (68 cm)

Produced for the budget-conscious rider, the
Davey's simple lug pattern and shot-in seat
stays kept the frame-build costs to a minimum.
The luxury of a rear brake or gears was not
available on this bicycle.

▷ **WEJ '59 Special Race Frame 1934**

Origin	UK
Frame	Steel
Gears	Single speed
Wheels	27 in (68 cm)

British frame-builder W.E.J. claimed its frames were
constructed with the precision of an aircraft and
featured a plane on the brass head badge. The
high-end frame featured shot-in stays that were
welded lower to the seat post, enabling a more
compact rear triangle to reduce flex.

Swept-back
handlebars

Leather toolbag
with tools for
changing the
rear sprocket

Compact frame

▽ **Baines Brothers VS 37 Whirlwind 1941**

Origin	UK
Frame	Steel
Gears	3-speed
Wheels	27 in (68 cm)

Baines created the unusual gate design to eliminate
whip when accelerating. The "37" in the model name
referred to the length of the wheelbase in inches and
gave an idea of this short bike's maneuverability.

Adjustable steel
seatpost

Down tube
gear-shifters

Bar-mounted
dual brakes

Alloy
mudguards

LETOURNEUR PACE BIKE 1941 (REPLICA)

The original bicycle was built by Schwinn for French-born
speed cyclist Alf "The Red Devil" Letourneur, to help him
break the motor-paced 100 mph (160.934 km/h) speed barrier.
He first achieved a record speed of 91.37 mph (147.04 km/h)
in 1938, which he bettered three years later in California,
reaching 108.98 mph (175.38 km/h) and becoming the first
person to exceed 100 mph (160.934 km/h) on a bicycle.

The Red Devil bicycle The enormous chainring and small
rear cog gave this bicycle incredibly high gearing, enabling
it to achieve high speeds from a rolling start.

Gino Bartali pulls
ahead of Stan
Ockers in the 1948
Tour de France

Great Manufacturers
Campagnolo

Of all the great names of cycling, Campagnolo is perhaps the brand most associated with the historic racing spirit of the bicycle. More than 85 years after it was founded, this family-run business, based in Vicenza, northern Italy, is still producing beautifully designed and highly-coveted components built to the most exacting standards.

Campagnolo

Company logo based on Tullio's signature

GENTULLIO "TULLIO" Campagnolo was an amateur cyclist who, in the 1920s, experienced first-hand the punishing reality of racing at a time when competitive cycling was viewed as a Corinthian endeavor in the purest sense. Although the details of the tale have been challenged by historians, the story of Tullio's company begins with him racing in a blizzard-swept competition in November 1927 in the Dolomite mountains of northern Italy. At the time, racing bicycles had only two gears—two cogs mounted on either side of the hub. In order to change gear, the rider had to dismount, remove the rear wheel from the bicycle, flip it 180 degrees, then reinsert it into the frame so that the other cog could engage with the chain. Tullio claimed that while leading the Gran Premio della Vittoria race up the Croce d'Aune pass, he was forced to stop to change gear, but his fingers froze on the wing nuts that secured the wheel to the bicycle frame. As a result, Tullio's chances of winning evaporated. Tullio, the son of a hardware store owner, was ideally placed to tackle the mechanical problems of the racing bicycle, which had changed little since the late 19th century. His solution to the wheel-change problem came in 1930, when he perfected a quick-release skewer that allowed the wheel to be removed from the bicycle frame with the turn of a lever. Tullio's

Hand in hand
Charly Gaul reaches back to Louison Bobet in the 1955 Tour de France. Pre-race favorite Bobet went on to win the overall victory on Campagnolo equipment.

Gran Sport derailleur 1953

Nuovo Record derailleur 1965

Super Record Signature derailleur 1983

Super Record EPS derailleur 2011

1930 Gentullio Campagnolo produces his first product, a quick-release skewer.

1933 Tullio registers his company name, Campagnolo SRL.

1935 The quick-release skewer is exported to the UK market.

1940 Campagnolo introduces the first item of gear componentry, the Cambio Corsa dual-rod derailleur.

1943 Logo showing a winged quick-release lever circled by a bicycle wheel appears on Campagnolo products.

1948 Campagnolo opens a factory in Cognin, France.

1950 Campagnolo's workforce grows to 123.

1953 The third-generation Gran Sport derailleur perfects Campagnolo's parallelogram-derailleur technology.

1958 Record groupset includes alloy hubs and a chainset with cotterless cranks.

1965 Nuovo Record groupset is introduced.

1973 Bianchi-Campagnolo rider Felice Gimondi wins the World Championships road race.

1981 New headquarters and production facility are built in Campagnolo's home city of Vicenza.

1986 The C-Record groupset, with aerodynamic, rounded styling, is released.

1989 Campagnolo produces an off-road groupset for the mountain-bike market.

1992 Ergopower combined brake and gear-levers released.

1998 A composites division is established to develop carbon-composite technology.

2005 Resisting pressure to outsource production to Asia, Campagnolo opens a factory in Romania.

2008 Campagnolo becomes the first brand to offer an 11-speed groupset.

2011 Campagnolo releases its electronic power shifting (EPS) system.

2014 Italian rider Vincenzo Nibali wins the Tour de France—the first outright victory on a bicycle using Campagnolo components since Marco Pantani's win in 1998.

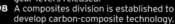

A market leader for decades
Left is a 1950s poster depicting Campagnolo-sponsored riders; on the right is the 2015 Super Record EPS groupset.

skewer was an ingenious product and is still standard-issue on all but the cheapest of mass-produced bikes. Its design encapsulates Campagnolo's ethos—to develop simple but elegant components that improve the riding experience of cyclists at all levels.

Tullio registered his company in 1933, and applied his quick-release concept to gear-changing technology. Derailleur devices had been invented in the late 19th century, but the idea did not catch on until touring cyclists began to use them in the 1930s. Campagnolo produced the Cambio Corsa in 1940, a dual-rod design that used two levers mounted on the bicycle's seat stay—the first lever disengaged the quick-release skewer, allowing the chain to be pushed across the cogs by the second lever. Because it was reliable and popular, although tricky to operate, the dual-rod *cambio* (changer) was used widely by racing cyclists, and was ridden to victory in the 1948 Tour de France by Gino Bartali.

Campagnolo secured its position at the top of the bicycle-component manufacturing industry with its Gran Sport derailleur. Inspired by a cyclo-touring derailleur made by French firm Nivex,

Tullio Campagnolo
(1901–1983)

Campagnolo developed a cable-actuated parallelogram design that allowed precise, reliable gear shifts every time. The prototype was demonstrated at a show in Milan in 1950 and went into production in 1951. It soon became the standard by which all rivals were judged.

Throughout the 1950s, Campagnolo made sure its products adorned the bicycles of the most successful racing cyclists. For the next 30 years its gears and brakes would be used by more than two-thirds of the winners of the Tour de France and Giro d'Italia. But as well as sponsoring elite professional cyclists, Campagnolo continued its drive to improve the ride of everyday cyclists. In 1956 it released a series of new products,

from pedals and a headset to a two-bolt seat post that allowed riders to finely adjust the position of their saddle.

Campagnolo also demonstrated an understanding of how customers—whether individual cyclists, or companies selecting parts to complete the bicycles they sold—interacted with its products. In the late 1950s the company introduced the "groupset" concept by developing an integrated collection of the parts required to make up a bicycle—pedals, brakes, gears, chain, and headset—designed to work perfectly with one another. Now commonplace in the cycling industry, at the time Campagnolo was challenging the existing pattern of mixing parts from several different manufacturers.

During the 1960s and 1970s, Campagnolo reigned more or less unchallenged over the high-end racing scene. It introduced the Nuovo Record groupset in 1965; then, in 1973, the Super Record set new standards of style, performance, and lightweight design. However, the influx into the world market of cheaper components from Asian competitors, notably Shimano of Japan, led to the loss of Campagnolo's market-leading position in the 1980s.

Campagnolo fought back in the 1990s by focusing on its core market of high-end road cycling. It became the first company to produce factory-built wheels, while in 2000 the 10-speed drivetrain was introduced—moves that were later copied by Shimano. Although Campagnolo no longer dominates the bicycle industry, it maintains its niche position as purveyor of the finest cycling components that money can buy, as well as its lineage as a family-run firm rooted in the history of cycle sports.

"The **history** of Campagnolo is the story of **modern cycling**."

MARKETING SLOGAN, 2008

Testing conditions
The Vicenza factory houses fatigue-testing equipment for all of Campagnolo's products, such as this carbon-fiber chainset.

Touring and Leisure Bikes

The popularity and increasing affordability of the automobile caused a decline in recreational cycling in the US, where bicycles were considered toys, and most were made for teenagers and children; cruisers imported from Germany with rugged balloon tires were fashionable. In Europe, cycling remained an adult activity and bicycles with multispeed gearing were increasingly common. Cyclo-touring became popular, and riders would explore the countryside on single- and multi-day trips.

Seat stuffed with sea grass

Brass carbide lamp

Treadle drive mechanism

△ Hesperus-Werke "J-Rad" 1922

Origin Germany

Frame Steel

Gears 3-speed

Wheels Front 20 in (50 cm), Rear 26 in (65 cm)

Zeppelin engineer, Paul Jaray, patented this recumbent machine when his children started cycling. Lever-driven via cables, rather than by pedals, the J-wheel was a precursor to the chopper-style bicycle of the 1970s. Its relaxed operation was popular with wealthier cyclists.

Seamless steel dual-top tube

Looped fork provides flex

Full-length mudguards

△ Alexander Rocket Bicycle 1930s

Origin US

Frame Steel

Gears Single speed

Wheels 26 in (65 cm)

Despite the curved metalwork, the Rocket was a heavy machine. Made in Texas, the bicycle was popular with paperboys and couriers. Few remain, as with the advent of WWII and the need for metal, Americans had to turn in bicycles for scrap.

Chrome-plated rear rack

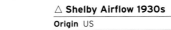

△ Shelby Airflow 1930s

Origin US

Frame Steel

Gears Single speed

Wheels 26 in (65 cm)

Manufacturers wanted to create a comfortable ride on unpaved 1930s roads. Shelby's solution was a front suspension system with sliding spring. The Airflow was made from seamless steel tubing; its joints were hand-filed.

Chrome-plated handlebar

Aero-styled rack

◁ Elgin Bluebird 1936

Origin US

Frame Steel

Gears 3-speed

Wheels 26 in (65 cm)

The Bluebird was equipped with built-in speedometer, headlight, fake "fuel" tank, sleek mudguards, and a chrome-plated handlebar. Produced in Massachusetts, its high cost meant it was never a big seller.

> " A **bicycle** goes nearly all the way towards making a **healthy man!**"
>
> CYCLE TRADES OF AMERICA, 1920

▽ Joe Cooke
Imperial Petrel 1938

Origin	UK
Frame	Steel
Gears	3-speed
Wheels	27 in (68 cm)

Joe Cooke, the owner of a custom bicycle shop in Birmingham, built the Imperial Petrel "Superigid," which had semicircular tubes at the front and chainstays for extra stiffness.

Handmade Brooks leather saddle

Pump mounted on frame

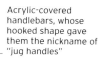

Head badge
The Imperial Petrel head badge has a striking design. The frame's name, "Petrel," after the bird, is picked out in dark blue. Joe Cooke chose the name because he thought the bird symbolized speed and grace.

Acrylic-covered handlebars, whose hooked shape gave them the nickname of "jug handles"

Alloy brake levers

Gears
Most hub gears at this time, such as this lightweight 2-speed, used a toggle chain to link the control cable to the gear lever, via the hollow wheel axle.

Reflector
Prismatic reflectors were invented in 1924. In the US today, all new bicycles must have reflectors as specified by the Consumer Product Safety Commission.

Gear-shifter
The Sturmey-Archer quadrant shifter was a shift lever mounted on the top tube. It connected the control cable to the toggle chain in the wheel axle.

Front lamp
This bicycle was ahead of its time as it was sold with lights. Today, many US states and municipalities require front and rear lights when riding after dark.

Diamant Model 67

A lightweight, steel-framed racing bicycle boasting an array of aluminum components, the Model 67 *Berufsfahrermodell* (professional racer's model) was the pinnacle of the Diamant stable in the late 1930s. The oldest German bicycle brand still in existence today, Diamant pioneered a range of technologies and manufacturing techniques—from chain design to metal-alloying processes—and enjoyed its glory years as the premium Eastern Bloc racing brand from the 1950s to the 1990s.

FOUNDED BY BROTHERS Friedrich and Wilhelm Nevoigt in 1882 to produce sewing machines, Diamant manufactured its first bicycle in 1895. With innovations such as the 1898 twin-roller chain—which was stronger and offered better gear-shifting than existing block-chain designs— the brothers earned a reputation for building high-quality, lightweight racing bicycles. The Model 67 was first produced in 1936 prior to the Berlin Olympics, where it was ridden to two gold medals by the German cycling team. Ernst Ihbe and Carl "Carly" Lorenz won the men's tandem 2,000 m, while Toni Merkens won the men's 1,000 m sprint.

Built around a lightweight yet stiff frame—made from thin-gauge steel tubes, joined with aluminum lugs—the Model 67 was finished to the highest possible standard. Production of the Model 67 continued until 1954, when the mantle of Diamant's flagship lightweight racing bicycle was passed to the new Model 167. As part of East Germany's centrally planned economy, Diamant produced racing bicycles for many Eastern Bloc cycle teams and academies. Diamant bicycles were used in a host of victories up until the 1990s, including Täve Schur's Peace Race triumphs in 1955 and 1959. The brand was acquired by the Trek Bicycle Corp. in 2002.

Lohmann leather saddle

Aluminum "bridge" saddle mount

Wooden rims made with laminated layers of wood, usually maple

SPORLUX caliper brakes

Fichtel & Sachs derailleur

SPECIFICATIONS	
Origin	Germany
Designer	Unknown
Year	c. 1939
Frame	Chromoly steel
Gears	3-speed
Brakes	Caliper
Wheels	28 in (70 cm)
Weight	Approx. 24 lb (11 kg)

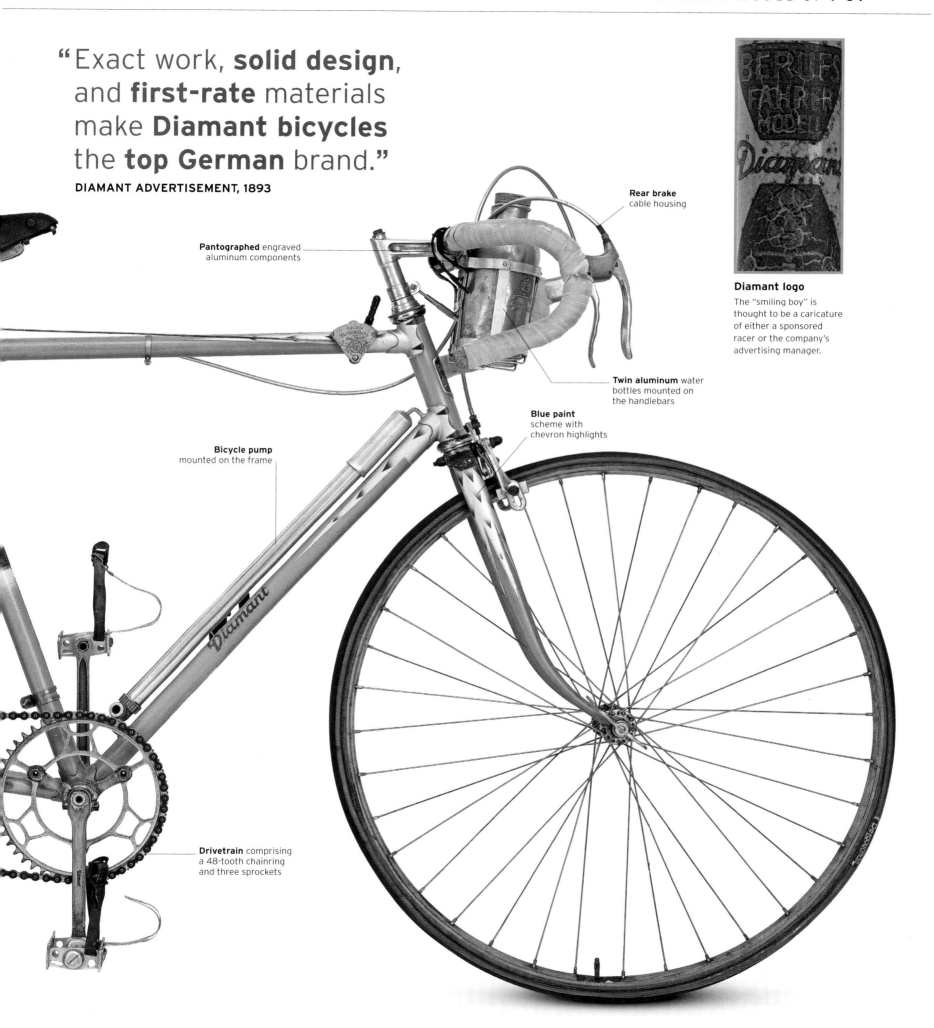

" Exact work, **solid design**, and **first-rate** materials make **Diamant bicycles** the **top German** brand."

DIAMANT ADVERTISEMENT, 1893

Rear brake
cable housing

Pantographed engraved
aluminum components

Diamant logo
The "smiling boy" is thought to be a caricature of either a sponsored racer or the company's advertising manager.

Twin aluminum water bottles mounted on the handlebars

Blue paint
scheme with chevron highlights

Bicycle pump
mounted on the frame

Drivetrain comprising a 48-tooth chainring and three sprockets

THE COMPONENTS

Diamant developed the equipment and in-house expertise to forge own-brand, aluminum-alloy components, allowing the pantographed pedals, cranks, stem, handlebars, seat post, bottle, and wheel wing nuts to take center stage on the Model 67. The wooden-rimmed wheels were the lightest and strongest racing rims available in the 1930s, while the Fichtel & Sachs 3-speed rear derailleur offered reliable, chain-activated gear-shifts.

1. Lohmann leather racing saddle **2.** Fichtel & Sachs 3-speed derailleur with short length of mini-pitch chain **3.** Handlebar with aluminum-alloy brake levers and Diamant-branded bottles **4.** 48-tooth chainring **5.** Fichtel & Sachs gear lever **6.** Aluminum stem with pantographed Diamant branding **7.** SPORLUX caliper brake mounted on front fork **8.** Aluminum-alloy wing nuts

Recumbents and Trikes

The first recumbents were developed soon after the advent of pneumatic-tired safety bicycles. Although the lower seating position meant they were more aerodynamic, they had little commercial impact until the 1930s, when there was a wave of interest, particularly in France. Interest in tricycles diminished rapidly once the safety bicycle became dominant. There was a US-led revival in the 1970s that spread across the Western world.

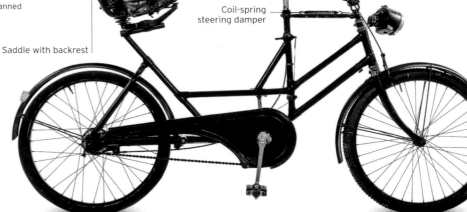

Chater Lea chainring

Toe clips with leather straps

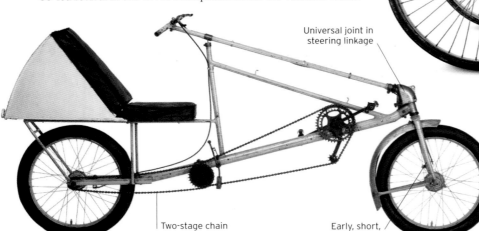

Universal joint in steering linkage

Two-stage chain drive to rear wheel

Early, short, straight front fork

△ Selbach Special Racing Tricycle 1932

Origin	UK
Frame	Steel
Gears	Single speed
Wheels	Front 26 in (65 cm), Rear 27 in (68 cm)

Maurice Selbach was a builder of high-quality lightweight cycles based in southeast London. Many Road Records Association milestones were broken on Selbach racing tricycles, which were very rigid and held the road well. They were also available with tapered tubing.

Wide, low-pressure balloon tire

△ Mochet Velocar 1933

Origin	France
Frame	Steel
Gears	Single speed
Wheels	20 in (50 cm)

French manufacturer Georges Mochet began producing recumbents in the 1930s. The aerodynamic advantage of these bikes was so great that even mediocre riders could win races. Consequently, they were soon banned from mainstream cycling events.

Saddle with backrest

Coil-spring steering damper

▷ Triumph Moller Auto-Cycle 1936

Origin	UK
Frame	Steel
Gears	Single speed
Wheels	22 in (55 cm)

Designed by Danish engineer Holger Møller, the Moller Auto-Cycle was made under license in the UK by Triumph. Like a car, it had a steering wheel, which operated a patented steering system. British champion cyclist Evelyn Hamilton promoted the bike, but few were sold.

Designed for Children

Despite the new vogue for balance bikes kicked by the feet, tricycles were still thought to be necessary to teach children vigorous pedaling. Reminiscent of the cranked Parisian velocipedes, their basic design has changed very little during the last 150 years, apart from "stand-on" models designed to accommodate passengers.

Grub screw to adjust saddle height

Cranks connect directly to front wheel

◁ Child's Tricycle 1913

Origin	UK
Frame	Steel
Gears	Single speed
Wheels	Front 14 in (35 cm), Rear 12 in (30 cm)

This child's tricycle is typical of its time. Like the French velocipedes of the 1860s, this tricycle is propelled via a pair of simple cranks attached to the front wheel. To minimize cost, this machine had solid rubber rather than pneumatic tires.

Gumwall, narrow-section tires

◁ Booth Gents Tricycle 1938

Origin UK

Frame Steel

Gears 3-speed

Wheels 26 in (65 cm)

At a time when most cycle components were made of steel, this high-quality, lightweight racing tricycle featured some aluminum alloy parts. Its Super Champion derailleur gearing was designed by record-breaking Swiss road racer Oscar Egg.

Gear-shift lever

Chain tension arm for derailleur gear

Battery-operated headlight

Wheels covered to match the design of a racing-style airplane

▷ Junior Toy Co. Sky King 1936

Origin US

Frame Steel

Gears Single speed

Wheels Front 15 in (38 cm), Rear 9 in (23 cm)

The concept for this tricycle came from a US radio and TV show based on the adventures of an aircraft pilot called Sky King. With its aerodynamic flair, the tricycle imitated the style of the hero's plane. The example shown here is a modern replica.

Solid rubber tires

In the late 19th century there were many political campaigns around the world led by women, demanding greater equality with men. This coincided with the spread of biking, and the two grew entwined, with the bicycle becoming emblematic of the drive for women's rights. Women took to biking as readily as men, and in 1895, American, Annie Kopchovsky became the first woman to cycle the globe. Women's riding clubs and races, such as this race in 1900s Paris, were common.

Women's Bikes

As bicycles became cheaper and increasingly available, more women gained access to them and the personal freedom they offered. The women's version of the safety bicycle was well established by the early 1900s. The position of its frame and handlebars gave the rider an upright riding position, and the frame's step-through design meant that a woman wearing a dress could easily mount and ride her bike. Additionally, these bicycles were often equipped with a skirt guard to prevent dresses from getting tangled in the rear wheel. Over time, women discarded their restrictive dresses and replaced them with divided skirts or bloomers for bicycle riding.

Elaborately decorated fabric skirt guard

Acetylene gas-operated front light

Enclosed chaincase

Patented kickstand

△ **NSU Damenrad Women's Bicycle 1915**

Origin	Germany
Frame	Steel
Gears	Single speed
Wheels	26 in (65 cm)

Originally a manufacturer of knitting machines, NSU (later renamed Neckarsulmer Fahrzeugwerke AG) began producing bicycles in 1892. Its Damenrad women's bicycle featured a reinforced step-through frame and large-section balloon tires.

◁ **Decker GMBH Edelweiss c. 1935**

Origin	Germany
Frame	Steel
Gears	Single speed
Wheels	26 in (65 cm)

This high-quality bicycle was designed using a twin step-through frame that featured a patented bicycle stand and an unusual "made to measure" leather suitcase attached to the rear carrier. It also had the Eidelweiss model emblem on the seat tube.

▷ **Dawes Efficiency Tourer 1935**

Origin	UK
Frame	Steel
Gears	3-speed
Wheels	26 in (65 cm)

This women's lightweight touring bicycle came with cable-operated caliper brakes. The long wheelbase and frame angles aided stability and the riding position enabled comfort over long distances. The chainguard and mudguards ensured rider protection.

Sports-type slim-cut saddle

Cyclo gear attached to chainstays

Semi-drop handlebars

Sports-type sprung saddle

◁ **BSA Women's Sport Petronella Bicycle 1936**

Origin	UK
Frame	Steel
Gears	3-speed
Wheels	26 in (65 cm)

Women competing in club racing and time-trialing events needed sports bicycles. The Petronella had a short wheelbase, lightweight frame, and 3-speed Sturmey-Archer gears. Its brakes were the powerful caliper-type design.

▽ **S H Cycles Women's Bike 1940s**

Origin	Japan
Frame	Steel
Gears	Single speed
Wheels	26 in (65 cm)

This high-quality women's roadster featured a reinforced step-through frame, with a bolt-on rear carrier and rear-mounted kickstand. The fully enclosed chaincase protected the rider and ensured a long chain life.

Company emblem
Just as many car manufacturers of the time affixed their logos to the front of their vehicles, so many bicycle companies followed suit. The front mudguard of this bike features a rocket-like design.

Wicker basket ensures ample cargo storage

Well-sprung saddle for a comfortable ride

Rod-operated front and rear brakes

Plastic skirt guard on seat stay

◁ **Semler Womens' 1942**

Origin	Netherlands
Frame	Steel
Gears	Single speed
Wheels	26 in (65 cm)

A typical women's roadster, this bicycle featured a cut-away diamond frame with parallel down tubes and a sprung saddle. The skirt guard, chaincase, and mudguards kept the rider safe, clean, and dry. The rack behind the saddle could be used for transporting items.

Coaster rear brake

Alloy chaincase

Great Races
Giro d'Italia 1909

The Giro d'Italia, like the Tour de France, was born out of a battle between two newspapers. From the outset it was a race of brutal distances, brave competitors, and passionate supporters.

Sports newspapers
Illustrated sports newspapers were the primary source of information from the late 19th century until 1960.

Luigi Ganna (left) after the 1909 race
The winner of the inaugural Giro d'Italia is seen here with seventh-place rider Dario Beni (next to him), a race official, and another competitor. The items looped around their shoulders are spare tires.

NEWSPAPERS WERE BIG BUSINESS at the turn of the 20th century since the press was the only way most people could find out what was happening in the world. The Tour de France (see pp.178–79) resulted from a circulation war between two sports newspapers, *L'Auto* and *Le Vélo*. *L'Auto* organized the first Tour in 1903 to boost its circulation, and, within a very short time, its sales outstripped its rival's.

In this case, the two rival Italian papers were the *Corriere della Sera* and *La Gazzetta dello Sport*. The *Corriere* had planned a race, but *La Gazzetta*'s editor, Tullo Morgagni, convinced the paper's owner, Emilio Costamagna, and its cycling editor, Armando Cougnet, to get in first, buoyed by the success of two single-day races the paper had organized: the Milan–San Remo and the Giro di Lombardia. On August 7, 1908, *La Gazzetta* announced its plan for a round-Italy race.

Covering long distances was a big draw in cycling in those days. Most people did not travel far, and in rural areas many rarely left their own villages. The fact that professional cyclists covered massive distances under their own power on relatively simple machines captured people's imaginations.

RIDERS PUSHED TO THEIR LIMITS
The first Giro d'Italia started in Milan on May 13, 1909, with a 248-mile (397-km) stage from Milan to Bologna, and ended on May 30 with a 128-mile (206-km) stage from Turin to Milan. There were six other stages in between: the shortest was 142.5 miles (228 km) and the longest a massive 235-mile (378-km) loop around the top half of the country, with the capital, Rome, at its southernmost tip; thus there were fewer but much longer stages

Crossing the finish line in Milan
Thousands of supporters watched riders complete the final, eighth stage of the first Giro d'Italia. Cyclists competed as independents or in teams. Not all competitors were Italian.

than there are today. Riders covered a total distance of 1,530 miles (2,448 km) in 18 days; 127 of them started, but only 49 made it to the final finish line.

The winner of the first Giro d'Italia was decided on points awarded in the finishing order on every stage. This was done to avoid problems that beset

"My **backside** is on fire."

LUIGI GANNA, WHEN ASKED WHAT HE FELT WHEN HE CROSSED THE FINISH LINE AFTER WINNING

the 1904 Tour de France when biased supporters stopped and held back riders to allow their favorites to gain time. Scoring on points rather than time meant there was no incentive for spectators to get involved in that way. However, it also meant that the winner, Luigi Ganna, was not the quickest rider over the entire course. If the 1909 race had been decided on time (as the race is today) then the third-place rider, Giovanni Rossignoli, would have won by quite a margin.

One issue did affect the first Giro d'Italia—cheating by the riders. Three of them were disqualified before the start of stage three because there was no record of their having passed through control points. It was later discovered that they had covered part of the route by train. However, the race was a great success overall. Huge crowds turned out to watch the riders: an estimated 30,000 watched the Milan finish. Ganna was a worthy winner. He had already won Milan–San Remo that year, and had been fifth in the 1908 Tour de France. His prize money helped him set up a bicycle factory in 1912. This inaugural race boosted *La Gazzetta dello Sport*'s circulation immensely, and it has been an annual event ever since, except during the two world wars.

Champion Felice Gimondi
Seen here in the 1976 Giro d'Italia, the Italian rider is on the final climb, the 9,045-ft (2,757-m) Passo dello Stelvio. Gimondi has won three times and been on the podium nine times.

KEY FACTS

RESULTS

First: Luigi Ganna, Italy
Second: Carlo Galetti, Italy
Third: Giovanni Rossignoli, Italy

THE COURSE

The first Giro avoided the high mountain ranges of Italy that the modern race passes, but there were still some stiff climbs, including the ascents to Roccaraso, Rionero Sannitico, and Macerone on stage three between Naples and Chieti, the steep Passo Bracco on stage six from Florence to Genoa, and the Colle di Nava on stage seven from Genoa to Turin. As well as top Italian racers, other competitors included the French rider Lucien Petit-Breton and the Belgian Cyriel Van Hauwaert, so the first Giro d'Italia was a truly international race.

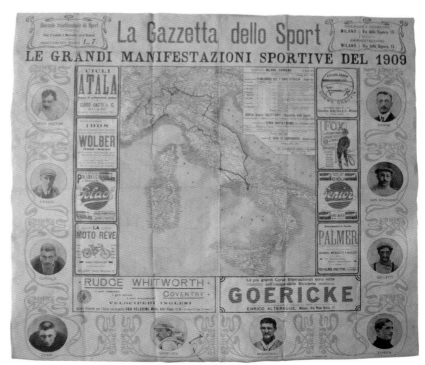

Front page of *La Gazzetta dello Sport*, August 7, 1908
To support the announcement of the new race, the paper also carried advertisements for the race sponsors, which were either bicycle or tire manufacturers.

Bikes for a Purpose

In the early 1880s, bicycles were already being used for utilitarian purposes by individuals, small businesses, and large organizations. As cycling became widespread, so the variety of purposes for which they could be used increased. Specialist machines were built for sports use, such as bicycle football and hockey. Individual designs for bicycles that could make work easier were also developed. Shopkeepers and service providers realized that they could use bicycles to market their goods over a wider area, thus increasing sales. Telephone orders could also be dispatched within hours with the use of bicycles.

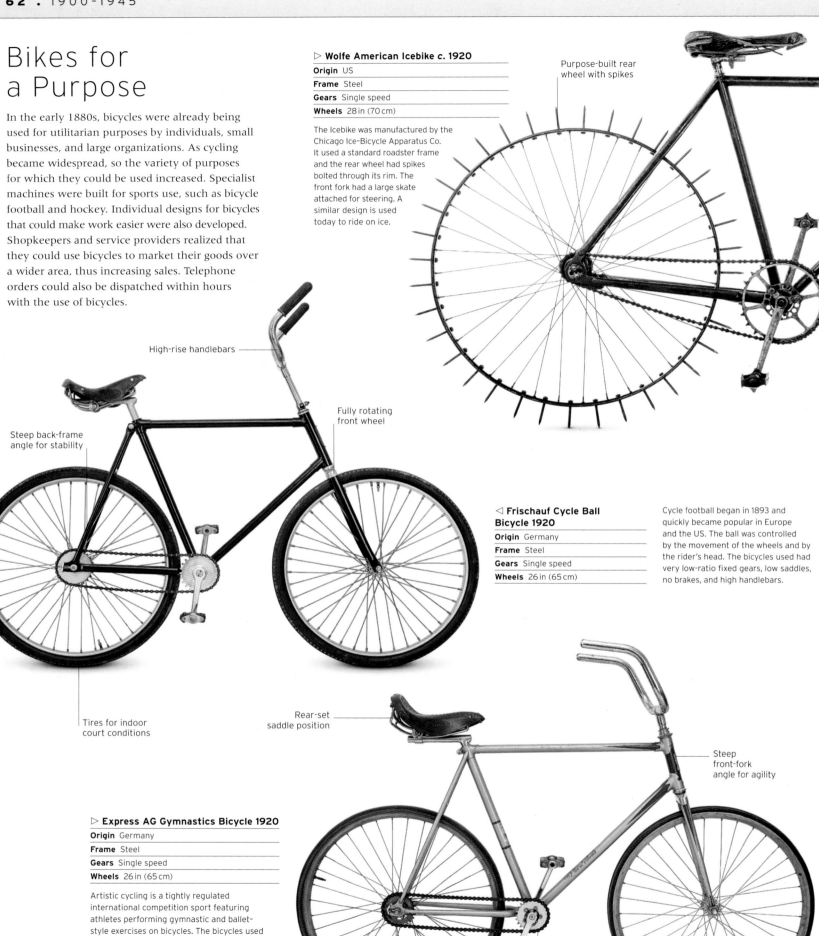

▷ **Wolfe American Icebike *c.* 1920**

Origin US

Frame Steel

Gears Single speed

Wheels 28 in (70 cm)

The Icebike was manufactured by the Chicago Ice-Bicycle Apparatus Co. It used a standard roadster frame and the rear wheel had spikes bolted through its rim. The front fork had a large skate attached for steering. A similar design is used today to ride on ice.

Purpose-built rear wheel with spikes

High-rise handlebars

Steep back-frame angle for stability

Fully rotating front wheel

Tires for indoor court conditions

◁ **Frischauf Cycle Ball Bicycle 1920**

Origin Germany

Frame Steel

Gears Single speed

Wheels 26 in (65 cm)

Cycle football began in 1893 and quickly became popular in Europe and the US. The ball was controlled by the movement of the wheels and by the rider's head. The bicycles used had very low-ratio fixed gears, low saddles, no brakes, and high handlebars.

Rear-set saddle position

Steep front-fork angle for agility

▷ **Express AG Gymnastics Bicycle 1920**

Origin Germany

Frame Steel

Gears Single speed

Wheels 26 in (65 cm)

Artistic cycling is a tightly regulated international competition sport featuring athletes performing gymnastic and ballet-style exercises on bicycles. The bicycles used must conform to an exact specification.

Very low-ratio fixed gear

Low handlebars to increase front-end grip

Handbrake for rear wheel

Rear mudguard

WAFER BISCUITS 1ᴰ

STOP ME AND BUY ONE

T. WALL & SONS LTD THE FRIARY, ACTON

T/65

WALL'S ICE CREAM

PURE DAIRY PRODUCTS
FRESH FRUIT JUICES
SOUND FOOD VALUE

LARGE BRICKS 1/6
SMALL BRICKS 9ᴰ
TUBS 4ᴰ
CHOC BARS 3ᴰ
BRICKETTES 2ᴰ
SNOFRUTES 1ᴰ

Large front skate rail

Solid front tires

△ **Wall's Ice Cream Delivery Tricycle** *c.* 1930

Origin	UK
Frame	Steel
Gears	Single speed
Wheels	28 in (70 cm)

The commercial tricycle was used by tradesmen of all types. Wall's introduced its first Ice Cream Delivery Tricycle in 1923, and by 1939 there were 4,000 on the road. There were two makers of these tricycles: Warrick & Co. and Alldays & Onions.

Fully sprung saddle for comfort

Strong, twin-tubed stepover frame

Large front carrier and wicker basket

HALFORDS CYCLES

Advertising panel

◁ **Halfords Vanette 1937**

Origin	UK
Frame	Steel
Gears	Single speed
Wheels	Front 18 in (45 cm), Rear 26 in (65 cm)

The Halfords Co. manufactured and distributed components for the auto trade. They also made bicycles and had a fleet of "Vanettes" to deliver their goods to customers. With its stepover frame, large front carrier rack, and comfortable saddle, this bicycle was used extensively in the UK.

Front rack for mailbag

Waterproof rubber saddle

Front and rear battery lights

▷ **G.P.O. Elswick Gents' Carrier 1938**

Origin	UK
Frame	Steel
Gears	Single speed
Wheels	24 in (60 cm)

The British red postman's bicycle was one of the best-known carrier cycles. Specially developed for its purpose, several manufacturers made them to the Post Office's specification. These bicycles were robust and made from durable materials.

Bicycles at War

Bicycle-mounted infantry messengers and ambulance carriers were used extensively during WWI. Bicycles were popular on account of the fact that they were light, quiet, and, unlike horses, did not require feeding. The models used at the time were normal roadsters, with front carriers, rifle clips, an inflator pump, and puncture repair outfits. Through WWII, bicycle use in Europe was limited mainly to messenger duties and air-drop operations, which involved paratroopers jumping out of planes with specially designed folded bicycles to reach comrades behind enemy lines. Bicycles continued to be used widely by the military after WWII, especially in Asia, and the last dedicated bicycle infantry unit, belonging to the Swiss army, was disbanded in 2003.

Detachable carrying case

Swiss army license plate

Toolkit bag

Rear coaster brake

△ **Militärvelo MO5 c. 1940**

Origin	Switzerland
Frame	Steel
Gears	Single speed
Wheels	26 in (65 cm)

First produced in 1905, this model was used by the Swiss army until 1989. Designed to carry equipment, it featured a heavy-duty frame onto which cases and racks were attached. In order to stop when loaded, it also had three types of brakes.

▽ **Royal Enfield Rifle Bike c. 1940**

Origin	UK
Frame	Steel
Gears	Single speed
Wheels	28 in (70 cm)

This special military model was basically a standard roadster bicycle with a rear carrier, rifle clips, and heavy-duty tires. It had a sprung saddle, stove-enameled paintwork, and rubber pedal grips. Gearing was limited to a single-speed freewheel.

Mounting clip for rifle

Heavy-duty tread tire

Rear carrier for small loads

Rear coaster brake

Battery-operated
dry-cell light

Heavy-duty tire

◁ Columbia Bike 1941

Origin	US
Frame	Steel
Gears	Single speed
Wheels	26 in (65 cm)

The Columbia featured heavy-duty spokes and wheel rims fitted with balloon tires. The twin top tubes gave the bicycle extra strength, enabling it to carry payloads weighing up to 200 lb (91 kg). The bike itself weighed 55 lb (25 kg).

BSA MK2 Para
Bike folded for
transportation

Cable operates
brakes

Folding frame
secured by
wing nuts

Heavy-duty wheel

△ BSA MK2 Para Bike 1943

Origin	UK
Frame	Steel
Gears	Single speed
Wheels	26 in (65 cm)

This model was specially developed for and used in all major airborne landings during WWII including D-Day and Arnhem. Paratroopers could fold the bicycle in half and carry it with them as they jumped from aircraft. Once on the ground, they could easily unfold the bike for use.

Rubber handlebar grip

Rear-mounted
kickstand

◁ Schwinn Military Touring WWII 1940s

Origin	US
Frame	Steel
Gears	Single speed
Wheels	26 in (65 cm)

Founded in 1895, the Schwinn Co. was noted for its high standards of bicycle construction. Its Military Touring model featured an all-welded frame, chainguard, and kickstand. Braking was provided by a rear coaster hub brake. Schwinn produced 10,000 of these bicycles per year during WWII.

Le Parisien *libéré*

LE FILM OFFICIEL DU

TOUR DE FRANCE 49

L'ÉQUIPE

THE GOLDEN AGE

In the wake of World War II, during which the bicycle had enjoyed a resurgence thanks to its affordability and practicality, sales of new machines rose throughout Europe in a brief wave of optimism. US soldiers returning home helped to spread new trends, bringing a taste for lightweight, geared European bicycles to a market unaccustomed to such quality. But the boom was dampened as postwar prosperity ushered in new forms of recreation—cars, shopping malls, and movie theaters all eroded the public interest in pursuits tinged with the austerity and hardship of those wartime years.

△ **1950 Cyclo-Cross World Championships**
Unlike traditional road racing, cyclo-cross requires riders to negotiate a variety of challenging surfaces, from grass to steps.

The bicycle's gradual decline in popular use contrasted with the road-racing scene, which entered its golden age. The centerpieces of the racing calendar—from hard-fought, one-day "classics," such as the cobbled, springtime Paris-Roubaix race, to excruciating, three-week "Grand Tours," foremost of which was the Tour de France—were by now well established. It was in the postwar era that the first superstars of the sport emerged, such as the flamboyant Italian Fausto Coppi. The young upstart to his elder rival Gino Bartali, Coppi rode with elegance and style, and celebrated success off the bike with similar panache, bringing Hollywood-style glamour to the world of cycling for the first time.

Around the world, the Japanese bicycle industry—long a skilled follower of overseas technological trends—began to challenge the powerhouses of Germany, the UK, and the US. The bicycle itself still carried European colonialist overtones, but its usefulness as a working tool was beginning to be appreciated by local populations in many developing countries.

> **"**He seems to **caress the handlebars,** while his torso seems **fixed by screws** in the saddle. His long legs **stretch** to the pedals like the **limbs** of a gazelle.**"**
>
> ANDRÉ LEDUCQ, FORMER TOUR DE FRANCE WINNER, DESCRIBING FAUSTO COPPI

Key Events

▷ **1940** Tungsten Inert Gas (TIG) welding, a precise method of joining metal tubing, is first used to build bicycle frames, following its invention in the aerospace industry.

▷ **1940s** Bicycles play a part in the steady sprawl of cities across Asia, providing transportation for workers and a means for businesses to operate.

▷ **1947** The first postwar Tour de France is won by a Frenchman, Jean Robic.

▷ **1950** Forty years after the birth of cyclo-cross in northern Europe, the first World Championships is held in Paris.

▷ **1951** Campagnolo releases the Gran Sport, a parallelogram-design rear derailleur that vastly improves on existing gear-shifting devices.

▷ **1956** Japanese manufacturer Shimano releases its first derailleur gear-shift mechanism after decades of producing 3-speed hub gears.

△ **Off-road racing**
BMX became a mainstream sport in the 1970s, but its origins can be traced back to the 1950s in the Netherlands, where organized races took place.

▷ **1958** Women's cycling is recognized at world championship level, with road and track events being contested.

▷ **1958** The Chinese bicycle industry reaches the Communist party's target of 1 million machines.

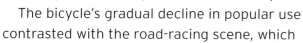
◁ **A poster for the 1949 Tour de France** won by Italian Fausto Coppi in a time of 145 hours and 36 minutes.

Racing Bikes

Postwar Europe witnessed a revival in bicycle racing despite austerity. Bicycles became lighter and stiffer, with nearly all high-end frames constructed from Reynolds 531—a type of steel tubing made by Reynolds in Birmingham. The tubing remained a standard of excellence for many decades and the choice of many high-quality frame-builders. Alloy component manufacturers refined their products, leading to a marked improvement in the reliability of gearing and braking. The resurgence of six-day racing across velodromes in Europe during the winter drew big crowds, and several manufacturers set up cycle teams to promote their products to the masses.

Cloth-taped, deep-drop handlebars

△ **Schwinn Paramount 1940s**

Origin	US
Frame	Steel
Gears	Single speed
Wheels	27 in (68 cm)

The Paramount was a highly sought-after model among American racers. The high-quality frames were handmade in Chicago and offered in a range of custom options including full chrome plating for a sparkling mirror finish.

Round-tubed Columbus steel

Slim race tires for reduced friction

Treaded tubular tires on cotton canvas

◁ **Cinelli Pista 1947**

Origin	Italy
Frame	Steel
Gears	Single speed
Wheels	27 in (68 cm)

Italian builders chose Italian tube-maker Columbus rather than British Reynolds. The result, they claimed, was a high-quality lightweight machine that offered a unique ride. Cinelli chose reinforced round chrome fork blades, providing additional stiffness.

Alloy brake levers

Center-pull alloy brake

▷ **Thanet Silverlight 1948**

Origin	UK
Frame	Steel
Gears	Single speed
Wheels	27 in (68 cm)

Expensive and slow sellers, Thanet's most famous model was the Silverlight frame with cradled bottom bracket and crossover seat stays. The early builds had silver-soldered brackets that proved to be weak, and later frames used lugs to strengthen the joints.

Police patrol bike 1940s

RSW Compact 1965

Chopper MKII 1972

Raleigh TI 1980s

1885 Richard Woodhead and Paul Angois open their workshop on Raleigh Street, Nottingham.

1888 Three Raleigh models—two roadsters and a tricycle—are exported for sale in France.

1889 The Raleigh Cycle Company is registered as the firm's official name.

1893 Raleigh's expansion is so rapid that it rents several premises on streets adjacent to its original Raleigh Street workshop.

1894 Company founders Woodhead and Angois leave Raleigh's board of directors, handing complete control of the company to Frank Bowden.

1901 Marketing slogan "The All-Steel Bicycle" is used for the first time.

1908 Sturmey-Archer hub gear introduced with combined coaster brake.

1926 3,000 bicycles are made every week at the Nottingham factory, which produces its own gas and electricity, and draws water from its own wells.

1939 British cyclist Tommy Godwin rides a Raleigh while covering 75,065 miles (120,805 km) in 365 days, a record that still stands.

1948 Raleigh factory opens in Boston, MA, followed by facilities in India, South Africa, Canada, West Germany, and Malaysia over the next 20 years.

1953 More than 100,000 bicycles are produced annually at Raleigh's Nottingham factories.

1963 The number of Raleigh employees around the world reaches 12,000.

1965 Raleigh Small Wheel developed in answer to the Moulton F-Frame.

1970 Raleigh Chopper launched in the UK.

1980 Raleigh becomes the first—and still only—UK bicycle brand to win the Tour de France.

1990s Raleigh's M-Trax mountain bikes cater to the growth in off-road cycling.

2012 Raleigh is acquired by Dutch bicycle group Accell.

children's bike—the Raleigh Chopper. It went on sale in the UK in 1970 and was an instant hit, selling 1.5 million units in the UK alone during the ten years of its manufacturing.

Raleigh's other headline-grabbing move in the 1970s was to sponsor a professional cycling team for the first time. The TI-Raleigh team won a phenomenal 50 races in its first season of 1974, and went on to win the Tour de France with Dutch cyclist Joop Zoetemelk in 1980—the only time that the race has been won on a British bicycle.

Raleigh found itself fighting decline in the 1980s as competition from cheaper Asian bicycle producers saw sales slide at home and abroad. TI sold the Raleigh brand in 1987 to the Luxembourg-based corporation Derby International, which sold the Nottingham factory site in 1999 without securing new premises.

Raleigh's UK-based frame-building operation ceased, and, four years later, bicycle assembly also came to a halt. The Raleigh division of bicycles is now owned by the Dutch bicycle group Accell. While its manufacturing heart is no longer located in Nottingham, Raleigh retains a design and distribution site in the former hub of the UK cycle industry.

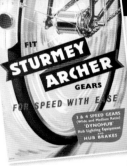

Raleigh's successes
Posters advertise the Sturmey-Archer hub gear and the children's Chopper.

Leisure and Utility Bikes

For European countries involved in World War II, the period from the end of hostilities until the end of the 1950s saw cycling boom and bust. Having satisfied pent-up demand in the immediate postwar period, the industry went into steep decline. As national economies improved, people turned to mopeds, scooters, and cars. Utility bikes were designed to be low-maintenance and to be ridden in ordinary clothes, for business or pleasure, but specifications and preferences varied widely from country to country. Europeans tended to use the same bike to commute, shop, or for leisure activities, while Americans cycled mostly for pleasure.

Kromegard luggage rack

Polished aluminum frame

Constant-tension, double-spring fork

Gear lever mounted on handlebar

Full chaincase

△ Monark Silver King 1948

Origin	US
Frame	Aluminum alloy
Gears	Single speed
Wheels	26 in (65 cm)

The Silver King bicycle had been around since 1934 and was made of heat-treated aluminum alloy. The 1948 version featured hex tubing, which made the bike stronger and lighter overall.

◁ Raleigh Roadster 1950s

Origin	UK
Frame	Steel
Gears	3-speed
Wheels	26 in (65 cm)

Roadster-style bicycles were Raleigh's best-selling bikes during this period, and it offered a wide range of models. The Sports Tourists featured Sturmey-Archer hub gears, Dynohub lighting, and a leather Brooks saddle. A women's model was also available.

Rear luggage rack

Dynamo driven by front wheel

▷ Miele Melior 1950

Origin	Germany
Frame	Steel
Gears	Single speed
Wheels	26 in (65 cm)

Miele started making bicycles in the 1920s, producing a wide range of models. Its 1950 Touring model was noted for strength and reliability. It featured a rear luggage rack, a chainguard, and a dynamo driven by the front wheel to power lighting.

"Bianchi Celeste is the most distinctive color scheme in the sport."

BIANCHI, ON ITS BLUE-GREEN LIVERY

Aluminum alloy brake lever

Bianchi logo

The Bianchi logo features the founder's name emblazoned across an eagle and crown, symbols of the House of Savoy, the Italian royal family.

Bianchi-made threaded headset

Bianchi Celeste paint scheme, said to derive from the eye color of Queen Margherita of Savoy

Chromium-plated lugs for the head tube

Custom-made steel crankset on the original Paris-Roubaix featured a trio of Bianchi "Bs" arranged around the chainring

Clips and straps to hold racer's feet to the pedals

THE COMPONENTS

Many of the original parts that adorned the Paris–Roubaix were custom-made for Bianchi by other Italian manufacturers. The stem and handlebars were produced by Ambrosio and engraved with the Bianchi name, while the hubs listed as Bianchi were almost certainly manufactured by either Campagnolo or Fratelli Brivio. The lightweight aluminum wheel rims were produced by Nisi of Turin.

1. Brooks leather saddle with spare tire   **2.** Campagnolo Paris–Roubaix derailleur and toothed rear dropout   **3.** Universal brake levers with rubber padded hood covers, mounted on Coppi steel handlebars with Bianchi stem **4.** Campagnolo gear-shifter   **5.** Down-tube-mounted pump   **6.** Bianchi racing pedals with clips and straps   **7.** Universal caliper brake   **8.** Front hub with Campagnolo quick-release lever

1

3

2

4

American Children's Bikes

Having eagerly adopted affordable cycling, the US then became the first nation to abandon the bike in favor of the automobile after World War II. Attempts to revive the American market for adult bicycles had little success, so the US cycle industry focused on selling machines as playthings for juveniles. Bikes became kinetic toys, sometimes cashing in on the popularity of cartoon characters and often imitating the motorcycles that young riders aspired to.

"It's **low-cost transportation** and it helps **boys make money."**

HORACE HUFFMAN ABOUT THE PAPERBOY'S BIKE

▽ **Huffy Radio Bike 1955**

Origin	US
Frame	Steel
Gears	Single speed
Wheels	26 in (65 cm)

Built by the Huffman Manufacturing Co. of Dayton Ohio, this bicycle had a tube-type radio in the "tank." The bike was available in red, blue, or green. It was dropped from the Huffy range after 18 months; around 8,500 were built.

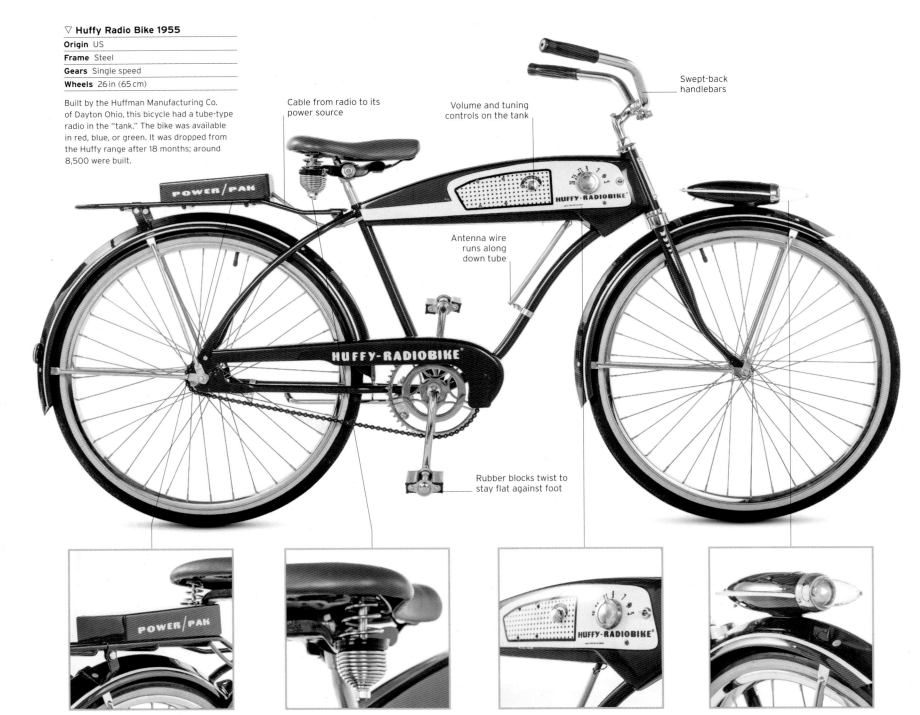

Cable from radio to its power source

Volume and tuning controls on the tank

Swept-back handlebars

Antenna wire runs along down tube

Rubber blocks twist to stay flat against foot

Radio power source
Made of thin metal, the radio's "Power/Pak" was attached to the rear rack of the bicycle and powered by triple-life A and B batteries.

Comfortable seats
Along with the large tires, the well-padded and fully sprung seat ensured a smooth and comfortable ride—ideal for cruising the streets.

Music on the move
A three-vacuum-tube radio was built into each bicycle. The radio featured a volume control, tuner, and powerful antenna that could tune in stations up to 100 miles (160 km) away.

Futuristic headlight
The battery-powered light attached to the front mudguard emitted a golden yellow light. Its design was reminiscent of the Space Age styling featured in *The Jetsons*.

Friction lock seat post

Back-pedal coaster brake

◁ **Huffy Convertible Super Girls' Model 1949**

Origin US

Frame Steel

Gears Single speed

Wheels 20 in (50 cm)

This was the first Huffman product to be called a Huffy and it had a huge impact on the US market for children's bikes. A key feature was the small-diameter balloon tire, which meant that the bicycle was in scale with its rider.

Decorative tank feature

Curved braces reinforced front fork

Coaster brake

▷ **Huffy Convertible Super Boys' Model 1949**

Origin US

Frame Steel

Gears Single speed

Wheels 20 in (50 cm)

This bicycle was called the Huffy Convertible because it could have training wheels bolted to the rear axle, which could then be removed when a child had learned to balance and cycle unaided by him- or herself.

One-piece crankset

Sprung and padded leather saddle

Eyes flashed at the touch of a button

◁ **Shelby Donald Duck Bicycle 1949**

Origin US

Frame Steel

Gears Single speed

Wheels 20 in (50 cm) or 24 in (60 cm)

This bicycle was a commercial success for the Shelby Cycle Co. A children's favorite, it was the first to tie in with Walt Disney's character of Donald Duck, whose head below the handlebars had a quack-quack horn and flashing eyes.

Chainguard painted to match

Spaceship-style headlight

Elaborate fake "fuel" tank

▷ **J C Higgins Girls' Balloon Tire Bicycle 1950s**

Origin US

Frame Steel

Gears Single speed

Wheels 20 in (50 cm)

J C Higgins was a brand name used by US mail order company, Sears Roebuck. This bicycle was built in girls' and boys' versions. The pseudo-motorcycle styling features front suspension, rear-wheel fairing, and streamlined rear rack.

Touring Bikes

From its very advent, the bicycle opened up the opportunity for independent travel. Over time, touring bicycles were included in the catalogs of all major manufacturers. Touring on two wheels rapidly gained popularity in Europe during the 1930s due to the rising affluence of the working classes and the influence of the Outdoor Movement. Touring bikes were designed to be ridden comfortably over extended distances and typically had a long wheelbase for stability. Front and rear mudguards were essential, as was the provision for carrying some luggage. These bicycles also had a wide range of gears to cope with different terrains.

Sturmey-Archer hub gear

Lightweight frame

Cable-operated caliper brakes

△ Maclean Club Model 1948

Origin	UK
Frame	Steel
Gears	3- or 4-speed
Wheels	Front 26 in (65 cm), Rear 27 in (68 cm)

The Maclean Co. was formed in 1922. Its Club Model frames were made using Reynolds 531 tubing—a combination of manganese, molybdenum, and carbon steel. The bicycles were built to the buyer's specification with either derailleur or Sturmey-Archer gears.

▽ R O Harrison 1950

Origin	UK
Frame	Steel
Gears	5-speed
Wheels	26 in (65 cm)

Founded in 1933, R O Harrison Cycles was a London-based manufacturer of high-quality, classic lightweight frames. Its 1950 model had a typical touring fork rake and frame angles, and came equipped with pump hanger pegs.

Twin tubes
Bicycle frames needed to be lightweight and rigid, and many manufacturers of the time produced frames with twin top-, seat-, or down tubes.

Battery power
The earliest lights were illuminated by a flame, fueled by oil or carbide, and could be dangerous. Battery-powered lights were not only safer, but also produced more light.

Saddlebag for carrying tools and refreshments

Alloy handlebar stem

Chrome-finished fork ends

Pedal clips prevent shoes from slipping

Double chainring crankset with cable-operated front derailleur

◁ Maclean Ekla 1949

Origin UK

Frame Steel

Gears 10-speed

Wheels 27 in (68 cm)

This top-of-the-line bicycle was made using high-quality Ekla decorative lugs and fork crowns brazed onto the Reynolds 531 tubes. It was equipped with 10-speed derailleur gears, a Brooks saddle, and Weinmann brakes with hooded levers.

▷ E & P Stricker 1950

Origin Germany

Frame Steel

Gears 3-speed

Wheels 26 in (65 cm)

Made by E & P Stricker of Bielefeld, Germany, this was a typical example of the Western European postwar touring bicycle. It featured a kickstand, an alloy chainguard, and a sprung seatpost for extra comfort when riding.

Toolkit clipped to frame

Pump pegs brazed onto seat tube

Front drum brake

Saddlebag

Battery-powered lamp

Rear derailleur

◁ Gillott Clubman Touring Bike 1951

Origin UK

Frame Steel

Gears 3-speed

Wheels 27 in (68 cm)

Renowned worldwide for high-quality craftsmanship and attention to detail, A S Gillott produced bicycles for competition, club riding, and touring from its shop in Camberwell, London. This Clubman model featured wheels with alloy rims and large flange hubs, as well as alloy brakes to reduce weight.

The Flying Pigeon, based on the UK's 1932 Raleigh Roadster, began production in July 1950. Workers had been asked to design a strong, durable, and light machine, and this one was the brainchild of a worker named Huo Baoji. It was adopted as the approved form of transportation within the People's Republic of China, and the country became known as the kingdom of bicycles. Bicycles were one of the three must-haves for every citizen, the other two being a sewing machine and a watch.

Bikes at Work

As early as 1881, tricycles were used by the British postal service to deliver packages and letters, and the bicycle too was quickly adapted to carry goods. Purpose-built designs were introduced, enabling bikes to deliver various types of goods, messages, and newspapers. Butchers and bakers delivered their products on bikes, craftsmen used them to carry their tools when they worked on customers' premises, and military forces adopted them for light transport duties. As cities grew congested with vehicles, bicycles became a convenient alternative because they were easy to maneuver, took up less parking space, and did not require costly fuel.

Pedal-powered grinding wheel
A stone grindwheel was driven by a secondary belt connected to the rear bicycle wheel. The wheel could be used to sharpen a range of tools, from knives to axes.

▷ **Knife Sharpener's Bicycle 1950s**

Origin	Germany
Frame	Steel
Gears	Single speed
Wheels	65 cm (26 in)

Knife sharpeners used special bicycles that not only helped them reach their customers but also powered grindstones. Used across the world, these bikes were based on normal roadsters but had an additional drive mechanism to rotate the grindwheel. They were also equipped with carriers for tools and water.

Drive mechanism for grindwheel

Grindwheel bolted to handlebars or stem

Sprung saddle

Hard-wearing pneumatic tires

Stand and rack
The rear rack was easily converted to a kickstand by the operator. The rack would swing around onto the floor and suspend the rear wheel, providing a stable base when sharpening tools.

Toolkit
A frame-mounted metal case was integrated into the shape of the bicycle frame. The box housed the worker's tools, and a hinge on the side of the box allowed easy access to the contents.

Chainring
This bicycle featured an ornate five-arm, chrome-plated chainring. The cover was designed to stop the rider's clothes, and any metal from the grinding wheel, from jamming the bicycle chain.

Bottle dynamo
This unit resembled a bottle and created power for a front light. A roller placed on the sidewall of the bicycle tire would engage when the wheel moved forward, generating electricity.

Frame-mounted gear lever

SOUTHERN RAILWAY PARCEL DELIVERY SERVICE FROM HORSTED KEYNES STATION

Heavy-duty wheel and tire

◁ **Pashley Delibike 1948**

Origin UK

Frame Steel

Gears 3-speed

Wheels Front 20 in (50 cm), Rear 26 in (65 cm)

This bicycle was designed for making deliveries, and featured a large wicker basket mounted above a small front wheel. It had a retractable front stand and a reinforced frame. Rider comfort was aided by a sprung saddle and rubber grips on the handlebar.

Small front wheel allows for basket

Rear carrier for patrolman's tools

▷ **Triumph RAC Patrolman's Bicycle 1950s**

Origin UK

Frame Steel

Gears Single speed

Wheels 26 in (65 cm)

This 1950s Triumph was used by patrolmen of the Royal Automobile Club (RAC), which provided roadside assistance to motorists in the UK. Based on heavy-duty roadster models, it had a rear rack for tools and displayed the organization's badge.

Heavy-duty wheel and tire

Rear luggage rack

◁ **Bismarck Cargo Bicycle 1950s**

Origin Germany

Frame Steel

Gears Single speed

Wheels Front 18 in (45 cm), Rear 26 in (65 cm)

This purpose-built carrier was produced by Bismarck, a renowned bicycle manufacturer known for its high-quality and durable machines. It featured a reinforced step-through frame, front and rear carriers, and a sprung saddle. The kickstand provided stability when loading.

Rear coaster brake

Kickstand

▷ **Schwinn Typhoon Circus High-Wire Bike 1959**

Origin US

Frame Steel

Gears Single speed

Wheels 26 in (65 cm)

Based on a Schwinn cruiser, this bicycle was adapted for high-wire circus riding. The wheels were made of solid wood with a slot running around the circumference to retain the wire. The fork and handlebars could be made immovable.

Grooved wheels
The wooden wheels featured deep grooves that helped the rider stay on the high-wire cable.

Fork and handlebars fixed in straight-ahead position

Low-ratio, fixed-gear drive

Great Races
Cyclo-Cross World Championships 1950

Modern cyclo-cross races are held in park or woodland circuits, but they once took place in the center of many towns and cities, where they were highly popular. One race held in Paris, France, the Critérium International de Cyclo-cross, became the first official cyclo-cross world championship event.

A poster advertising the 1954 cyclo-cross championships in Geneva

THE SPORT OF CYCLO-CROSS began in the early 1900s as a winter activity for road racers. The races were single-lap courses that took in several villages over a wide area. Riders were left to find their own route, and the only rules were that they had to go through the villages in a specified order and that they were not allowed to use roads. As the riders navigated between places using the church towers or spires, the races became known as steeplechases. As the sport developed, with more competitors joining in, and spectators wanting to watch, organizers started using circuits in woods and parks, and even towns and cities, where street obstacles mixed up the terrain. The latter proved very popular because they were accessible to spectators.

The famous Critérium International de Cyclo-cross was introduced in 1924 in Lille, northeastern France, but moved to Paris in 1934 and became an annual event until 1939, when, like many cycling races in France and French-speaking Belgium, including the Tour de France, it was suspended with the start of World War II because it was too difficult to organize. However, once the Germans had gained control of occupied France, they encouraged some racing, hoping that it might help win over local hearts and minds. The Critérium International de Cyclo-cross was one of the races allowed, and it started again

Robert Oubron

French rider Oubron (right) won the Critérium International de Cyclo-cross a record four times between 1937 and 1942. He was cyclo-cross champion of France five times, but missed out in the first-ever world championships.

in 1941 and was held on a circuit in the Montmartre district of Paris. The circuit itself was around 4,921 ft (1,500 m) long and very hilly—there were no flat sections. It included city streets, a strip of off-road through Square Willette, and the steps that lead up to the famous Basilica de Sacré Coeur. The riders raced over a total distance of 10.5 miles (17 km) and had to run up and down some 1,400 stone steps, carrying their bicycles on their shoulders. The race was suspended again in 1942, but returned in 1947.

In 1949 the race was switched to the Plateau de Gravelle, still in Paris, but this time in an area that provided more off-road riding in the Bois de Vincennes. As before, it was a multi-lap course and, apart from the road start and finish, it used woodland trails and open parkland, with one very steep descent into and out of the *Trou du Diable* (Devil's Hole). It was quite a tough course, with a lot more natural obstacles than are found on a modern cyclo-cross course, including large boulders that riders had to scramble up and down.

The Critérium International de Cyclo-cross had long been regarded as an unofficial cyclo-cross world championship

and it became the official World Championships in 1950. Ridden on the Plateau de Gravelle course in Paris, it was won by a Frenchman Jean Robic, who knew the course well because he had raced on it the previous year. Robic led a clean sweep of four French riders to take the second biggest victory of his career after the 1947 Tour de France.

> "**I knew I would win.** Roger Rondeaux offered a certain **resistance**, but I was **confident** I would **beat him.**"

JEAN ROBIC, NEVER A BELIEVER IN FALSE MODESTY

Carrying the bikes up the steps to Sacré Coeur
Cyclo-cross riders have to carry their bicycles along the
sections that they cannot ride, even in modern races.
On every lap of the 1950 Montmartre circuit, riders were
faced with several long flights of stone steps. The longest
was the stretch that runs parallel to the funicular railway
that climbs to the Basilica of Sacré Coeur.

Champion Erwin Vervecken leads the 2008 Belgian championship
Belgians dominate the world in men's cyclo-cross racing to such an extent
that it can be as hard to win their national cyclo-cross championship titles
as it is to win the world title. In the last 20 years, Belgium has won a total
of 12 men's world titles, while the Netherlands (in second place in the
ranking) has won four.

KEY FACTS

RESULTS
First: Jean Robic, France
Second: Roger Rondeaux, France
Third: Pierre Jodet, France

RACE EVOLUTION
The Critérium International de Cyclo-cross moved from Lille,
in eastern France, to Paris in 1934. The race was held on a variety
of circuits until 1941, when the street circuit in the spectacular
Montmartre district was first used. This area remained home to
the race until 1949, when it switched to the Plateau de Gravelle
circuit near the Bois de Vincennes in southeastern Paris because
this location provided more off-road riding. It was on this circuit
that, when the Union Cycliste Internationale began to regulate the
event, the Critérium International de Cyclo-cross was designated
the first official cyclo-cross world championship in 1950.

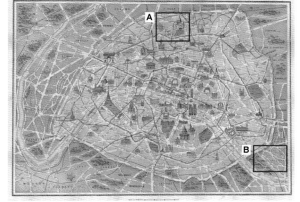

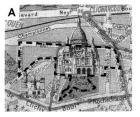

The two courses
Map A (inset) shows the early route around Montmartre and the
Sacré Coeur. Map B (inset) shows the area covered by the Plateau
de Gravelle circuit in southeastern Paris.

Tandems

In the UK and other European countries involved in World War II, the period from the end of hostilities until 1959 saw a cycling boom-and-bust: having initially satisfied the pent-up demand put on hold by the war, the bicycle industry then went into steep decline. As the economy improved and people turned to motorized transport—mopeds, scooters, motorcycles, and cars—struggling British cycle-makers were not interested in tandems, though a few specialists did build custom machines. In Germany and the US, major manufacturers also produced a few tandems, since it was thought riding two-up could be fun for couples and kids.

Curved seat tube allows shorter wheelbase

Two sets of twin lateral braces

Full coverage front and rear fenders

Twin chainring

Powering a tandem
Having two riders means there is twice the leg-power to drive a tandem, but also a greater weight to propel. To overcome this, many touring tandems featured gears.

△ **Rensch Curved Seat Tube Tandem** *c.* 1948

Origin	UK
Frame	Steel
Gears	5-speed
Wheels	27 in (68 cm)

Harry Rensch started building bikes under his own name in London in the 1930s. By 1940, he was producing tandems with a curved ST to enable a short wheelbase and two pairs of thin lateral frame braces. Rensch launched Paris Cycles in 1943.

▷ **Bauer Women's Tandem 1949**

Origin	Germany
Frame	Steel
Gears	3-speed
Wheels	26 in (65 cm)

The Bauer-Werke company was founded in 1911 by Ludwig Bauer in Frankfurt-Heddernheim, Germany, and it began producing bicycles in 1922. Bauer offered a complete range of models from everyday bikes and tandems like this one to racing machines.

Sprung saddle for extra comfort

Hub dynamo

Sprung rear saddle
for extra comfort

Twin lateral bracing
from head tube to
rear dropout

Drop handlebars

Both chains on
same side of bike

△ Paris Touring Tandem 1950

Origin	UK
Frame	Steel
Gears	10-speed
Wheels	27 in (68 cm)

Paris was a brand name used in the 1940s
and 1950s by Harry "Spanner" Rensch.
Deeply influenced by French lightweight
bicycle design, his Paris touring tandem
is fillet-brazed, which avoids the need for
lugs to join the tubes together.

▽ Child's Tandem c. 1950

Origin	UK
Frame	Steel
Gears	Single speed
Wheels	14 in (35 cm)

This rare tandem tricycle was made by an
unidentified maker. The British toy brand
Triang made a similar machine in the early
1950s. Unlike the Triang, this tandem has
bolt-on top tubes. The machine has been
repainted and the saddles are not original.

Braking system
With the additional
weight of two riders,
tandems needed
very effective brakes.
This Rensch model
features an early
form of V-brake.

Top tubes
bolted on

Cross-over drive

Rear coaster
brake

Front rack

◁ Schwinn AS Tandem 1955

Origin	US
Frame	Steel
Gears	Single speed
Wheels	26 in (65 cm)

The Schwinn AS (Arnold-Schwinn) tandem featured
heavy-duty spokes and frame. The chainguards
protected the rider's clothing from grease and
snagging. The curved tubing under the rear
seat added to the overall style of this machine.

Drum brake
in front wheel

Single chainguard

The 1960s
CYCLING GOES POP

CYCLING GOES POP

△ **A Christmas advertisement published by Schwinn in 1967** featured its Sting-Ray model, the must-have kids' bike of the year.

With the age of the automobile in full swing, bicycle manufacturers looked to the auto industry for ways to popularize their products. First to capitalize on the youth-centered trend of customizing bicycles with motorcycle parts was Schwinn, who released the Sting-Ray children's bike in 1963. With its motorcycle-style, top-tube-mounted gear lever, high-backed "banana" saddle perched over a larger rear wheel, and swept-back handlebars, the first "wheelie bike"—so called for the ease with which its rider could lift the front wheel—was instantly popular and much copied.

The popularity of wheelie bikes in the 1960s contributed to a resurgence in the bicycle industry around the world, with sales in the US topping 4 million that decade for the first time. Demand spread to other sectors of the market, with 10-speed racing cycles becoming popular in the US, where sales of European imports and homegrown imitations both blossomed.

A completely new concept was born when the Moulton F-Frame was introduced in 1962 in the UK. Designed by the engineer who had developed the rubber suspension of the radical Mini car, the F-Frame was a complete rethink of all the principles that shaped the bicycle, from the conventional diamond frame to the size of the wheels. The result was a small-wheeled bicycle with suspension and a step-over frame aimed squarely at the popular market. Ideal for short trips, easy and comfortable to ride, and especially appealing to women, the F-Frame soon became a fashionable icon for the new Pop era.

Key Events

▷ **1960** Racing is televised live for the first time at the Tour de France, increasing the appeal—and advertising potential—of the sport.

▷ **1960s** The bicycle is fully assimilated in many parts of Africa and Asia, becoming an important economic asset in local cultures.

▷ **1964** Jacques Anquetil becomes the first cyclist to win five Tours de France.

▷ **1965** The resurgence in US cycling is marked by the revival of the League of American Wheelmen, founded in 1880 but dormant since the early 1950s.

▷ **1967** The issue of drug-taking comes to prominence after the death of British star Tom Simpson, who had taken amphetamines, during the Tour de France that year.

△ **Death on the Tour de France** Following an autopsy of his body, it was found that as well as taking amphetamines, Tom Simpson had also consumed alcohol. He died of heart failure.

▷ **1968** Cycling's greatest endurance record, the Hour Record, is pushed to a distance of 30.25 miles (48.653 km) by Ole Ritter of Denmark.

▷ **1968** In honor of her dominance of women's cycling, Beryl Burton (UK) is invited to compete in the male-only Grand Prix des Nations in France.

> "The bicycle is the **most civilized** conveyance known to man. Other forms of transport grow **more nightmarish.** Only the bicycle **remains pure** in heart."

IRIS MURDOCH, *THE RED AND THE GREEN*, 1965

◁ **How many Bee Gees can you fit on a Moulton Standard?** The three Gibb brothers and Colin Peterson in London, 1961

Cruiser Bikes

Designed in the US, the cruiser has its origins in the 1933 Schwinn B-10E. Aimed at the youth market, it was styled to look like a motorcycle. It also introduced low-pressure balloon tires to the US. Cruisers had an upright riding position, robust construction, and a soft ride. Their heavy weight and single-speed transmission made them unsuitable for hill climbing but ideal for cruising along beaches and riding on suburban streets. These bikes were spopular in the US until the 1960s, when imports of lighter European machines made them unfashionable. Since the late 1990s, there has been a resurgence in popularity of cruisers.

Built-in headlight

Sweeping, space-age lines

Built-in taillight

△ **Bowden Spacelander 1960**

Origin	US
Frame	Fiberglass
Gears	Single speed
Wheels	26 in (65 cm)

The Bowden Spacelander featured an unusual bike design. It was made of molded fiberglass and was expensive for its time. Only 544 Spacelanders were ever made and its rarity makes it a collectible bike.

▽ **Bowden 300 1961**

Origin	US
Frame	Fiberglass
Gears	Single speed
Wheels	26 in (65 cm)

The Bowden 300 was a follow-up to the Bowden Spacelander. It too had a fiberglass frame, and with only 8–10 bikes ever made, it is even rarer than the original Spacelander.

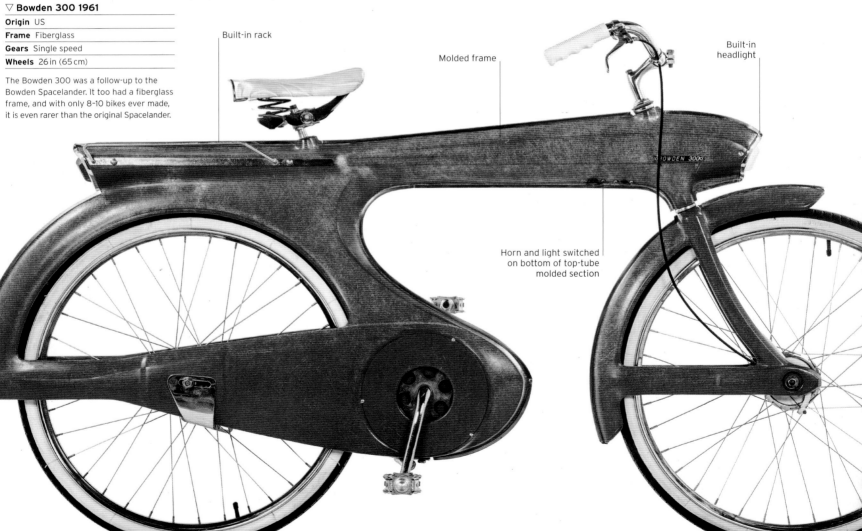

Built-in rack

Molded frame

Built-in headlight

Horn and light switched on bottom of top-tube molded section

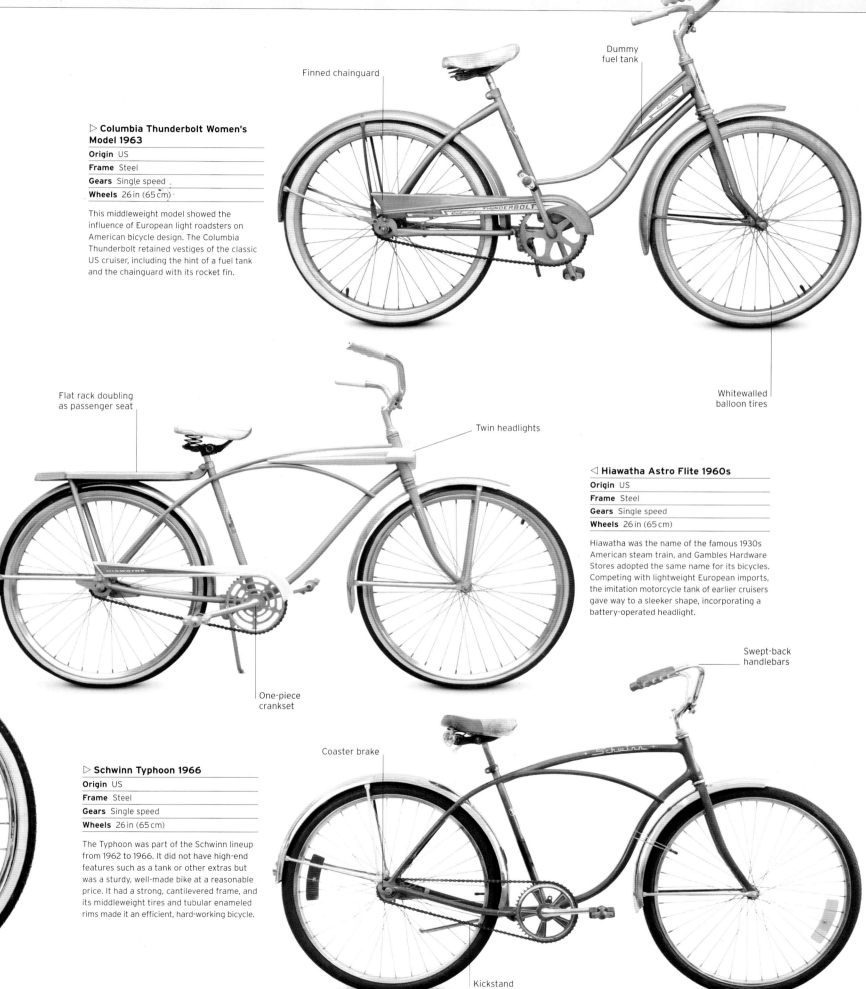

Finned chainguard

Dummy fuel tank

▷ Columbia Thunderbolt Women's Model 1963

Origin	US
Frame	Steel
Gears	Single speed
Wheels	26 in (65 cm)

This middleweight model showed the influence of European light roadsters on American bicycle design. The Columbia Thunderbolt retained vestiges of the classic US cruiser, including the hint of a fuel tank and the chainguard with its rocket fin.

Whitewalled balloon tires

Flat rack doubling as passenger seat

Twin headlights

◁ Hiawatha Astro Flite 1960s

Origin	US
Frame	Steel
Gears	Single speed
Wheels	26 in (65 cm)

Hiawatha was the name of the famous 1930s American steam train, and Gambles Hardware Stores adopted the same name for its bicycles. Competing with lightweight European imports, the imitation motorcycle tank of earlier cruisers gave way to a sleeker shape, incorporating a battery-operated headlight.

One-piece crankset

Swept-back handlebars

Coaster brake

▷ Schwinn Typhoon 1966

Origin	US
Frame	Steel
Gears	Single speed
Wheels	26 in (65 cm)

The Typhoon was part of the Schwinn lineup from 1962 to 1966. It did not have high-end features such as a tank or other extras but was a sturdy, well-made bike at a reasonable price. It had a strong, cantilevered frame, and its middleweight tires and tubular enameled rims made it an efficient, hard-working bicycle.

Kickstand

Workers leaving
the Peugeot
factory, 1886

Great Manufacturers
Peugeot

Peugeot has been at the heart of the French transportation industry for more than two centuries, and its story traces the evolution of vehicle technology in the late 19th century. One of the most distinctive racing teams from the 1960s to the 1980s, Peugeot's successes included a record ten Tour de France wins.

BICYCLE PRODUCTION was a logical step for a family of industrialists that had made its fortune in steelmaking. Founded in 1810, the Peugeot company produced everything from tools and clock springs to razor blades and coffee grinders from the steel made at its factories in the Doubs region of eastern France.

The first Peugeot bicycle was built in 1882 by Armand Peugeot, grandson of company co-founder Jean-Pierre II. Made to the "ordinary" or high-wheeler design—known as Le Grand Bi in French—it led to the mass-production of bicycles under the Cycles Peugeot name. Production began at the company's Beaulieu factory, which had been purchased in 1857 to produce fine steel hoops for ladies' skirts—a product that gave Peugeot the technology and expertise to produce the fine steel spokes for making bicycle wheels. The first tricycles and "safety" bicycles were

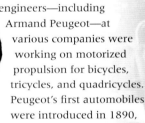

Armand Peugeot
(1849–1915)

released to the public in 1886, resplendent with the distinctive Peugeot lion motif.

The 1880s and 1890s were a time of rapid technological progress, and Peugeot was typical of many engineering firms of the time. The bicycle had not yet been pigeonholed as being powered by human legs alone, and engineers—including Armand Peugeot—at various companies were working on motorized propulsion for bicycles, tricycles, and quadricycles. Peugeot's first automobiles were introduced in 1890, and over the next 100 years the company's vehicle range included bicycles, mopeds, motorcycles, and automobiles. By the late 19th century, Peugeot's range of bicycles included tandems, tricycles, quadricycles, and a road bike available in 12 different models, and at the turn of the century the company was building around 20,000 bicycles a year. Peugeot was ideally poised to capitalize on France's new national race, the Tour de France, and entered a team in the second staging of the event in 1904. The following year brought the first of four consecutive victories for Peugeot: Louis Trousselier won in 1905, René Pottier in 1906, and Lucien Petit-Breton in 1907 and 1908, all on Peugeots.

Following the expansion of automobile production owing to the needs of the French military in World War I, in 1926 Peugeot's motorcar and two-wheeler—including both

Manufacturing breadth
As well as producing bicycles, Peugeot made a range of tricycles in the early 20th century.

Climbing high
Pictured in Peugeot's distinctive checkerboard team kit, Bernard Thévenet rides a mountain stage in the 1975 Tour de France. He won the race two years later, putting Peugeot at the pinnacle of racing success.

Grand Bi high-wheeler 1882

Peugeot vintage tandem 1926

PX10 with ornate Nervex lugs 1968

PY-10FC with carbon-fiber tubes 1985

1858 Peugeot's lion logo—standing for strength, suppleness, and swiftness—is trademarked.

1882 Armand Peugeot builds the company's first bicycle, a Grand Bi high-wheeler.

1886 Peugeot's first production bicycles and tricycles are released for sale.

1890 Paul Bourillon wins the sprint World Championships on a Peugeot bicycle.

1890s Peugeot offers prizes for the development of flying bicycles. The Wright brothers later use bicycle

technology in the first powered flight.

1913 Oscar Egg sets a new Hour Record of 24.045 miles (43.525 km) on a Peugeot.

1914 Around 63,000 Peugeot bicycles are produced up to 1918 for use in WWI.

1958 Peugeot begins making components for the auto industry to counter falling bicycle sales.

1967 In the Peugeot team's racing season, Eddy Merckx wins Milan–San Remo and the World Championships, and

Roger Pingeon wins the Tour de France.

1972 The opening of a new factory makes Peugeot the largest producer of racing bicycles in continental Europe.

1974 Peugeot's worldwide sales peak at around 900,000 units.

1977 Bernard Thévenet wins the last of Peugeot's ten Tour de France titles.

1983 Peugeot releases the CPX range, which includes wheelie bikes fitted with front- and rear-wheel suspension, as well as BMX bikes.

1980s The Peugeot team's "Foreign Legion" of anglophone riders—including Stephen Roche and Robert Millar—wins a series of major races, raising the global profile of professional cycling.

1987 Cycles Peugeot is absorbed into Peugeot's vehicle components division, ending in-house bicycle manufacturing.

2010s Four ranges are offered today via the Peugeot Automobiles division and selected bicycle retailers: off-road, hybrid, road, and junior.

Peugeot poster art
Printing became an art form in the Belle Époque due to advances in color lithography. These early advertisements reflect Peugeot's appeal to leisure and racing cyclists.

"Peugeot ... **winning** on the roads and tracks of **Europe since 1894.**"

ADVERTISING SLOGAN, 1970

bicycles and motorcycles—divisions separated. The P-10 bicycle, equipped with both front and rear brakes, wooden rims, Dunlop tires, and a tool kit, arrived in 1927. The P-10 designation remained in Peugeot's range for decades, always signifying the top-of-the-line model.

Despite the disruption of World War II, during which Peugeot's output was commandeered by the occupying German forces, production jumped from 162,000 bicycles in 1930 to 222,000 in 1955, by which time around 3,500 workers were employed in the Beaulieu factory.

Lion motif
The Peugeot lion, 1970s

New technology was introduced in the form of stainless-steel bicycle frames for the PX-10 road-racing model, which featured French-only components from companies such as Mafac, Simplex, and Stronglight.

The 1960s marked an upturn in the fortunes of the Peugeot brand, largely thanks to the high-profile successes of its professional cyclists. In 1963 the Peugeot team wore a new black-and-white grid-patterned strip, designed to be more visible in the monochrome photography and TV pictures used to report on the major races.

A new wave of riders became household names: Charly Gaul (Luxembourg), Tom Simpson (UK), Eddy Merckx (Belgium), and Roger Pingeon (France) all won major races for the team. By 1977 the Peugeot team had won the Tour de France ten times.

The brand's strong performance continued into the 1970s, as Peugeot benefited from the US-led bicycle boom that saw lightweight, 10-speed European racing bikes become highly sought after. Global supply of Peugeot bicycles increased when the company moved production to a new state-of-the-art manufacturing plant in Romilly, near Paris, in 1972.

In 1983 Peugeot introduced the PY-10FC, one of the first mass-produced bicycles to use carbon fiber as a frame material. Claimed to be 30 percent lighter and eight percent stiffer than a steel-framed equivalent, it had carbon-fiber tubing

bonded to aluminum lugs, with front forks and rear stays also made from lightweight aluminum. And technological innovation was not restricted to road cycling—in 1984 Peugeot released the VTT1, the first production mountain bike to be built specially for the French off-road market.

However, Peugeot was losing ground to its competitors, as its policy of using only French-made components was proving expensive at a time when cheaper parts made in Asia allowed it to be undercut. The professional cycling team was disbanded in 1986, and soon after that, Peugeot ceased in-house production of bicycles. The Peugeot name lived on as a brand licensed to various companies around the world, but the once-great pillar of French bicycle manufacturing was no more.

Brand reborn
Aluminum-framed Peugeot bicycles are assembled at the Romilly-sur-Seine factory, which is now owned by Swedish company and license-holder Cycleurope.

Track and Road Racers

Spurred by increasing awareness of the value of exercise and interest in professional bike racing, bicycle sales boomed in the late 1960s. American manufacturers such as Schwinn began producing their own versions of lightweight racing bikes. Roadsters and beach cruisers were abandoned in favor of models with lightweight frames and drop handlebars. Bicycles continued to evolve over the course of the decade, and the number of gears increased to seven, with the option of two or three chainrings in front. The average speed at races increased thanks to the availability of lighter components and narrower tires, as well as the improved reliability of the machines.

▽ Torpado 1960s

Origin	Italy
Frame	Steel
Gears	6-speed
Wheels	28 in (70 cm)

First launched in 1908, Torpado soon earned a reputation for making highly capable performance racing bicycles. These were painted in signature pearlescent turquoise. Top models featured internally routed cables.

Torpado head badge
The metal head badge is made from brass or alloy, and features the Torpado logo set in front of a globe motif. Detail was picked out in enamel paint.

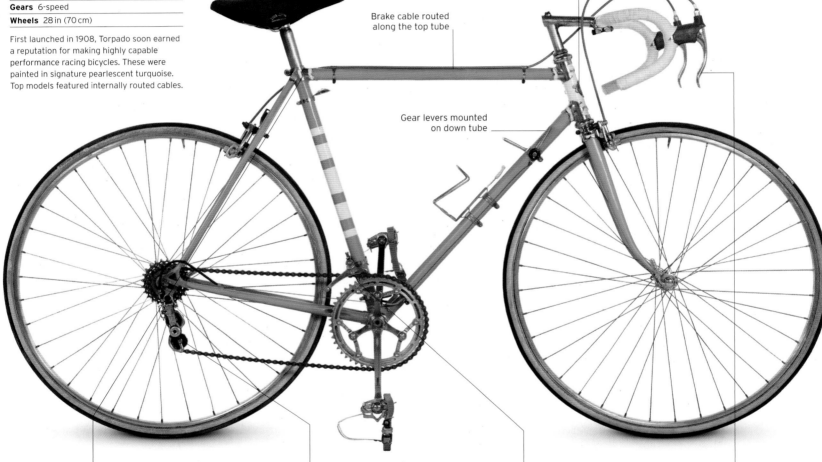

Brake cable routed along the top tube

Gear levers mounted on down tube

Seat cluster
Each lug was individually chromed for a polished finish. The seat stays featured scalloped top eyes, creating a carved-away appearance.

Rear derailleur
The Campagnolo Gran Sport rear derailleur was one of the more expensive components. The Campagnolo range was popular because it offered reliable shifting.

Front derailleur
Campagnolo founder Tullio Campagnolo named this part after his son, Valentino. The steel-based component shifted the chain from the big chainring to the smaller inner ring.

Brake levers and brakes
A classic example of a "non-aero" lever, the brake cable was routed externally rather than hidden under the tape. Often riders would hand-drill holes along the steel lever to reduce weight.

5-speed
cassette

Water bottle
cage mounted
with clips

◁ **Verhoeven Type
Competition 1960**

Origin Germany

Frame Steel

Gears 5-speed

Wheels 28 in (70 cm)

Constructed from Reynolds 531 steel,
the Verhoeven was one of the mid-range
road bikes available to amateur racers.
Its cables were held in place by chrome
clips. The gear-shifter was located at
the end of the handlebar for ease of
use when riding "in the drops."

Cable stops brazed
to the frame

Forward-facing
dropout allows
quick wheel
change

▷ **Hetchins Magnum
Bonum 1962**

Origin UK

Frame Steel

Gears 6-speed

Wheels 28 in (70 cm)

Hetchins was a high-end
British manufacturer known
for its racing and performance
machines. It was famous for its
curly lug patterns, which made
the frames unmissable even
from a distance.

Clincher-style
tire with
inner tube

Front mudguard
made from thin
shaped metal

◁ **Condor Professional 1963**

Origin UK

Frame Steel

Gears 6-speed

Wheels 28 in (70 cm)

Condor established a reputation for
quality lightweight builds and many
competitive racers aspired to ride its
professional model. This London-
based brand is one of few to have
survived to the modern day.

Pale metallic blue is
a classic Cinelli color

▷ **Cinelli Super Corsa 1968**

Origin Italy

Frame Steel

Gears 6-speed

Wheels 28 in (70 cm)

With their high-qualityColumbus Italian
tubing, Cinelli bikes drew the attention
of riders worldwide. Their beautifully
crafted frames featured Campagnolo
components. The Super Corsa was
favored by the Italian Olympic team.

Bicycles were manufactured on an industrial scale in many countries by the 1960s, such as at the Raleigh factory in Nottingham, England, which was capable of producing a new bike every minute. Despite being mass-produced on such a scale, and in modern factories, all bicycles of the era were still assembled by hand, with workers systematically adding the many components to the frame.

Track-Racing Bikes

Outwardly, bicycles built for 1960s track racing looked very similar to the machines of the early 20th century. On closer inspection, however, the quality, weight, and design had changed a great deal. Lower front ends created more aerodynamic riding positions. Stiffer frames handled better at high speed and resisted the lateral stress generated by riders accelerated from a standing start. Lugs became less ornate as complex construction used more material, which increased weight; by simplifying the lug pattern, builders could make lighter bicycles. The heavier leather and copper-rivet saddles went too, riders preferring plastic or lighter synthetic perches for their machines.

BERYL BURTON

Despite a childhood plagued by health problems, Yorkshire-born cyclist Beryl Burton went on to become one of the world's most successful female cyclists of the 20th century. She not only won over 90 races and achieved seven world titles during her career, but also set the women's 12-hour time-trial world record in 1967, which at 277.25 miles (446.20 km) still stands in 2016. She even handed fellow competitor Mike McNamara a candy as she passed him.

Beryl Burton was a household name in 1960s Britain and was awarded the OBE and MBE. She is seen here at a champions' meeting in London. She died in 1996 at age 58.

Hand-built wheels

△ **Carlton Fixed-Wheel Racer 1962**

Origin	UK
Frame	Steel
Gears	Single speed
Wheels	28 in (70 cm)

Purchased by Raleigh in the 1960s, Carlton made affordable, good-quality bicycles. The frame featured complicated lug work similar to famous Hetchins designs. The mirrorlike finish was achieved by building the bicycle from chrome-plated Reynold 531 steel tubing.

Lightweight plastic saddle

▽ **Viking Vitesse 1963**

Origin	UK
Frame	Steel
Gears	Single speed
Wheels	28 in (70 cm)

Viking shot to prominence when champion cyclist Beryl Burton rode this Vitesse to win Gold in the 1963 World Championships. Viking's range of machines was aimed squarely at the competitive cyclist, and included variations for racing and track.

Handlebars half-covered with synthetic tape

Frame built with Reynolds 531 round steel tubing

48-tooth alloy chainring

Alloy seatpost
with pinch bolt

Steel headset
allowed forks
to move freely

▷ **Tommy Godwin 1964**

Origin UK

Frame Steel

Gears Single speed

Wheels 28 in (70 cm)

A specialist track cyclist in the 1940s and
1950s, Godwin won double bronze for Great
Britain in the 1948 London Olympics. He
worked for bicycle-maker BSA and built
many of his racing bicycles himself, so he
could choose the best components.

Campagnolo Record
high-flange wheels

Lugged steel
frame

◁ **Goldia Bahnrad 1965**

Origin Switzerland

Frame Steel

Gears Single speed

Wheels 28 in (70 cm)

Offered with the ubiquitous Reynold 531 tubing, Goldia
bicycles were refined and elegantly finished. Always
completed with the best components, the bicycles were
ridden by world-class cyclists during the six-day track
racing series. This machine had a Campagnolo Record
crankset and wheels and a Cinelli bar and stem.

Lowered
handlebars

▷ **Faliero Masi Special 1968**

Origin Italy

Frame Steel

Gears Single speed

Wheels 28 in (70 cm)

In his workshop beneath the Vigorelli velodrome
in Milan, Italy, ex-pro racer, Faliero Masi, crafted
bicycles that were stylish and truly exceptional.
Although the machines were very expensive,
Masi always had a long waiting list that included
professional cyclists. He once proudly claimed,
"I have no competitors, only copiers."

Chromed wheel
dropouts

Sprung, chromed-
steel top clips

Moulton Deluxe

A radical redesign that marked a departure from the traditional diamond-frame bicycle, the Moulton Deluxe boasted comfort, sturdiness, and practicality that belied its miniature stature. The archetypal F-Frame model in Moulton's five-bike range at the 1962 launch, the Deluxe was designed as a utility bike capable of around-town urban use and fully loaded cycle touring. Its head-turning modern looks were intended to appeal to a new swath of bicycle users, including female riders.

SPURRED ON BY THE 1956 Suez Crisis, when car owners increasingly looked to the bicycle as a form of transportation because of high gas prices, British engineer Alex Moulton set about rethinking bicycle design for the modern age. His solution was to create the unisex F-Frame, which dispensed with the traditional top tube and seat stays in favor of a more rider-friendly, stepover frame design.

In common with all the original F-Frame Series 1 models, the Deluxe featured a horizontal steel beam projecting over the rear wheel for carrying luggage, since practicality was an integral part of the Moulton design concept. Smaller wheels with high-pressure tyres gave better maneuverability and less aerodynamic drag than standard-size bicycle wheels, and also lowered the Moulton's center of gravity to improve its stability when riding with luggage attached. Rubber suspension on the front and rear forks counteracted the harsh ride of the small wheels.

The Deluxe continued to be produced until 1966 and was one of the bestsellers of the original Moulton range. Still in production today, the original Moulton design has been overhauled and refined numerous times, with models ranging from the separable-frame Stowaway and drop-handlebar Speedsix series to the AM Spaceframe design and lightweight New Series, all achieving a loyal following.

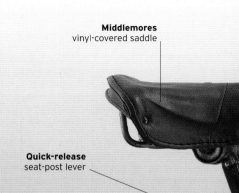

Middlemores
vinyl-covered saddle

Quick-release
seat-post lever

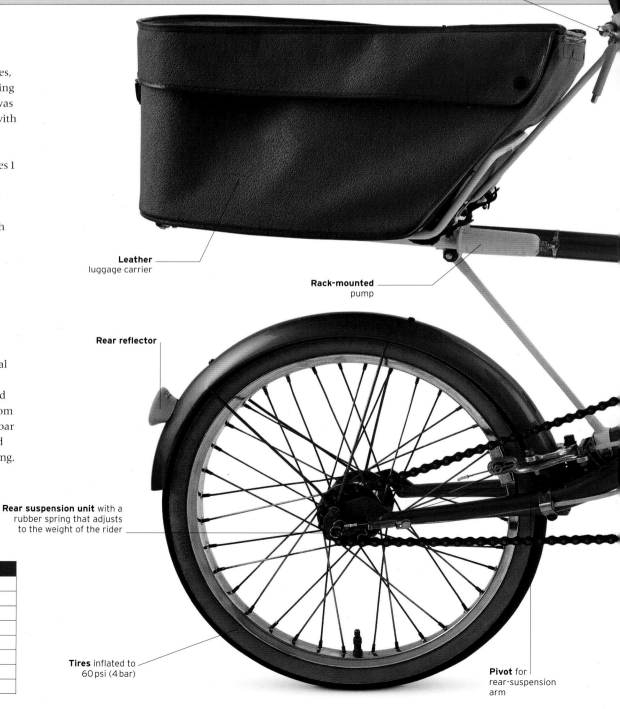

Leather
luggage carrier

Rack-mounted
pump

Rear reflector

Rear suspension unit with a
rubber spring that adjusts
to the weight of the rider

Tires inflated to
60 psi (4 bar)

Pivot for
rear-suspension
arm

SPECIFICATIONS	
Origin	UK
Designer	Alex Moulton
Year	1962
Frame	Steel
Gears	4-speed
Brakes	Caliper
Wheels	16 in (40 cm)
Weight	Approx. 30 lb (13.6 kg)

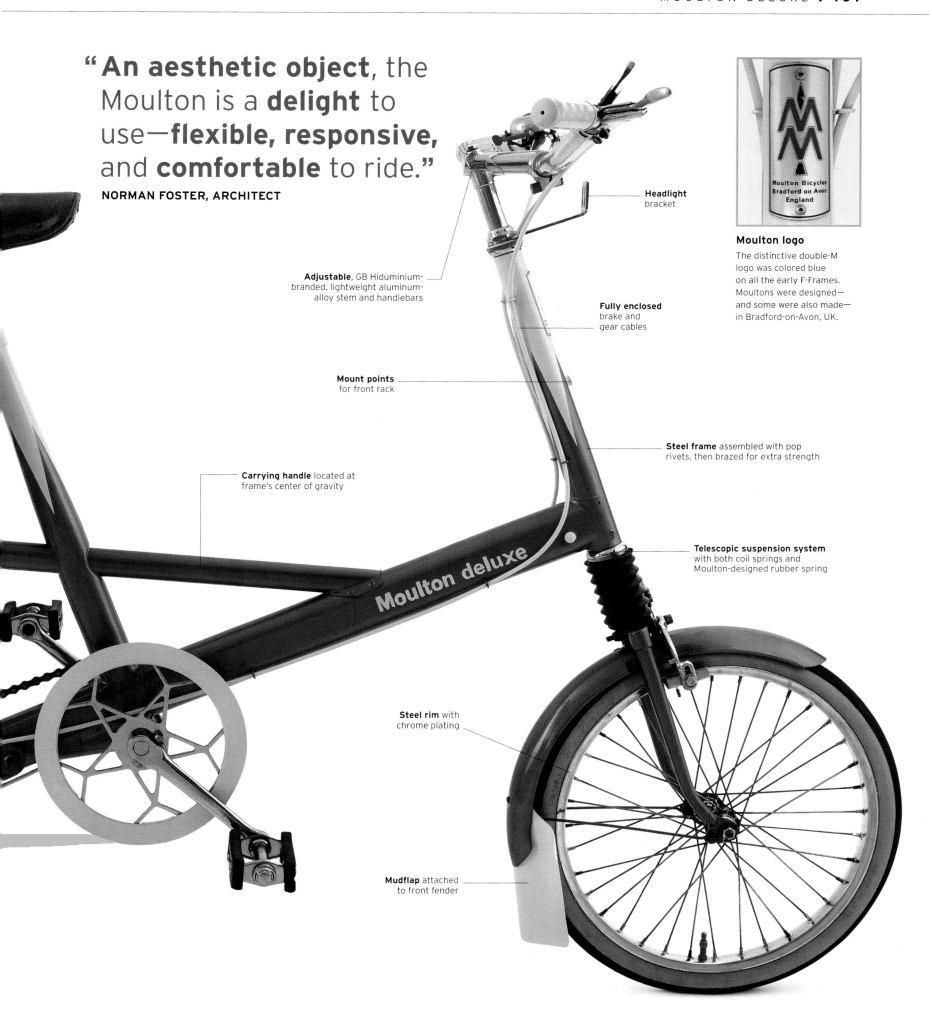

"**An aesthetic object**, the Moulton is a **delight** to use—**flexible, responsive,** and **comfortable** to ride."

NORMAN FOSTER, ARCHITECT

Headlight bracket

Moulton logo
The distinctive double-M logo was colored blue on all the early F-Frames. Moultons were designed—and some were also made—in Bradford-on-Avon, UK.

Adjustable, GB Hiduminium-branded, lightweight aluminum-alloy stem and handlebars

Fully enclosed brake and gear cables

Mount points for front rack

Steel frame assembled with pop rivets, then brazed for extra strength

Carrying handle located at frame's center of gravity

Telescopic suspension system with both coil springs and Moulton-designed rubber spring

Moulton deluxe

Steel rim with chrome plating

Mudflap attached to front fender

THE COMPONENTS

The Moulton Deluxe featured higher-quality components than most other models in the Series 1 range. Aluminum parts were lighter than steel components, while a four-speed Sturmey-Archer hub gear offered extra power. Although the exact parts varied as the Moulton range evolved, customers could choose from a range of options, such as a front-wheel, hub-mounted dynamo to power a headlight.

1. Middlemores vinyl-covered saddle **2.** Seat-tube junction with quick-release lever for height adjustment **3.** Rack-mounted pump **4.** Sturmey-Archer FW four-speed hub gear **5.** White polythene chainguard **6.** Front fork with GB aluminum caliper brake **7.** Moulton-branded Adie bell **8.** Brazed cross tube with pop rivets **9.** Rubber "bellows" for front suspension **10.** Front-wheel fender with mudflap

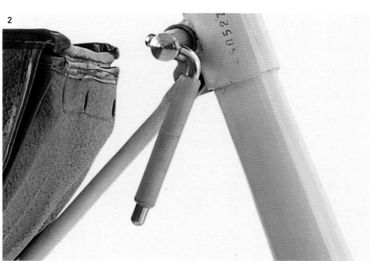

6

7

8

9

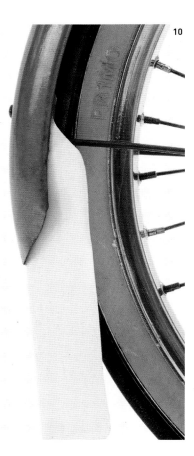

10

Small-Wheeled Bicycles

The Moulton bicycle, introduced in the UK in 1962, was a revolutionary development of the classic bicycle, aimed at commuters. It quickly became another symbol of the Swinging Sixties, along with miniskirts and Mini cars, and several other manufacturers followed Moulton and brought out their own small-wheeled models. A key aspect of the Moulton was its rubber suspension, which meant it handled far better than versions made by other manufacturers. The small-wheeled bicycles became popular for short-distance riding in town. Some were also designed to be folded small enough that they could be transported in a car or bus.

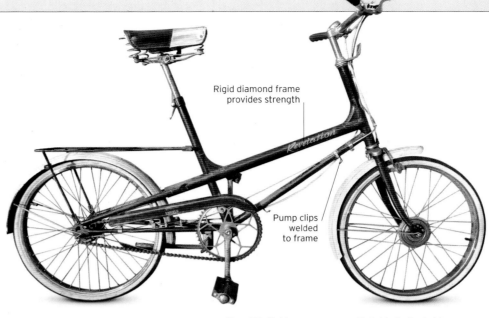

Rigid diamond frame provides strength

Pump clips welded to frame

△ Royal Enfield Revelation 1965

Origin	UK
Frame	Steel
Gears	3- or 4-speed
Wheels	20 in (50 cm)

Probably the best of the non-Moulton small-wheeled bicycles, the Revelation had a rigid frame and the same wheelbase as a standard bicycle. It was supplied with front and rear racks.

High handlebar

Frame secured by bottom brace

Folding bracket secured by lever

◁ Raleigh Twenty 1968

Origin	UK
Frame	Steel
Gears	3-speed
Wheels	20 in (50 cm)

This bestseller addressed the problems of the RSW 16. Its larger wheels gave it a smoother ride and improved steering. It was sold in fixed and folding "Stowaway" versions.

Wheels had road tires

▽ Helkama Jopo 1960s

Origin	Finland
Frame	Steel
Gears	2-speed
Wheels	24 in (60 cm)

The Jopo small-wheel featured a strong pressed-steel frame that was welded together for durability. The main down tube was hinged so that the bicycle could be folded easily. The seat and head-tube angles offered a comfortable ride.

Integral rear rack

Strong, steel-plate frame

Hinged to fold

▷ Moulton Bicycle 1962

Origin	UK
Frame	Steel
Gears	3-speed
Wheels	16 in (40 cm)

In 1962 Moulton launched its small-wheel bicycle. It was an overnight sensation, and triggered a small-wheeler boom that helped to reverse the postwar decline in bicycle sales. In 1967 the company was taken over by Raleigh, and in 1971 it launched this Mk3 model.

Middlemores saddle

Rubber suspension for back wheels

Large holdall
secured to rear rack

◁ Raleigh Small-Wheel (RSW) 16 1965

Origin	UK
Frame	Steel
Gears	3-speed
Wheels	16 in (40 cm)

This bicycle, unlike the Moulton, did not have any
suspension and relied on wide balloon tires for a
soft ride, but they were slow and hard to pedal.
The large rear holdall and hub dynamo- powered
lighting were popular accessories.

Tires designed to
run at low pressure

Kickstand

▽ Sears Tote 1960s

Origin	US
Frame	Steel
Gears	3-speed
Wheels	20 in (50 cm)

This was a small-wheeled bicycle
manufactured by the Sears Co. of New
York. It featured an unusual triple-tubed
frame that could be split into two parts.
The chainguard and chainring were
made of pressed metal.

Unisex "one-size-
fits-all" frame

Front suspension

Rear rack
integral to frame

Small-diameter
frame tubing

Frame "splits"
at midpoint

Pressed metal
chainring

Touring Bikes

From the late 1960s, demand for bicycles increased across Europe and the US. Manufacturers responded with a wider choice of models aimed at both the conventional adult market and younger riders; mass-production techniques enabled them to build good-quality bicycles at affordable prices. Component and accessory suppliers also increased the range of gears, brakes, stems, and hubs available to meet riders' needs. The use of light alloy components was commonplace, and improved performance and durability. The design of derailleur gears developed, and a 10-speed gear range became standard for touring bicycles.

Long wheelbase for stability at high speed

Mounting lugs for rear rack

Brakes removed for racing

Rear derailleur and cassette removed

△ Puch Bergmeister 1960s

Origin Austria

Frame Steel

Gears Single speed

Wheels 27 in (68 cm)

This was a premium lightweight model aimed at sports tourers and club riders. In standard form, it featured a leather saddle, center-pull brakes, derailleur gears, and lightweight wheels. This example has been stripped down for racing.

Ribbed tires for grip on surfaces with loose stones

Braced forks for extra strength

◁ Edward O'Brien's Tracker c. 1968

Origin UK

Frame Steel

Gears Single speed

Wheels 26 in (65 cm)

Built by O'Briens of Coventry, this model was aimed at the teenage rider. It was designed to resemble a US speedway bike, and featured a dropped seat tube, chrome plated front-fork bracing, large-section tires, and high-rise handlebars.

Lightweight frame made of Reynolds or Vitus tubing

Center-pull alloy brakes

▷ Bertin C37 c. 1968

Origin France

Frame Steel

Gears 10-speed

Wheels 27 in (68 cm)

André Bertin was a successful professional racer who founded a bicycle manufacturing business that built a range of high-quality, lightweight cycles that could be adapted for touring. The C37 model featured open cable guides, a lugged frame, and alloy components.

▽ **George W Stratton Mixte 1969**

Origin	UK
Frame	Steel
Gears	5-speed
Wheels	27 in (68 cm)

This George W Stratton was a top-of-the-line bike. Its mixte-style frame meant it had twin tubes running from the headset to the rear axle. This provided a low stepover height while retaining the rigidity of the diamond frame.

Sprung saddle for long-distance comfort

Reynolds 531 tubing

Lightweight wheels

Large-capacity tire pump

Brooks B17 saddle

Frame made of Reynolds tubing

Simplex gearing

Aftermarket light

Downtube shifters

◁ **Dawes Galaxy 1969**

Origin	UK
Frame	Steel
Gears	10-speed
Wheels	26 in (65 cm)

A lightweight touring bike introduced as a standard production model at a time when most touring bicycles had to be custom-made and were very expensive, this bicycle quickly became popular and is still in production.

Great Races
Tour of Flanders 1969

This race, also known as the *Ronde van Vlaanderen*, or De Ronde, is, like the Paris–Roubaix, one of the cobbled classics. It is the biggest race in Flanders, the cycling-crazy region of Belgium that has produced more road-cycling champions than any other country.

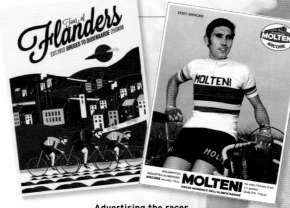

Advertising the races
Posters advertise the annual race (left) and others promote riders. On the right is Merckx in 1972 wearing the world champion's rainbow jersey.

INAUGURATED IN 1913 as a result of newspaper circulation wars, this famous race takes place annually in the spring. The 53rd Tour of Flanders, in 1969, is famous for the virtuoso performance of Belgium's Eddy Merckx. He had already won many road races, but a win in this, his "home" race, had so far eluded him. It is hard to say which one of Merckx's 500-plus victories in men's professional cycling was his greatest, but this is definitely a candidate.

The race took place in April. Conditions were dry at the start, but there was a strong wind blowing across the route. The cyclists started by riding west from Ghent to the Belgian coast, then went inland to the Flemish Ardennes—the hills where the race is decided.

Eddy Merckx was backed by one of the greatest-ever teams—Faema. Races may have one winner, but team members work together to ensure that it is one of their members. Faema made the race hard

Felice Gimondi of Italy
Although second in the 1969 Tour of Flanders, Gimondi won all three Grand Tours: Tour de France, Giro d'Italia, and Vuelta a España.

from the start, using the coastal stretch to split the peloton. A large group formed at the front, which was reduced to 12 men, including Eddy Merckx and three of his teammates (Jos Spruyt, Julien Stevens, and Bernard Van de Kerckhove—all Belgians) after the first climb. Also in the group were Italians Felice Gimondi, Franco Bitossi, Michele Dancelli, and Marino Basso, two more Belgians (Frans Verbeck and Georges Claes), a Dutchman (Eef Dolman), and a British rider (Barry Hoban). Merckx set an incredible pace on all the hills, and one or two riders dropped away from the front group on almost every climb. When it was down to six riders, Eddy Merckx made his attack.

MERCKX BREAKS AWAY

With 43 miles (70 km) to go, Merckx hit the front on one of the final climbs and accelerated. At the summit, he was five seconds clear of the next rider,

> "When **Merckx attacked** I kept thinking he's got to **ease** at the **top**, but he didn't, he just **kept going faster.**"
>
> BARRY HOBAN, 1969

who was five seconds clear of the one behind him, and the gaps continued to grow on the way down. The group had been broken by Merckx's acceleration, and it was several seconds before they were organized enough to chase him. But Merckx had the scent of victory and was pulling away fast. With 31 miles (50 km) still to go and fearing Merckx had made his move too early, his team manager drove alongside and asked him if he was sure he was doing the right thing. Merckx made it clear that he was.

The weather worsened throughout the day. By this stage it was pouring rain and the temperature had dropped to near freezing. But Merckx was oblivious to it. He crossed the finish line in Meerbecke 5 minutes and 36 seconds ahead of the next rider, Felice Gimondi. The following rider finished a couple of minutes behind Gimondi. Merckx never won the Tour of Flanders again.

A grueling race
The Tour of Flanders is one of the five one-day road races known as the "monuments" of the sport. They are the oldest, toughest, and most prized races of their kind. Eddy Merckx is one of only three men—all of them Belgian—to have won all five races.

Merckx in his bid for victory
By the time Merckx began to break away from the main group, conditions were terrible, with driving rain making the cobblestone surface of the climb very slippery. But he brushed it all aside and rode hard all the way to the finish.

KEY FACTS

RESULTS
First: Eddy Merckx, Belgium
Second: Felice Gimondi, Italy
Third: Marino Basso, Italy

THE ROUTE
The route varies slightly from year to year. Eddie Merckx's 1969 race began in Ghent and finished in Meerbecke, in eastern Belgium. In 2009 (the race shown in the map below), the Tour of Flanders race began in Bruges (Brugge in Flemish). Parts of the route are completely flat, but it includes a number of *hellingen* (hills)—indicated by the green triangles—which are where this race is won and lost. Each of the *hellingen* is short, but steep, and most have a cobblestone surface. The modern race still begins in Bruges, although it now finishes in Oudenaarde. In 2015 the riders covered a distance of 165 miles (264.9 km).

Route map for the 2009 Tour of Flanders This race covered 161 miles (259.7 km) and included 16 *hellingen*. It was won by the Belgian rider, Stijn Devolder, who also won in 2008.

Children's Bikes

In the 1960s, there was a huge difference between children's bikes on either side of the Atlantic. Most British and European bikes designed for children were scaled-down versions of adult machines, and included everything from miniature racing bikes in Italy to junior Moultons in the UK. Americans had more disposable income than Europeans, which is reflected in the styling of the children's bicycles built for the US market. The banana-seat-bike craze started in 1963 in the US and dominated for the rest of the decade, but these bicycles were not popular in UK and Continental Europe. This changed with the launch of the Chopper bicycle at the end of the decade. It was designed for the American market but not heavily promoted in the UK and Europe until 1970.

Decorative tank feature

Whitewall tires

△ Columbia Thunderbolt 1960

Origin	US
Frame	Steel
Gears	Single speed
Wheels	26 in (65 cm)

By 1960, the design of Columbia's children's bicycles, with their lighter construction, showed a definite European influence. However, the cruiser heritage was still evident in the dummy fuel tank in the frame.

Schwinn-style "cantilever" frame

Front rack, rarely seen on British bicycles

Whitewall tires

◁ BSA Santa Fe 1960s

Origin	UK
Frame	Steel
Gears	3-speed
Wheels	26 in (65 cm)

This was an American-style, middle-weight bike built by Raleigh with the export market in mind. The distinctive Schwinn-style frame, swept-back handlebars, and semi-balloon tires were novelties in the UK.

Rear rack attached to saddle

▷ Schwinn Street 1964

Origin	US
Frame	Steel
Gears	Single speed
Wheels	Front 20 in (50 cm), Rear 24 in (60 cm)

Based on a standard Schwinn design, the Street was quickly modified to reflect the aesthetics of its day, taking inspiration from low-rider cars and drag-strip bikes. It featured Schwinn's head badge, distinctive spring fork, and seat, but comfort and rideability were not a concern.

Coaster brake
The coaster brake, developed in around 1900, allowed the rider to freewheel, while back-pedaling applied an all-weather brake in the hub.

Faux exhaust pipes

Kickstand

Chrome-plated,
swept-back handlebars

◁ **Sears Spaceliner 1966**

Origin	US
Frame	Steel
Gears	Single speed
Wheels	26 in (65 cm)

The Sears Roebuck mail-order company had Spaceliners built for them by the Murray Ohio Manufacturing Co. The bikes had a distinctive fake fuel tank that looked like the number "7." The Spaceliner was available in adult and children's versions.

Sprung "sissy bar"
supported rear of seat

"Stik-shift" for
derailleur gear

Schwinn "springer"
suspension forks

Handlebars and
steering wheel

Extended forks

△ **Schwinn Lemon Peeler 1968**

Origin	US
Frame	Steel
Gears	5-speed
Wheels	Front 16 in (40 cm), Rear 20 in (50 cm)

Schwinn's Sting-Ray, launched in 1963, was the market leader in the banana-seat-bike craze. In 1968 Schwinn followed this up with the Krate series, which included the "Lemon Peeler." This clearly influenced Raleigh's Chopper design.

As the amount of traffic increased in towns and cities during the 1960s, bicycle safety, especially for the young, became a concern. In the UK, the Cycling Proficiency Test was first launched in 1947 and gradually introduced across the country. Children were given lessons in how to ride safely, usually at their school, after which there was a test. The program still exists and is now called Bikeability.

Leisure Bikes

The postwar decline in European cycle commuting led manufacturers to concentrate on the adult leisure market. Colorful sporty roadsters replaced robust but antiquated utility bicycles. British three-speed racers had impressed the American troops stationed in the UK during World War II and, as cruisers went out of fashion, large consignments of these bikes were exported to the US. Professional club cyclists still bought high-quality lightweights, but many more people purchased cheaper, mass-produced "English racers." By the end of the 1960s there was a "10-speed" boom in the US, with drop-handlebar sports bikes selling in huge numbers.

Wired rear light

Sturmey-Archer Dynohub

△ **Triumph Palm Beach 1964**

Origin	UK
Frame	Steel
Gears	3-speed
Wheels	26 in (65 cm)

Designed for everyday cycling, the Palm Beach was built by Raleigh and sold under the Triumph brand, which had long been associated with the manufacture of motorcycles. It featured a two-tone color scheme, a Sturmey-Archer three-speed hub, and dynamo-powered lights.

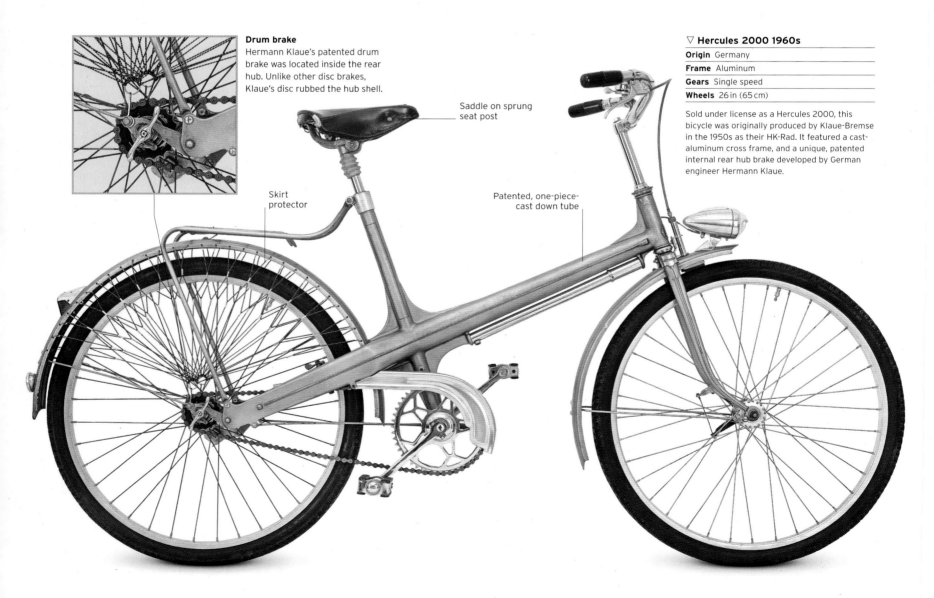

Drum brake
Hermann Klaue's patented drum brake was located inside the rear hub. Unlike other disc brakes, Klaue's disc rubbed the hub shell.

Saddle on sprung seat post

Skirt protector

Patented, one-piece-cast down tube

▽ **Hercules 2000 1960s**

Origin	Germany
Frame	Aluminum
Gears	Single speed
Wheels	26 in (65 cm)

Sold under license as a Hercules 2000, this bicycle was originally produced by Klaue-Bremse in the 1950s as their HK-Rad. It featured a cast-aluminum cross frame, and a unique, patented internal rear hub brake developed by German engineer Hermann Klaue.

Standard step-through frame

One-piece crankset

◁ Schwinn Breeze 1965

Origin US

Frame Steel

Gears 3-speed

Wheels 26 in (65 cm)

The Schwinn Breeze was a budget lightweight with a standard Schwinn frame, tourist handlebars, and nylon sports touring tires. Combined with a 3-speed hub and caliper brakes, the Schwinn Breeze had a transatlantic feel.

Removable wire netting basket

▷ Schwinn Town & Country 1967

Origin US

Frame Steel

Gears 3-speed

Wheels 24 in (60 cm)

The Schwinn Town & Country tricycle was built to be sturdy. It had lots of carrying capacity in the rear basket, a heavy-duty contoured saddle with spring support, and a multispeed gear system for scooting around town or heading to the country.

Caliper brake on front wheel

Narrow tires for less rolling resistance

Rear coaster brake

Step-through frame

Front caliper brake

◁ Western Galaxy Flyer 1969

Origin US

Frame Steel

Gears Single speed

Wheels 26 in (65 cm)

After President Eisenhower's doctor promoted cycling for health and fun, American adults became interested in bikes again. They wanted lighter machines and, by the 1960s, Western Auto Supply Co. had slimmed down their cruisers, removing the iconic fake fuel tank.

Narrow whitewall tires

The 1970s
NEW
WAVES

NEW WAVES

The 1960s had seen the bicycle's fortunes revived by an influx of mostly youthful riders, who took to two wheels in greater numbers than ever before. A decade later, many of those who had been hooked by the thrills of the wheelie bike began to shape the bicycle into still more forms and variations, as a new wave of creative energy gave rise to the sports of BMX (bicycle motocross), mountain-biking, and triathlon (cycling, running, and swimming).

Although riding customized bikes around motocross-style tracks occurred in multiple places and at different times around the world, the movement that gave rise to BMX sprang to life in the US. Among the teenagers who experimented on BMXs was Scot Breithaupt, a motocross rider who began to hold contests on full-size motocross tracks in California in 1970 for youngsters riding modified wheelie bikes. At around the same time, a group of enthusiasts began riding modified 1930s Schwinn cruisers, which they christened "clunkers," down off-road trails in Marin County, CA. Their development of bicycles that could withstand the punishment of steep downhills and bumpy terrain gave rise to the fat-tired machines that became known as "mountain bikes" from the late 1970s.

Companies sprang up to cater to these new forms of cycling. US start-ups led the way, from Trek's high-quality tourers and Gary Fisher's early mountain bikes, to Cannondale and Klein, who innovated with aluminum frames. Low-cost Japanese components and bicycles also broadened the choices available to cyclists.

△ **Cycling off the beaten track**
The first mountain bikes, such as those produced by Joe Breeze, appeared in the 1970s. The sport was rapidly established over the following decade.

Key events

▷ **1970** Cinelli releases the M71 clipless pedal, the first ski-binding-type system to attach the rider's foot to the pedal.

▷ **1971** A UK-made Carlton Cycles prototype features the first use of carbon fiber on a bicycle frame.

▷ **1972** Shimano launches its top-of-the-line Dura-Ace groupset of components.

▷ **1974** The first modern triathlon is held In Mission Bay, CA.

△ **Eddy Merckx's winning year**
After breaking the Hour Record in 1972, Eddy Merckx completed a triple in 1974, winning the Giro d'Italia, Tour de France, and Union Cycliste Internationale World Championships.

▷ **1974** Shimano releases the Positron rear derailleur, its first gear system to use indexing—one click of the gear lever moves the chain by one ratio.

▷ **1975** Recumbent bicycles enjoy a revival, marked by the formation of the International Human Powered Vehicle Association.

▷ **1976** The first organized mountain bike race, known as "Repack," is held in Pine Mountain, Marin County, CA. Alan Bonds wins it.

▷ **Mid-1970s** The Flying Pigeon bicycle is distributed in every town and city in China as part of a Communist drive for modernity.

▷ **1978** In the US, bicycle sales overtake those of automobiles.

" You **won't believe** what kids can do with bicycles! They do **everything** grown-up **motocross** racers do, except they do it with **pedal power.** "
PROMOTIONAL POSTER FOR YAMAHA GOLD CUP BMX RACE, LOS ANGELES, 1974

◁ **Poster published by Shimano to promote** the manufacturer's Dura-Ace Light Alloy Hub, 1970

Early 1970s Racers

Improvements in the quality of materials available to frame-builders and manufacturers resulted in some of the finest traditional racing bicycles. Europe remained the heartland for frame-building and components through the 1970s, with the British company Reynolds leading the way for frame tubing and the Italian manufacturer Campagnolo for essential components and drivetrains. Many Italian and French brands, too, gained popularity with discerning cyclists. However, being able to stroll into a bike shop and walk out with a top-end machine was still some years off: quality racers still had to be constructed by hand and each component specified and installed by a skilled mechanic.

Flawless paint finish

Plain steel-lugged frame

Wheels with high flange hubs

Original chainset

▷ **Jacques Anquetil 1970**

Origin	France
Frame	Steel
Gears	10-speed
Wheels	28 in (70 cm)

A five-time Tour de France winner in the 1960s, Anquetil was a big name in the racing world and his bikes were popular with recreational riders. The bikes used affordable Huret gears and featured fashionable Mafac center-pull brakes.

Front derailleur
This is a 1970 Huret Luxe. Based in France, Huret was a major manufacturer of bicycle derailleurs, with a model to suit every budget.

Original saddle replaced with a Selle San Marco Regal

Reynolds 531 frame

Half-chrome forks and stays

◁ **Carlton Truwell-Campagnolo Team Bike 1971**

Origin	UK
Frame	Steel
Gears	12-speed
Wheels	28 in (70 cm)

Raleigh acquired Carlton bicycles in 1960. Its Special Bicycle Development Unit continued making bikes under the Carlton name. This model had stylish "shot-in" stays and a Campagnolo Record groupset with bar-end shifters to minimize reach for fast shifting.

Minimalist cantilever brakes

Campagnolo rear derailleur

▷ **Carlton John Atkins Pro Cyclo-Cross 1971**

Origin	UK
Frame	Steel
Gears	6-speed
Wheels	28 in (70 cm)

British cyclist, John Atkins, was the leading cyclo-cross rider of the era and is still considered the best British cross racer of all time. His Carlton was made using Reynolds tubing, with generous clearances for his favored Clement Grifo tubular tires.

Single-ring Stronglight crankset to keep weight down

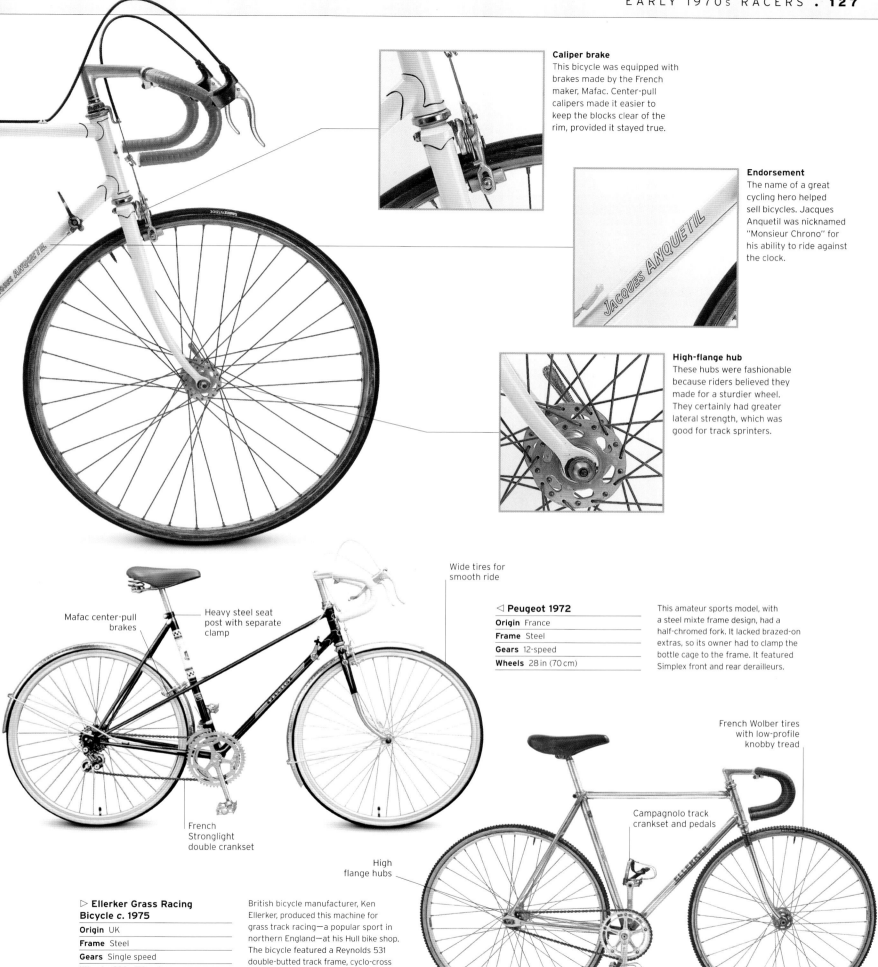

Caliper brake
This bicycle was equipped with brakes made by the French maker, Mafac. Center-pull calipers made it easier to keep the blocks clear of the rim, provided it stayed true.

Endorsement
The name of a great cycling hero helped sell bicycles. Jacques Anquetil was nicknamed "Monsieur Chrono" for his ability to ride against the clock.

High-flange hub
These hubs were fashionable because riders believed they made for a sturdier wheel. They certainly had greater lateral strength, which was good for track sprinters.

Heavy steel seat post with separate clamp

Mafac center-pull brakes

French Stronglight double crankset

Wide tires for smooth ride

◁ **Peugeot 1972**

Origin	France
Frame	Steel
Gears	12-speed
Wheels	28 in (70 cm)

This amateur sports model, with a steel mixte frame design, had a half-chromed fork. It lacked brazed-on extras, so its owner had to clamp the bottle cage to the frame. It featured Simplex front and rear derailleurs.

French Wolber tires with low-profile knobby tread

Campagnolo track crankset and pedals

High flange hubs

▷ **Ellerker Grass Racing Bicycle c. 1975**

Origin	UK
Frame	Steel
Gears	Single speed
Wheels	28 in (70 cm)

British bicycle manufacturer, Ken Ellerker, produced this machine for grass track racing—a popular sport in northern England—at his Hull bike shop. The bicycle featured a Reynolds 531 double-butted track frame, cyclo-cross tires, and a chrome finish.

Late 1970s Racers

From the beginning of the 1970s through the end of that decade, there was little change in the evolution of top-end, high-quality bicycles. Apart from an experiment or two with titanium frames, steel remained the manufacturers' metal of choice for all models—from traditional roadsters to the most expensive racing bikes. As roads improved, however, the geometry of the bike developed, resulting in livelier handling and a stiffer frame. The number of sprockets on the freewheel also went up from five at the beginning of the decade to six by the end.

Steep head tube and tight frame geometry

Chrome fork crown

Gipiemme chainrings with SG logo

△ Sesia 1976

Origin	Italy
Frame	Steel
Gears	12-speed
Wheels	28 in (70 cm)

The Sesia was a classic Italian custom-made bike with a steel frame, elegant cutout lugs, and chrome stays. The side-pull brake calipers were the Flash model by Italian brand Modolo.

Unicanitor thin leather saddle

Manufacturer's GPT stamp

Campagnolo Record low flange hubs

◁ Pinarello Special 1976

Origin	Italy
Frame	Steel
Gears	12-speed
Wheels	28 in (70 cm)

Giovanni Pinarello of Treviso made sought-after racing bicycles built with Columbus tubes and understated finishes. Campagnolo's Super Record crankset was the pros' choice.

Frame painted in Mercier's trademark pink

Cinelli stem and bar

Christophe toe clips

▷ Mercier Service des Courses 1976

Origin	France
Frame	Steel
Gears	12-speed
Wheels	28 in (70 cm)

The Mercier Services des Courses was an iconic 1970s racing bicycle, and this example was similar to the bikes ridden by Joop Zoetemelk and his Gan-Mercier team in the 1975 Tour de France. The French-built frame used Reynolds 531 tubing and forks, with stylish cutout long-point lugs. It featured a full Campagnolo Nuovo Record groupset with Mavic rims, and would not have looked out of place in the pro peloton.

Stripped frameset
with no braze-ons

Lightweight Huret
shifters

Drilled-out
chainrings

◁ **Schwinn Paramount
Titanium 1970s**

Origin US

Frame Titanium

Gears 12-speed

Wheels 28 in (70 cm)

Schwinn's Paramount models
had been the US firm's flagship
racing bikes since the 1930s. This
model was pared down for lightness
with a Huret Jubilee rear derailleur
and Campagnolo chainset with
intricately drilled chainrings.

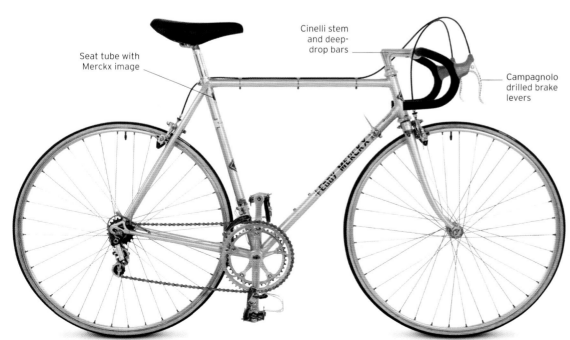

▽ **Kessel Eddy Merckx 1978**

Origin Belgium

Frame Steel

Gears 10-speed

Wheels 28 in (70 cm)

Belgian bike retailer Kessel marketed its
own Eddy Merckx models as the great
champion was coming to the end of his
racing career. The bicycles were built
with Reynolds double-butted tubes and
fork, and a Campagnolo groupset.

Seat tube with
Merckx image

Cinelli stem
and deep-
drop bars

Campagnolo
drilled brake
levers

BIRTH OF TITANIUM FRAMES

Bicycle frames made of titanium are stronger and lighter
than their steel counterparts. Titanium has inherent
shock-absorbing properties, and is resistant to fatigue and
corrosion, so frames do not need to be painted, allowing
the beauty of the finished metal to shine through. The
first titanium bicycle frames were produced in the 1960s
by British company Speedwell, which manufactured them
in small numbers. By 1974, Teledyne of the US was
producing them in larger quantities. After the collapse
of the Soviet Union, Russia released large amounts of
titanium, which contributed to a substantial drop in price.

Most titanium frames are assembled using tungsten
inert gas (TIG) welding. This is necessary because it protects
the weld from atmospheric pollution, which can weaken it.

Joop Zoetemelk, 1985 road world champion

Great Manufacturers
Colnago

One of the most prestigious names in cycling, Colnago combines the master craftsmanship of its founder with more than 60 years of racing success at the highest level. Ernesto Colnago experimented with frame geometry, aerodynamic designs, and titanium and carbon-fiber materials long before rivals saw their potential.

FROM ITS ORIGINS in the workshop of the young mechanic Ernesto Colnago, who built frames for amateur racers, to its current position as a premium cycling brand, Colnago has always made bicycles for the performance market. Ernesto Colnago's grounding as a frame-builder and mechanic for professional cycling teams imbued his company with a strong ethos of functionality, innovation, and elegance from the very beginning.

Ernesto began his career in 1945 at the age of 13 as a welder's assistant at the Gloria cycle factory in Milan. An avid amateur racer, he accrued a succession of wins before breaking his leg in a crash after sprinting to fourth place at the Milano–Busseto race in 1951. Ernesto's resulting immobility led to a period in which he built

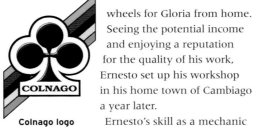

Colnago logo

wheels for Gloria from home. Seeing the potential income and enjoying a reputation for the quality of his work, Ernesto set up his workshop in his home town of Cambiago a year later.

Ernesto's skill as a mechanic shone through despite his youth. He received commissions from top Italian racers of the day, including Fausto Coppi, and made simple adjustments to frame geometry—such as making smaller, more compact frames—to improve rigidity and rider comfort. Ernesto was also lauded as the key factor in the 1957 Giro d'Italia triumph of Gastone Nencini, who told journalists that "the credit must go to Ernesto Colnago, a young mechanic from Lombardy who has built me an unbeatable bicycle."

With such praise issuing from the highest echelons of the sport, demand

Hour Record ride
Although the bicycle ridden by Merckx for his 1972 record was branded with the Belgian's name, it was custom-made by Colnago.

replacing the company's original eagle logo. The ace symbolized the blooming of the spring flowers by the roadside of the Milan–San Remo spring classic, which had just been won by Italian Michele Dancelli on a Colnago bike—an all-Italian victory

the cutting edge of cycling technology. In return, his profile as the most successful cyclist of the era—and arguably, of all time—also lent further prestige to the Colnago brand.

While Colnago was founded on racing success, the survival of the business depended on appealing to recreational cyclists and amateur racers. Colnago offered "off-the-rack" racing bicycles in around 15 sizes— far more than most other companies—but could build made-to-measure bicycles for customers too. Extra details, such as chromed

Creative tools
Ernesto Colnago, seen here in 1960 in the Cambiago workshop with brother Paolo, deploys artistry and a mechanic's touch.

"For me, the **whole** thing **revolves** around **my love** for bicycles."

ERNESTO COLNAGO

for Colnago's expertise grew quickly. Ernesto was soon working with the Italian national team, and in 1960 one of his bicycles was ridden to a gold medal at the Rome Olympics.

The 1970s cemented Ernesto's reputation as a master craftsman of racing bicycles of the highest quality. Colnago's distinctive ace-of-clubs motif was developed in 1970,

that led Ernesto to joke, "I had an ace up my sleeve that day."

The following year Eddy Merckx joined the Molteni team and brought his racer's instinct to the Colnago design and construction process. Fastidious in his scrutiny of every measurement and component of the bikes he rode, Merckx partnered with Ernesto to take Colnago bicycles to

Carbon revelation
Italian Franco Ballerini won the Paris-Roubaix race twice, in 1995 and 1998, on Colnago's flagship carbon-fiber race bike, the C40.

Mexico Oro with gold-plated parts 1979

C35 Oro with Ferrari wheels 1989

C40 with Spinergy wheels 1994

Master 55 limited edition 2008

1952 Ernesto Colnago opens his own workshop in his home town of Cambiago, near Milan.

1954 Colnago produces his first complete bicycles, and experiments with a cold-forging process for making steel bicycle forks.

1960 Colnago works with Italian racing team.

1962 Colnago starts working as a mechanic for the Molteni team. Gianni Motta wins the Giro d'Italia in 1966.

1972 Colnago designs and builds the bicycle

for Eddy Merckx's Hour Record ride in Mexico City. It features a custom-made titanium stem and drilled components and weighs just 12.68 lb (5.75 kg).

1974 Branded Colnago bicycles appear in the professional peloton for the first time, ridden by the Scic team.

1987 The Precisa straight-bladed front fork is developed after Ferrari advises that straight steel blades offer improved shock absorption compared with traditional curved blades.

1991 Italy wins the World Championships team time trial, riding Colnago bikes with smaller front wheels that improve aerodynamics and allow team members to ride close together for better drafting.

1991 Colnago debuts its Master BiTitan titanium frame, with a twin down tube.

1994 The Mapei team rides Colnago bikes to 58 wins in its first season. In 1996, 1998, and 1999, Mapei riders finish first, second, and third in the Paris-Roubaix.

1998 Colnago becomes one of only a few bicycle manufacturers to seek and be awarded ISO 9001 certification for its frame manufacturing process.

2000s Colnago continues sponsorship of professional road, cyclo-cross, and mountain-bike teams.

2002 The CF2 carbon-fibre, full-suspension mountain bike is released with Ferrari.

2012 Colnago becomes the first company to release a production road bike equipped with hydraulic disc brakes.

lugs, subtle ace-of-clubs cut-outs on the frame, and "pantographed" engravings on components, soon drew a loyal following.

The 1980s saw innovations come thick and fast. First Colnago launched the Master racing bicycle, built with custom-drawn, crimped steel tubes—giving an indented tube profile rather than the standard circular or elliptical cross section—to increase frame stiffness. In 1987, Colnago produced a collaboration with Ferrari: a concept bike with a car-style gearbox instead of derailleurs, and hydraulic brakes. Two years later the Ferrari relationship gave rise to the C35, a hand-wrapped, carbon-fiber monocoque bicycle that was 20 years ahead of its time.

Colnago has a long history of sponsoring professional racers. It entered its most celebrated phase of team sponsorship in the 1990s when it became bicycle supplier to

the Mapei team. This period coincided with the Colnago C40, the first all-carbon-fiber bicycle frame to be ridden in the punishing conditions of professional cycling. The Mapei riders found that, particularly in races over cobblestones—a terrain in which short-travel suspension forks were popular at the time—the carbon-fiber frames produced a noticeably more comfortable and stable ride than their steel counterparts.

As Colnago entered the 21st century, the realities of global manufacturing forced a change in the long-held policy of construction solely on Italian soil. From 2005, mid-range Colnago bicycles were made in Taiwan by the A-Team, a grouping of Taiwanese firms including Giant and Merida. Yet Colnago's creative center and design heartbeat remains at its Italian headquarters in Cambiago, where all of its top-end bicycles are still produced.

Groundbreaking designs
This roadworthy version of the C42 time-trial bike had its aerodynamic rear-wheel fairing removed to meet UCI regulations.

Touring Bikes

The fitness boom in the US and beyond influenced cycling with new models aimed at those who wanted to ride for fun and exercise. The traditional touring scene remained strong, especially in Europe, where hand-built custom frames continued to be the only choice for a quality load-bearing machine. Innovation of parts and materials, and multiple bike types, were some years off, but by the end of the 1970s the nascent mountain bike scene in the US was creating waves that would finally drag the cycling world into the modern era. Touring bikes would benefit greatly, in time. Until then, however, racing-bike frames were commonly adapted for touring purposes, and equipped with optional or aftermarket mudguards, water-bottle holders, and luggage racks.

Chainguard kept clothes oil-free

Steel-cottered cranks with a single ring

French Huret Svelto rear derailleur

△ Val de Loire 1970

Origin	France
Frame	Steel
Gears	5-speed
Wheels	26 in (65 cm)

This charismatic French touring or city bike had wheels with *ballon* (balloon) tires, giving a cushioned ride. The brake levers were fixed to the center or underside of the bars, and there were dynamo-powered front and rear lights.

▽ Schwinn Varsity Sport 1972

Origin	US
Frame	Steel
Gears	10-speed
Wheels	27 in (68 cm)

The Varsity was a versatile American sports and commuting bike. The handmade steel frame, with lugless front end, was equipped with fenders, rack, dynamo lights, and additional horizontal brake levers. Gear levers were clamped to the stem and could be operated without taking hands off the bar.

Drivetrain
At the front, this model featured one-piece cranks with double chainrings and guard, with a derailleur at the rear.

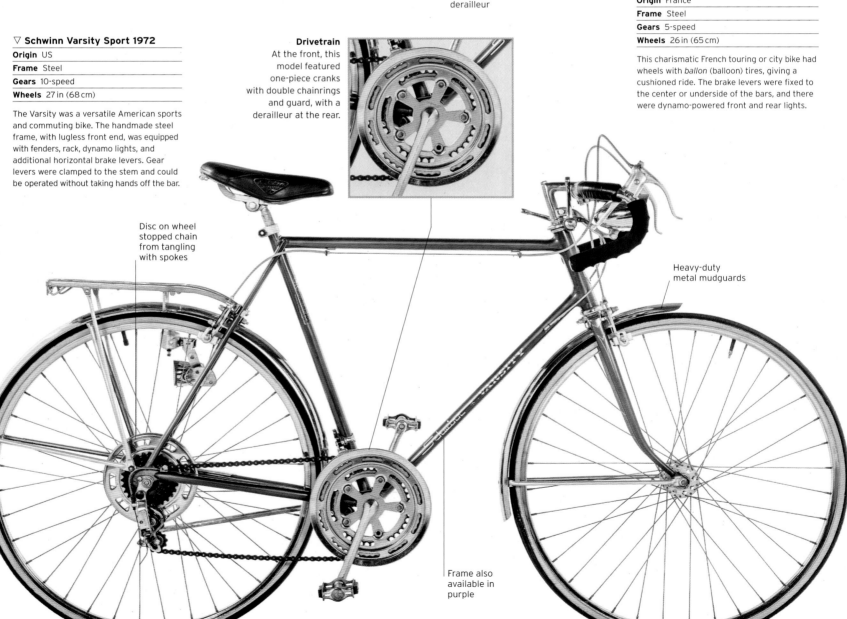

Disc on wheel stopped chain from tangling with spokes

Heavy-duty metal mudguards

Frame also available in purple

Minimalist
fenders

Chrome highlights
on the fork crown

◁ **Schwinn Sport Tourer 1976**

Origin	US
Frame	Steel
Gears	10-speed
Wheels	27 in (68 cm)

"Sports touring" was a term aimed at the
recreational rider who might ride only on
weekends for short periods. Schwinn's answer
was a hand-finished chromoly frame with many
unbranded alloy parts resulting in a machine
weighing some 30 lb (14 kg). Handlebar-mounted
gear-shifters offered fast thumb shifts.

Crankset
with ring-style
chainguard

▷ **Peugeot UE-8 1970s**

Origin	France
Frame	Steel
Gears	10-speed
Wheels	28 in (70 cm)

This classic French touring bike had a steel
frame decorated with Peugeot's familiar
checkered-flag graphics. The extravagantly
raked, half-chromed fork promised lazy
steering for relaxed outings. The UE-8
came equipped with a rack, fenders,
and substantial dynamo-powered lights.

Light, powerful
Mafac center-
pull brakes

Gear levels
on downtube
shifters

Steel cottered
crankset

Lugged frame with
flawless, hand-
finished joints

Standard
drop bars

Mounts for fenders

◁ **Jack Taylor Tour of Britain 1979**

Origin	UK
Frame	Steel
Gears	12-speed
Wheels	28 in (70 cm)

Jack Taylor Cycles was a well-respected
manufacturer of touring bicycle frames in the
UK, and was noted for its finely crafted lugs.
This model featured oval-section front forks
and Campagnolo gears. It was suitable for
road racing or touring, when equipped with
fenders and racks.

Long reach rear derailleur
for wide-ratio freewheel

Raleigh Chopper

One of the style icons of the 1970s, the Raleigh Chopper brought motorcycle-inspired cool to a generation too young for motorized two-wheelers, injecting irreverence and exuberance into a previously conservative area of bicycle design. Drawing directly from the US craze for Easy Rider–style bikes, such as the Schwinn Sting-Ray, Raleigh repackaged the wheelie bike for the UK market and then exported the Chopper design around the world to many of its overseas markets.

WHEN THE FIRST RALEIGH CHOPPER children's bikes appeared in UK bicycle shops in late 1969, the effect was dramatic. With its hot-rod-inspired looks and components, from the "ape-hanger" swept-back handlebars to the curved "sissy bar" seat rail, the Chopper was so popular that it rapidly sold out of its initial release of 500 units—a sign of the success that was to follow over the next 10 years.

Just as the Schwinn Sting-Ray had done in the US six years earlier, the Chopper struck a chord with the youth bicycle market in the UK and elsewhere. Raleigh already had some experience of the wheelie-bike craze—its North America division brought out the Rodeo (1966) and Fireball (1968) in an attempt to take on Schwinn, whose Sting-Ray dominated the sector. Many of the Chopper's design features first appeared on these two models, including the top-tube-mounted gear-shifter and padded vinyl seat.

The feature that set the Chopper apart was its straight-tubed frame, which differed from the curving cruiser-style tubes of its US precursors. In other ways it shared the precarious riding characteristics of most other wheelie bikes, with the rear-slung saddle and small front wheel combining to place the rider's weight over the rear wheel, making wheelies and skittish front-wheel handling inevitable.

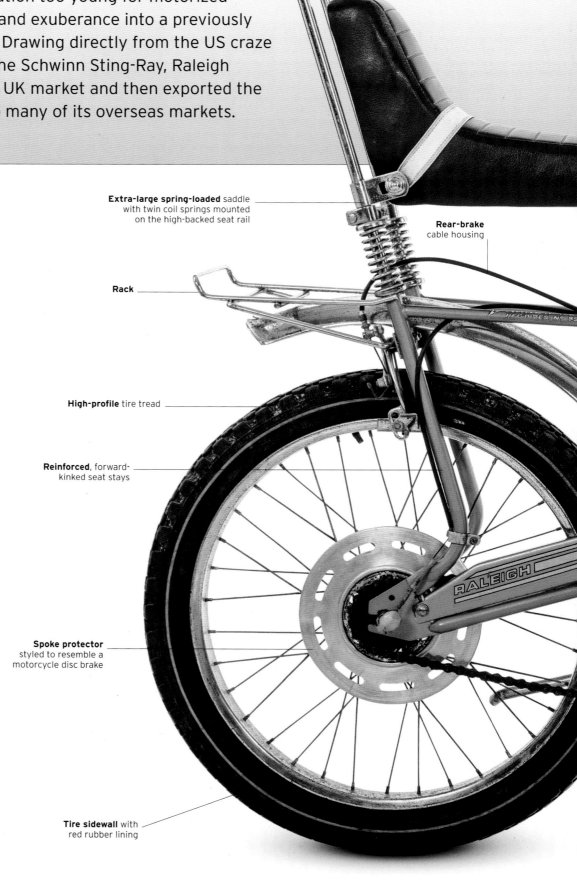

Extra-large spring-loaded saddle with twin coil springs mounted on the high-backed seat rail

Rear-brake cable housing

Rack

High-profile tire tread

Reinforced, forward-kinked seat stays

Spoke protector styled to resemble a motorcycle disc brake

Tire sidewall with red rubber lining

SPECIFICATIONS	
Origin	UK
Designer	Ogle Design/Alan Oakley
Year	1979
Frame	Steel
Gears	3-speed
Brakes	Caliper
Wheels	Front 16 in (40 cm), Rear 20 in (50 cm)
Weight	Approx. 41 lb (18.5 kg)

High-rise handlebar
welded to the stem

"**Chopper**—a machine inspired by the **screaming rubber** and **roaring fantails** of the dragster racing bike."
RALEIGH CHOPPER AD, 1970

Raleigh logo
First used in the early 1900s, the Raleigh logo's heron motif came from the family crest of company chairman Frank Bowden.

Car-style
gear-shifter

Parallel top tubes
welded to either side of the head tube

Chainguard

Front mudguard

CHOPPER

Branded crankset featuring Raleigh logo in the form of three Heron head crest cutouts

Center-mounted
kickstand

THE COMPONENTS

The Chopper was available in several different models and
component packages during the course of its 10-year production
run. Single-speed, hub-gear, and derailleur-gear versions were
released, while a drop-handlebar model—the Sprint—was also
introduced. The biggest overhaul of components was for the
MK II Chopper in 1972, which featured a redesigned frame
to counter the MK I's tendency to suffer snapped seat tubes.

1. Padded-vinyl, high-backed saddle **2.** Rear-facing reflector mounted
behind saddle **3.** Kinked seat stay for improved frame strength, and
drivetrain featuring Sturmey-Archer hub gear, mock disc-brake spoke
protector, and chainguard **4.** Coil-sprung saddle suspension **5.** T-bar
gear-shift lever **6.** Transmission console with gear indicator **7.** Raleigh's
own-brand brake lever mounted on swept-back "ape-hanger" handlebar
8. Battery-powered front light **9.** Flat pedal

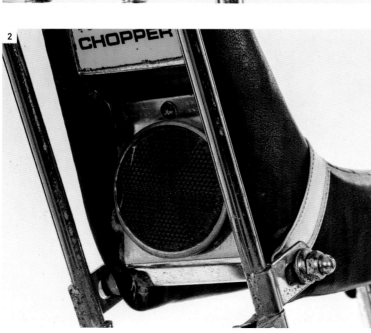

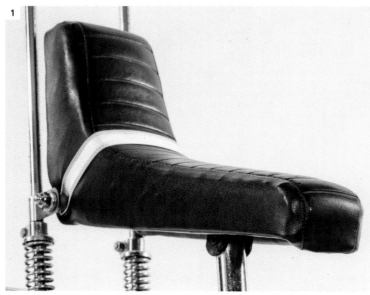

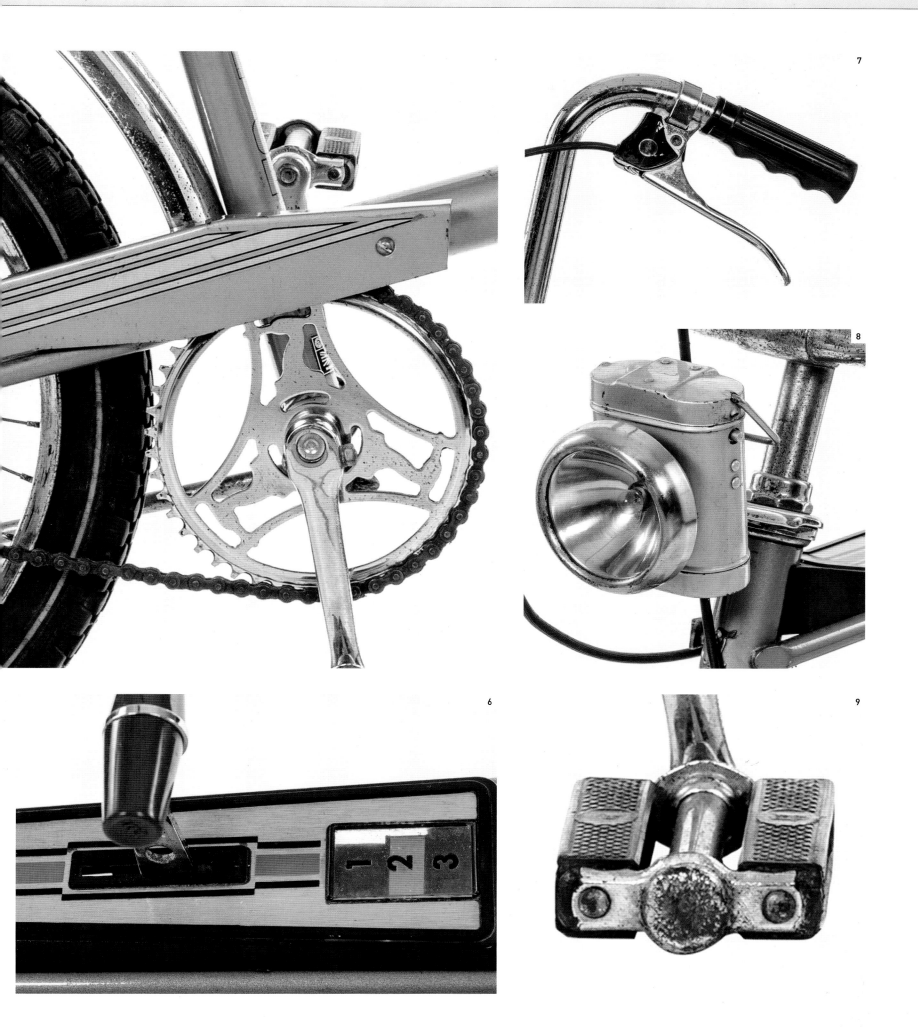

7

8

6

9

Mountain biking became a global phenomenon in the 1980s, but had its roots in the previous decade. It was pioneered by a group of thrill-seeking cyclists in California, USA, who rode their modified "klunkers" on the dusty trails of Mount Tamalpais in Marin County. These pioneers included Joe Breeze, shown here (far right) on his hand-built Breezer #1, the first modern, all-new bike designed specifically for the sport. Almost 40 years on, Breezer bikes are still available.

BMX Bikes

BMX is an abbreviation of "bicycle motocross." The modern form of the sport as recognized today began in California in the late 1960s. BMX was an instant hit with the youth of the day, and by 1974 there were 130,000 BMX bikes in California alone, and 100 dedicated tracks. The bikes were simple, with squat diamond frames often reinforced with gussets, and 20-in (50-cm) wheels with wide tires. For strength, manufacturers welded the fork blades directly to the steerer tubes. They used one-piece cranksets. BMX bikes soon spread around the world. A sport that many commentators thought would be a flash in the pan, BMX is still popular 50 years later.

Robust steel frame for jumps and stunts

BMX suspension
The Monoshock was developed for dirt racing, not stunts, and the suspension was designed to help the bike cope with harsh off-road conditions.

△ **Huffy Thunder**
1970s

Origin	US
Frame	Steel
Gears	Single speed
Wheels	20 in (50 cm)

American maker Huffman produced many bikes under the Huffy name. Early 1970s' versions still showed the influence of Sting-Ray design, and had a sturdy steel frame to sustaint jumps and stunts.

Front fork with suspension

▽ **Webco Monoshock**
mid-1970s

Origin	US
Frame	Steel
Gears	Single speed
Wheels	20 in (50 cm)

Webco Inc. was an early BMX bike maker that operated out of Venice, CA between 1974 and 1980. Some of its bikes had distinctive five-spoke, Motomag magnesium alloy wheels made by Skip Hess.

Shock absorber for rear wheel

Pivoting rear stays

Stem pad protects rider from edges in a crash

Colored BMX tyres

◁ Skyway 1974

Origin	US
Frame	Steel
Gears	Single speed
Wheels	20 in (50 cm)

Skyway was best known for producing BMX wheels, having introduced its eponymous five-spoke Tuff Wheel in 1974. However, the company also developed and manufactured complete bikes up until the late 1980s.

Rubber grips for better grip on handlebars

Frame pad also hides brake

▷ Schwinn Sting 1978

Origin	US
Frame	Steel
Gears	Single speed
Wheels	20 in (50 cm)

The Sting was a premium hand-built BMX bike and one of Schwinn's top-of-the-line models until the 1980s. The "tri-oval" chromoly frame was unique to Schwinn, with oval-shaped ends at the joints for greater strength. The bike was available with red or blue accessories.

Knobby tires for good traction

Color-coded wheel rims

Motomag alloy wheels

Twin-frame gusset for strength

◁ Mongoose Motomag 1970s

Origin	US
Frame	Steel
Gears	Single speed
Wheels	20 in (50 cm)

Having started out producing Motomag wheels, Skip Hess diversified by making entire BMX bikes under the Mongoose brand name. At its peak, the company made about 600 frames a day at its factory in Chatsworth, CA. The Motomag model featured Hess's trademark wheels and was produced from 1975 until 1981.

Great Races
Ironman Triathlon 1979

The Ironman triathlon—a 2.4-mile (3.8-km) swim, followed by a 112-mile (180.3-km) bicycle ride, then a full 26.2-mile (42.2-km) marathon run without a break—started as a friendly challenge between a small group of people in Hawaii.

The Kailua-Kona Ironman is still number one
Faris-Al-Sultan (left) won the men's 2004 Ironman title and Nina Kraft (right) the women's in 2005. Ironman has become a massive brand, and there are many triathlons worldwide.

THERE IS A LOT OF DEBATE about when the first swim–cycle–run event took place. There was a well-documented run–cycle–swim event in Mission Bay, CA, in 1976, while there were three-sport events in France as long ago as the 1920s. These

events consisted of the three triathlon disciplines, but the order varied. The first recorded swim–cycle–run sequence took place in Marseilles in 1927, and may have been the first-ever triathlon as we know the sport today.

The idea for the Ironman Triathlon came about in Hawaii in 1977, when a group of friends were chatting at the awards ceremony following the round-Oahu running race (Oahu is the third largest of the Hawaiian Islands). The friends

had different sporting interests and were debating who were the fittest: swimmers, cyclists, or runners. US Navy Commander John Collins suggested they have a race that combined three established endurance challenges: the Waikiki Roughwater Swim, the Oahu Bike Ride, and the Honolulu Marathon.

The Oahu Bike Ride is in fact 115 miles (185 km) long, but to make the start of the cycle

Competitors in the first ever Ironman
John Dunbar (left), a former Navy SEAL, is seen overtaking a competitor on his way to second place. Dunbar led after the bike section, but his support crew ran out of water and gave him beer to drink instead, so he slowed dramatically.

"Sometimes **ignorance is bliss**. It never occurred to me something could be **difficult** or **challenging** or whether I'd **win or lose.**"

TOM WARREN, 1979

race coincide with the end of the swim and the finish dovetail with the start of the marathon, Collins cut its distance to 112 miles (180.25 km). The Waikiki Swim is 2.4 miles (3.9 km) and a marathon is 26.2 miles (42.2 km), and so that is how the distances were decided upon. The name Ironman then came about because Collins wrote some basic rules that ended with: "Whoever finishes first, we'll call him the Ironman."

THE EARLY RACES

On February 18, 1978, 15 men started the first-ever Ironman and 12 of them finished. The winner was American Gordon Haller, with a time of 11 hours, 46 minutes, and 58 seconds.

The following year, 1979, saw 50 athletes sign up to take part, but the race was postponed for a day because of bad weather. The seas were still very rough the following day, so only 15 competitors were willing to go ahead, including former national cycling champion Lyn Lemaire, the first woman to compete. Tom Warren, a fitness enthusiast from San Diego, led out of the swim stage by four

minutes. It took him only four minutes to change into his cycling kit, then he really stretched his lead. Warren was 21 minutes clear by the end of the cycle leg. He had a big margin to play with during the marathon, but that in itself caused him problems. "Knowing I'd won and had only to go through the motions was difficult at one point," he explained. He also said that he had not found the shift between disciplines such a problem, because it was something he had been doing for years. At the time Warren was swimming 5 miles (8 km) and running 13 miles (21 km) a day, and cycling whenever he could. Warren won the 1979 event, cutting half an hour off Haller's 1978 time. Lemaire finished fifth overall in a time of 12 hours 55 minutes. Speaking after the race, Warren said: "There's normally a tailwind around the back of the bike course, so I pushed the

World champion Australian Craig Alexander (right)
Alexander won the world title in 2008, 2009, and in 2011, when he set a record of 8 hours, 3 minutes, and 56 seconds (with changes): a 51-minute, 56-second swim; a 4-hour, 24-minute, 5-second cycle; and a 2-hour, 44-minute, 3-second run.

first third really hard in anticipation of that tailwind, but when I got around the back side the wind had shifted, so it was just hard all the way… "

The Ironman grew fast, and in 1981 it moved to the Big Island of Hawaii, where it has been held since. Owned by the World Triathlon Corporation (WTC), the Hawaii Ironman is its world championship, with qualifying events around the world.

The start of the 2010 Ironman
The Ironman swim start is an incredible sight as hundreds of competitors battle to get clear of their rivals. Competitors start in four "waves." The professional men start first, with the pro women next. They are followed by the age-group men's race, then the women's. Each "wave" is separated by five minutes.

KEY FACTS

RESULTS
First: Tom Warren, US
Second: John Dunbar, US
Third: Ian Emberson, US

THE MODERN COURSE
The Ironman begins with the swim section in Kailua Bay. The transition between swimming and cycling and the final marathon stage are in Kailua-Kona. The map here shows the modern cycling route, rather than the original round-Oahu route. After cycling, the athletes have to climb up Palani Road to the Queen Ka'ahumanu Highway to run their marathon—an extreme test of fitness.

Coastal cycle route
The athletes ride out and back along the Queen Ka'ahumanu Highway—the Hawaii Island Belt Road. This route is very exposed and windy, with no shelter; the conditions can be extremely hot and humid.

Town and Leisure Bikes

The 1970s witnessed the biggest boom in bicycle purchases since the 1890s. Across the globe, people were hit by pedal-powered fever, and it resulted in a new wave of bicycle designs, some more successful than others. The traditional roadster remained popular, but the boom welcomed all sorts of bicycles of different shapes and wheel sizes. The 1973 oil crisis saw an increase in the cost of driving a car and made bicycle commuting a more attractive option. Low-priced town bikes, which were increasingly manufactured in Asia, offered inexpensive transportation for recreation and exercise.

Low-quality, faux-leather saddle

Quick-release lever unlocked the fold hinge

△ Hercules Auto Velo 1973

Origin	Germany
Frame	Steel
Gears	Single speed
Wheels	16 in (40 cm)

Designed to help industrial workers get from A to B, this was an early version of a folding bike. The bicycle had a robust chromoly-steel frame and a quick-release lever hinging the down tube. The fold method was clunky and did not catch on.

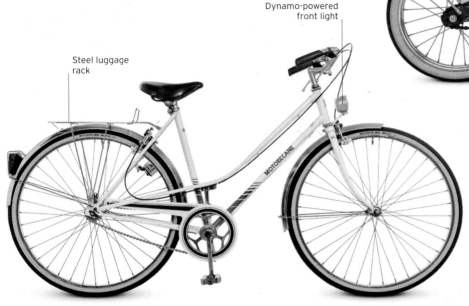

Dynamo-powered front light

Steel luggage rack

△ Motobécane Tourer Women's Model 1974

Origin	France
Frame	Steel
Gears	Single speed
Wheels	26 in (65 cm)

French manufacturer Motobécane enjoyed a good reputation as a builder of lightweight, quality racing bikes. During the bicycle boom of the 1970s, the brand stretched its wings and capitalized on the market's desire for easy, fuss-free town bicycles, which it sold at very reasonable prices.

▽ Mercier Step-through Tourer Women's Model 1970s

Origin	France
Frame	Steel
Gears	Single speed
Wheels	26 in (65 cm)

This classic women's town bike sold by the thousand to riders in suburbia. The Loop featured a basic steel frame with tubes joined by lugs. A chainguard stopped the rider's pants from getting caught in the chainrings. The rear wheel powered dynamo lights.

Simple saddle with synthetic upper and steel rails

Dynamo lamp powered by rear wheel

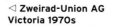

Extra-long seat post to compensate for compact frame

Chainguard

◁ Zweirad-Union AG Victoria 1970s

Origin	Germany
Frame	Steel
Gears	Single speed
Wheels	16 in (40 cm)

Sold in many West German department stores, the Victoria had a crude fold system: a single lever was released and the frame hinged back on itself. The chopper-style handlebar gave an upright riding position, and a rack over the back wheel was provided for cargo.

Canvas bag to hold shopping

Synthetic saddle with springs for comfort

Detachable wire basket

▽ BSA 20 Shopper 1970s

Origin	UK
Frame	Steel
Gears	Single speed
Wheels	20 in (50 cm)

The BSA Shopper mobilized people in British towns during the 1970s and sold by the thousand. Scaling down the bike to a simple frame with a short, low down tube and small wheels made it easy to maneuver and just light enough for day-to-day errands.

Wide pedals with plastic base

Motorcycle-style, padded saddle

Chainring powered by pivoting frame

Brake cables connect to chainstay-mounted brake

◁ Hercules Cavallo 1970s

Origin	Germany
Frame	Steel
Gears	Single speed
Wheels	24 in (60 cm)

Cavallo, Italian for "horse," was a bicycle based on the movement of a jockey. The riders placed their feet on platforms and moved their body up and down, activating the hinged frame and driving power to the rear wheel. German manufacturer Hercules produced the Cavallo, but needless to say, the new system of bike riding did not catch on—adults were too shy to use it in public.

Plastic wheel reflectors

Fixed pedals

Children's Bikes

Traditionally, children's bicycles had been smaller versions of adult roadsters. The 1970s saw a new craze for children—the chopper bike. American manufacturer Schwinn was the first to mass-produce the bike, and by the mid-1970s Raleigh had several chopper models to its name. The popularity of the style was overwhelming. For the next two decades, children played around on nothing else but these pedal-powered, miniature, motorbike-inspired bikes, which evolved into the 1980s' must-have bike, the BMX.

▽ **Schwinn Sting-Ray Apple Krate 1973**

Origin	US
Frame	Steel
Gears	3-speed
Wheels	Front 16 in (40 cm), Rear 20 in (50 cm)

With its central gear-shifter, motor-cycle-style seating, and unique front suspension, the Schwinn Sting-Ray was coveted by many North American children. Ads proclaimed the Sting-Ray was "the bike with sports-car styling." Britain's version of the bicycle was the Raleigh Chopper.

Front suspension
The Sting-Ray featured unique front suspension. At the front, a steel coil spring attached at the headset, while hinges on the front fork absorbed the shocks from the front wheel.

Rear derailleur
Schwinn made its own components for its bicycles; the rear derailleur used rollers or jockey wheels to keep the chain in line while a sprung mechanism pushed the chain up and down the rear cogs.

Rear caliper brake
A dual-pivot, side-pull caliper brake was one of the most popular bicycle brake designs. One arm pivoted at the center and the other at the side, pulling the brake pads onto the rim.

Gear-shift
The Apple Krate was unique because it was one of the first bikes to have 5-speed gearing. The chrome-finished lever, with its larger rubber handle, looked similar to a car gear lever.

Front drum brake
Braking at the front was controlled by a large aluminum drum brake in the center of the wheel. When the brake cable was pulled, it pushed two pads in the drum against the braking surface.

Rear rack ideal for backpacks

Rubber suspension

◁ **Moulton Junior 3 1973**

Origin	UK
Frame	Steel
Gears	3-speed
Wheels	17 in (44 cm)

British designer Alex Moulton famously created the rubber suspension system for the Mini motorcar. His revolutionary bikes used rubber springs and small wheels, and became incredibly popular, spawning several models, including bicycles for children.

Padded, curved saddle

Throttle-style gear-shifter

Seat with backrest

Dynamo-powered front lamp

△ **Raleigh Grifter 1977**

Origin	UK
Frame	Steel
Gears	3-speed
Wheels	20 in (50 cm)

At the top of every child's Christmas list in the UK when production started in 1976, the Grifter was heavily influenced by motocross bikes of the time, with its chunky off-road tires, extra-wide handlebar, and even a throttle-style, 3-speed grip twist shifter.

Balloon tires

△ **Bonanza Super de Luxe 1978**

Origin	Germany
Frame	Steel
Gears	3-speed
Wheels	Front 18 in (45 cm), Rear 20 in (50 cm)

After the launch of the Raleigh Chopper, manufacturers around the world followed suit, creating their own chopper bikes. The Bonanza, inspired by the US television series, had dynamo-powered front and rear lighting and a drum brake.

Step-over frame

Aluminum mudguards

▷ **Flandria F8 Girls' Model 1970s**

Origin	Belgium
Frame	Steel
Gears	Single speed
Wheels	20 in (50 cm)

Flandria was known for its prowess in making first-class adult racing bikes; aspiring young champions could also get a slice of the action with Flandria's range of smaller road bikes. These models were often equipped with a coaster brake and dazzling white tires.

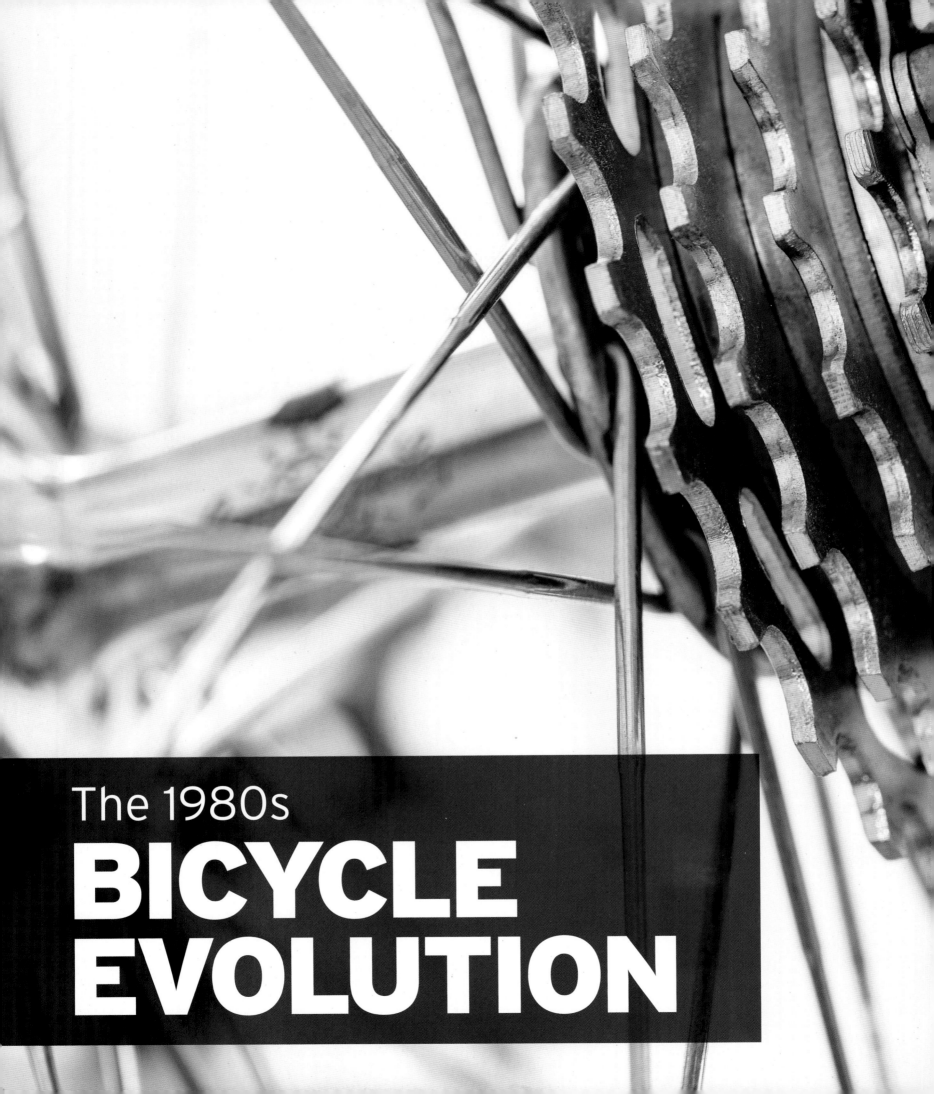

The 1980s
BICYCLE EVOLUTION

BICYCLE EVOLUTION

By the early 1980s the experimentation and ingenuity of the "clunker" riders was beginning to bear fruit, yielding a new breed of bicycle that would take the world by storm. Stronger, straight-tubed frames, custom-brazed from chromoly steel, replaced the organic curves of the modified cruisers of the 1970s, which had proved unable to withstand the bumps and drops of off-road riding. With the addition of 18-speed derailleur gears and knobby tires, the mountain bike was so named because of its ability to be ridden on harsh off-road terrain.

Away from the California cottage industry that created the mountain bike, a new trend was spreading among road and track cycling: aerodynamics. Due to the slowing effect of wind resistance—which at speeds of more than 15 mph (24 km/h) is estimated to require 90 percent of a rider's energy output to overcome—reducing and shaping the front profile of rider and machine had long been recognized as a holy grail that could increase speed while reducing effort.

In 1984, aerodynamic improvements were among the factors that enabled Italian Francesco Moser to smash the 14-year-old Hour Record of Eddy Merckx, which many had considered unbreakable, by 4,521 ft (1,378 m). Because he was riding a low-profile bicycle with a cow-horn handlebar and carbon-fiber disk wheels, and wearing a skinsuit, helmet cover, and overshoes made from Lycra, Moser's ride heralded a new era in scientific training and equipment refinement that would shape the development of cycling.

△ **An unfair advantage**
Moser's bicycle gave him such an advantage during his Hour Record that the organizers, the Union Cycliste Internationale, banned it.

Key Events

▷ **1980** Pioneers Gary Fisher and Charlie Kelly sell off-road bicycles under the company name "MountainBikes," using frames built by Tom Ritchey.

▷ **1981** Specialized commissions received for first mass-produced mountain bike, the Stumpjumper (see pp.162–65), based on Tom Ritchey's frame design.

▷ **1982** Race Across America (RAAM) is held for the first time, covering 2,968 miles (4,777 km) from Santa Monica, CA, to the Empire State Building in New York City.

▷ **1982** Shimano realizes the potential of the mountain bike, and so releases the Deore XT groupset for off-road use.

▷ **1984** Women's cycling events appear at the Olympic Games, held in Los Angeles, for the first time.

▷ **1984** US sales of mountain bikes reach one million.

▷ **1986** Pete Penseyres wins RAAM using aero-bars—a handlebar extension developed for triathlons.

△ **Moulton mountain bike**
In 1988 the small-wheeled Moulton Space-Frame AM-MTB full-suspension mountain bike is launched.

▷ **1989** Greg LeMond wins the Tour de France on the final day's time-trial, using the aerodynamic gains of aero-bars, a teardrop-shaped helmet, and a disc rear wheel to overhaul a 50-second deficit.

> "I'm lucky that **mountain biking** wasn't around when I was 20, because I wouldn't have won the **Tour de France**. It's **my kind** of sport."

GREG LEMOND, THREE-TIME WINNER OF THE TOUR DE FRANCE

◁ **The LA Summer Games of the Olympics in 1984** included three road races and five track events.

Early 1980s Racing Bikes

The 1980s was the final decade of the traditional all-steel bicycle, with frame-builders using the same working practices as previous generations. Tubes were lugged or lugless, both employing skilled brazing techniques. Everything from the choice of the paint to the wheels was specified by the customer, and the hubs, spokes, and rims were assembled by a trained wheel-builder. Derailleur gears operated by friction levers remained the norm, but the number of available gears went up to eight sprockets on the multiple freewheel by the end of the 1980s.

Lightweight racing wheels

High flange hub typical of the period

Concor saddle was a popular choice

Eye-catching chrome lugs

Lightweight Campagnolo front derailleur

△ Fuji Racer c. 1980

Origin	Japan
Frame	Steel
Gears	10-speed
Wheels	28 in (70 cm)

An example of Japanese bicycle-making at its finest, the Fuji had a beautifully crafted steel frame and finely pinstriped chrome lugs. The home-grown Sugino chainset was drilled for lightness. The bike had quality SunTour gears and brakes.

◁ Colnago Superissimo 1982

Origin	Italy
Frame	Steel
Gears	12-speed
Wheels	28 in (70 cm)

With its eye-catching chrome lugs, fork, and rear dropouts, the Colnago Superissimo had all the hallmarks of classic Italian style. Its Campagnolo groupset and Vittoria tires made it a very desirable bicycle.

▷ Raleigh Team c. 1980

Origin	UK
Frame	Steel
Gears	12-speed
Wheels	28 in (70 cm)

Modeled on the Dutch TI-Raleigh team cycles, the team replica machines built at the Nottingham factory for retail could almost pass for the real thing. Both were handcrafted from Reynolds tubing, with Campagnolo gears; the customer version had Nuovo components.

Deep drop Cinelli bars

Paint colors matched TI-Raleigh pro-team's livery

Lightweight chainring drilled with many holes

Unicanitor racing saddle

Chrome fork crown on Columbus forks

◁ CBT Italia c. 1980

Origin	Italy
Frame	Steel
Gears	12-speed
Wheels	28 in (70 cm)

The Italian bicycle by Construction Bicycles Tardivo (CBT) was the ultimate racing machine. The frame was made with Columbus tubes, the groupset by Campagnolo, and the bars from Cinelli. It had a chrome fork crown and delicate cutouts on the head-tube lugs.

Bullhorn handlebars
for time trialing

◁ **Colnago Speciale Competizione 1983**

Origin Italy

Frame Steel

Gears 12-speed

Wheels 28 in (70 cm)

Italian legend Ernesto Colnago added his own
creative touches to the classic lines of the steel
diamond frame. The bike had engraved chainrings
and stem, and a bottom bracket shell cut out in
the shape of the Colnago cloverleaf.

Chrome fork with
steep rake for racing

Rear wheel components
The bike has Mavic
components from the
pioneering French
bike manufacturer.

▽ **Vitus 979 Dural 1985**

Origin France

Frame Aluminum-magnesium alloy

Gears 12-speed

Wheels 28 in (70 cm)

Introduced in the late 1970s, by the
mid-80s the Vitus 979 was a proven race
winner under Irish pro Sean Kelly. The
aluminum-magnesium alloy frame was
much lighter than steel and the bike was
equipped with French Mavic components.

**One-piece alloy
head tube**
The aluminum-
magnesium alloy
head tube was made
in one piece for
greater strength.

Aero levers
with hidden
cable routing

Cables run
along the bar

Late 1980s Racing Bikes

The introduction of different materials to make bicycle frames, combined with exciting new technology, heralded the start of a new era in cycling. At the start of the decade, racing cyclists' only option was to commission an artisan-built steel frame. By the end, the choice had expanded to factory-built frames made from materials as diverse as magnesium and carbon fiber. The days of the universal lugged-steel frame, assembled by individual craftsmen, were coming to an end with astonishing speed.

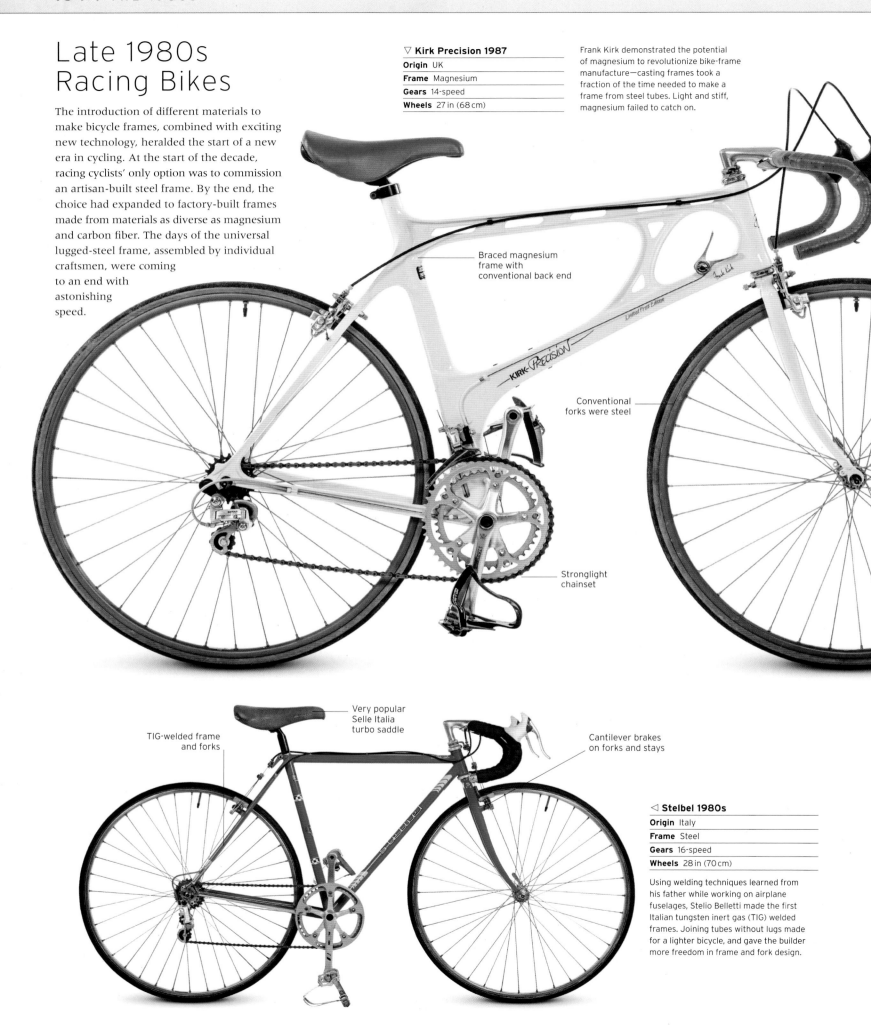

▽ **Kirk Precision 1987**

Origin	UK
Frame	Magnesium
Gears	14-speed
Wheels	27 in (68 cm)

Frank Kirk demonstrated the potential of magnesium to revolutionize bike-frame manufacture—casting frames took a fraction of the time needed to make a frame from steel tubes. Light and stiff, magnesium failed to catch on.

Braced magnesium frame with conventional back end

Conventional forks were steel

Stronglight chainset

TIG-welded frame and forks

Very popular Selle Italia turbo saddle

Cantilever brakes on forks and stays

◁ **Stelbel 1980s**

Origin	Italy
Frame	Steel
Gears	16-speed
Wheels	28 in (70 cm)

Using welding techniques learned from his father while working on airplane fuselages, Stelio Belletti made the first Italian tungsten inert gas (TIG) welded frames. Joining tubes without lugs made for a lighter bicycle, and gave the builder more freedom in frame and fork design.

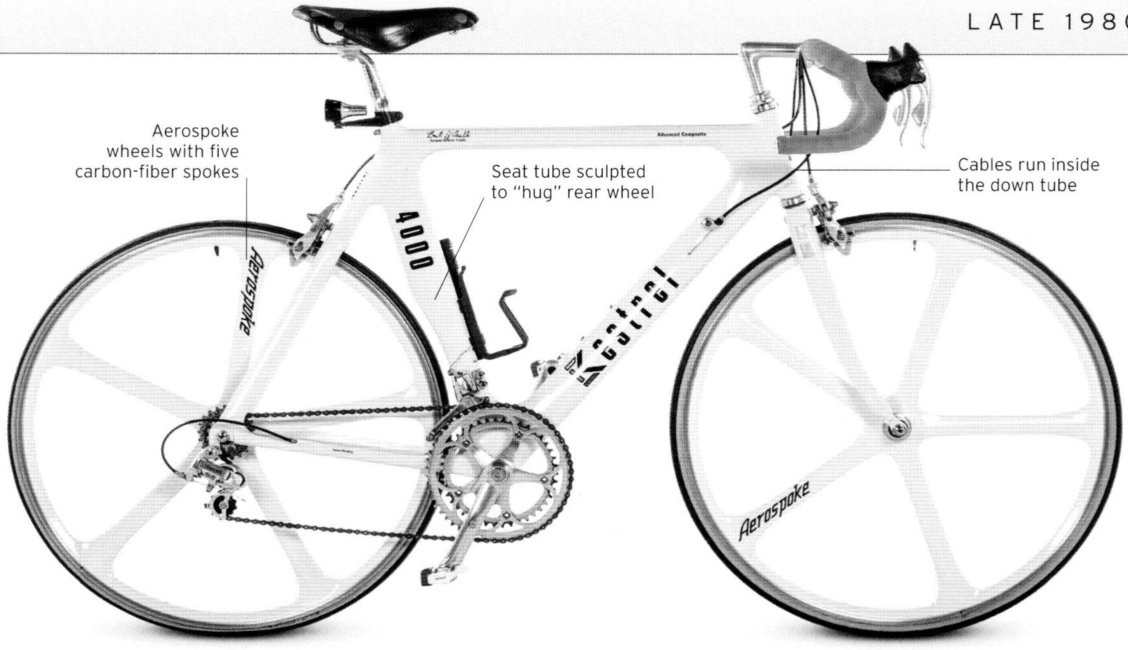

Aerospoke
wheels with five
carbon-fiber spokes

Seat tube sculpted
to "hug" rear wheel

Cables run inside
the down tube

◁ **Kestrel 4000 1987**

Origin US

Frame Carbon fiber

Gears 16-speed

Wheels 28 in (70 cm)

Claimed to be the world's first all-carbon-fiber bicycle frame, the Kestrel 4000 was aimed at the burgeoning triathlon market. Designed as a fast road bike for solo rides, the Kestrel was ahead of its time in employing an aerofoil down tube and seat stay, and a rear-wheel-hugging seat tube.

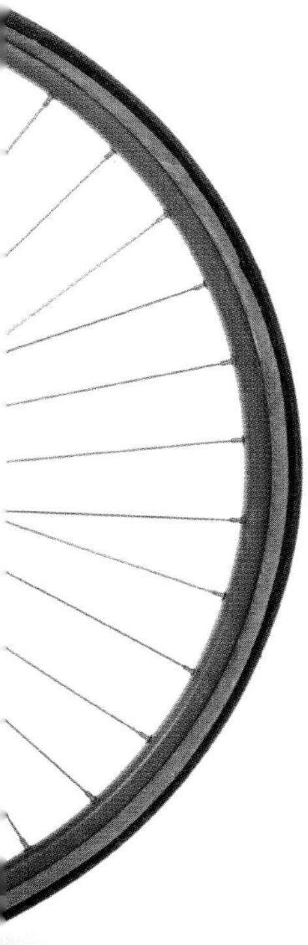

Lightweight
Flyte saddle

▷ **Rossin Neri 1989**

Origin Italy

Frame Steel

Gears 18-speed

Wheels 28 in (70 cm)

The Rossin road frame, named for the shop where it was built, was made with Italian Columbus tubes using a combination of smooth fillet-brazing and lugs. The influence of aerodynamic design was seen in Campagnolo's C-Record oval seat post, radical Delta center-pull brakes, and Cinelli's titanium handlebar stem.

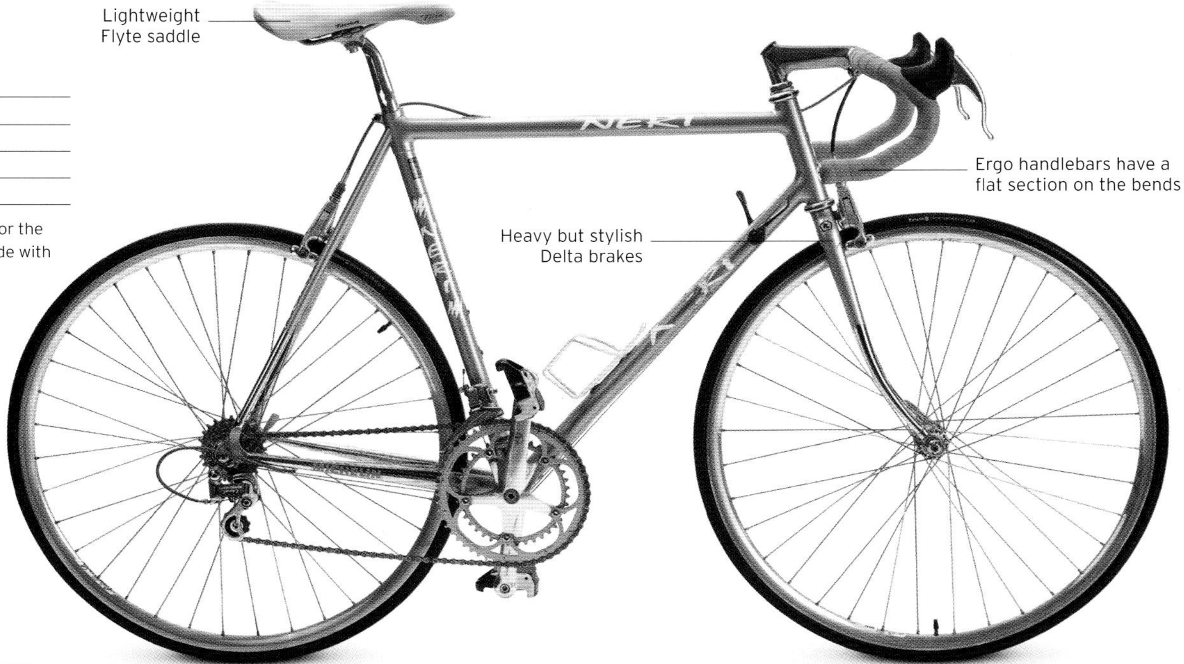

Ergo handlebars have a
flat section on the bends

Heavy but stylish
Delta brakes

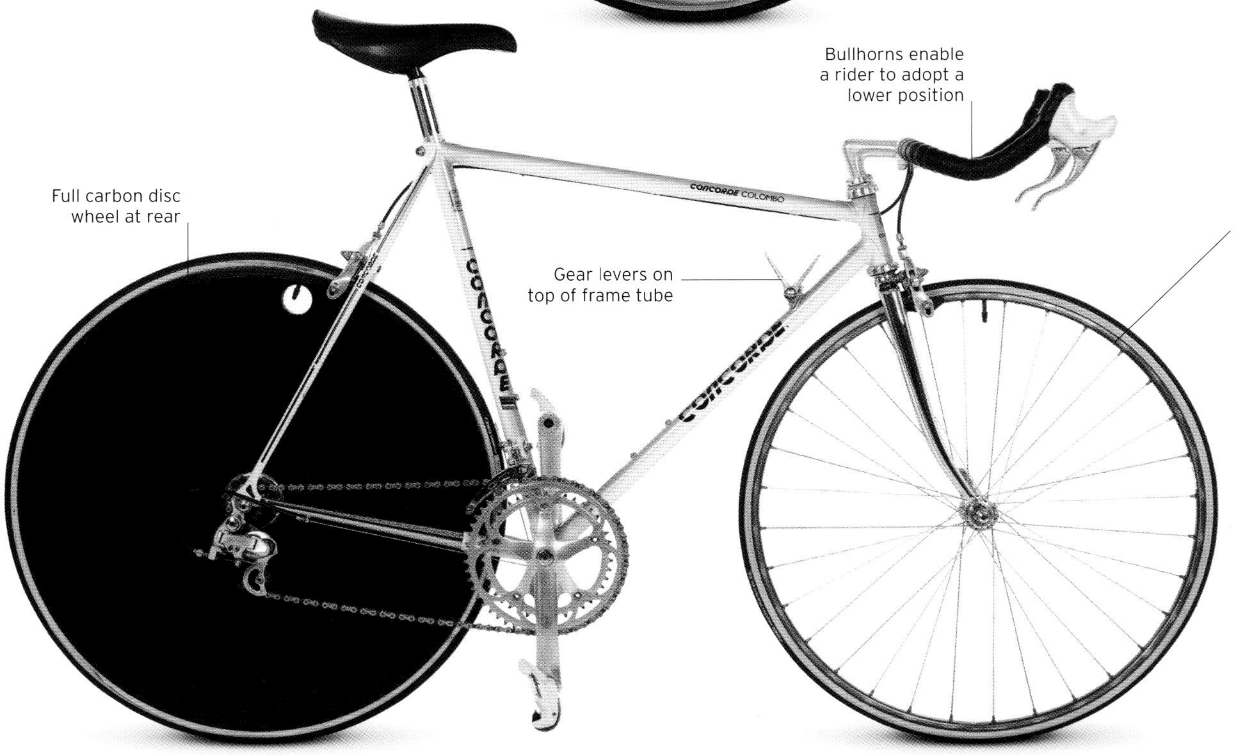

Bullhorns enable
a rider to adopt a
lower position

Full carbon disc
wheel at rear

Gear levers on
top of frame tube

Spoked front wheel

◁ **Concorde Columbo 1989**

Origin Italy

Frame Steel

Gears 12-speed

Wheels 28 in (70 cm)

Typical of the low-profile time-trial bikes of the time, the Concorde was designed to position the rider very low down to increase aerodynamic efficiency. The disc wheel and the centrally CBT mounted gear levers on the down tube also improve airflow.

Marco Aurelio Fontana rides the Lefty-equipped Cannondale F-Si

Great Manufacturers
Cannondale

One of the world's most innovative bicycle companies, Cannondale—which was founded in 1971, but produced its first bike in 1983—has often caused a stir with its eye-catching designs, new technology, and bold marketing. Best known for pioneering high-performance aluminum bikes, the US brand has gained a global reputation for staying at the cutting edge of bicycle and component design.

CANNONDALE WAS FOUNDED on a single guiding principle: that products offering tangible, real-world advantages over existing technologies will succeed. This insight came to co-founder Joe Montgomery in 1970 as he watched a cyclist struggling under the heavy load of a backpack while pedaling uphill. In 1971, Montgomery, along with Ron Davis and Jim Catrambone, launched their enterprise. The first year also saw their first product—a lightweight, two-wheeled trailer that could be attached to the rear of any bicycle, allowing the rider to haul heavy loads with minimal effort.

From the beginning, the small company did things differently. In the early years, it catered chiefly to the outdoor luggage market, with cycling equipment as its focus. Everything was designed and made in a makeshift workshop above a pickle shop in Wilton, CT. The Metro-North train station near the workshop, Cannondale, gave the company its name. Its products soon gained a following, as the Cannondale brand began to be associated with quality, durability, innovation, and the latest in design and technology.

The company's steady growth meant that it soon outgrew the pickle-shop loft, and a production plant was opened in Bedford, PA, in 1977. "Handmade in the USA" was a badge of honor for Cannondale products, and local production allowed tight control over quality, since the company could respond quickly to market changes.

Cannondale spent 12 years developing outdoor products before, in 1983, it announced its arrival as a full-fledged bicycle company with the ST-500 tourer. Cycle-touring equipment had come to dominate its output, so it was fitting that its first bike was a touring machine. A glossy, TIG-welded aluminum frame, with an oversized, large-diameter down tube and ovalized chain and seat stays, ensured that the ST-500 immediately stood out from the crowd of lugged, narrow-tubed steel frames. The use of aluminum was far from a publicity stunt: because of its lighter weight, it could be rolled into larger-diameter tubes, thereby creating a frame that was stiffer than steel, and would not rust. Oversized aluminum tubing also produced an immediate transfer of the rider's energy to the rear wheel, as compared to the softer, springier qualities of a steel bicycle frame.

The following year, Cannondale introduced a road bike—the SR-900, equipped with 12-speed Campagnolo Nuovo Record gears—and the SM-500 mountain bike, which had 15-speed Shimano Deore XT gears. These lightweight, advanced bicycles were aimed squarely at the higher echelons of the market. In the years that followed, tandem, BMX, hybrid, and triathlon/time-trial bikes were all added to Cannondale's stable. As well as building its own frames (protected by a US patent), from 1993 the company designed and produced a range of components.

From the late 1980s through the 1990s, mountain biking proved to be the field in which Cannondale's technological improvements won the strongest following. In 1991, one of the first rear-suspension mountain bikes, the Elevated Suspension Technology (EST), was introduced. The EST frame was paired with a Girvin Flexstem handlebar-mounted shock unit. In 1992, Cannondale replaced the Flexstem with a redesigned frame that featured the Headshok suspension fork. This was unique in that it paired rigid fork blades with a telescoping shock that ran on precision needle bearings in the frame's head tube. The design was lighter, better at absorbing bumps, and offered

cannondale

"It has **never** been our goal to produce **huge numbers** of bicycles. **Just the best bicycles**."

JOE MONTGOMERY, CANNONDALE PRESIDENT, 1991

Early innovation
Cannondale's first two-wheeled product, the 1971 Bugger bicycle trailer, showcased the young company's expertise in designing and producing high-quality cycling equipment and outdoor accessories.

ST-500 Sport-Touring bicycle 1983

Delta-V 2000 with Headshok 1993

Cipollini's CAAD3 time-trial bike 1997

SuperSix EVO Hi-MOD 2016

1971 Cannondale is founded by Joe Montgomery, Jim Catrambone, and Ron Davis in Wilton, CT.
1983 The company produces its first bicycle, the aluminum ST-500 touring bike.
1989 Cannondale Europe is founded in the Netherlands for distribution and sales.
1991 Cannondale introduces its first full-suspension mountain bike, the EST.
1992 Headshok front suspension is released.
1994 The CODA Magic crankset, with an external-bearing bottom bracket,

is produced 10 years prior to its industry-wide adoption.
1995 A short-travel version of the Headshok suspension unit is added to a road bike.
1997 While leading the Tour de France for three days, Mario Cipollini rides a customized yellow Cannondale race bike to match his leader's jersey.
2000 Lefty suspension fork launched.
2001 Cannondale introduces the BB30 bottom bracket, a large-diameter aluminum spindle design that is

both lighter and more resistant to flex under the rider's pedal strokes. It soon becomes an industry standard.
2003 After a bold but ill-fated attempt to expand into high-performance motor-cycles and all-terrain vehicles (ATVs), Cannondale seeks bankruptcy protection and is acquired by one of its creditors, Pegasus Partners.
2004 "Legalize my Cannondale" campaign is launched to promote the carbon-aluminum-framed Six13 road bike,

which weighs less than the legal minimum for a competition road bike.
2008 Cannondale is acquired by Dorel Industries, a sports-recreation conglomerate; investment in product development, testing, and manufacturing continues. In 2009, production moves to Taiwan.
2011 The SuperSixEVO carbon road frame is released. With exceptional stiffness-to-weight, it is named "Best Bike in the World" by Germany's *Tour* magazine.

Italian flair
The exuberant, irreverent personality of Mario Cipollini, seen here riding the CAAD3 in 1997, was a perfect match for Cannondale's colorful marketing style.

Headshok logo

more precise steering than anything else at the time. When mated with the new Delta-V rear-wheel suspension, this provided not only a comfortable ride, but also a mountain bike that could be ridden aggressively fast over steep, rocky terrain.

In 1994, Cannondale co-sponsored one of the most successful professional mountain-bike teams ever. The team won a host of women's and men's cross-country and downhill races on Cannondale bicycles, providing vital product feedback. One of the flagship products to come from such testing was the Lefty, an evolution of the Headshok that moved the shock absorber from the frame's head tube into a light-weight, single-bladed telescopic fork.

Cannondale moved into pro road cycling sponsorship in 1997 with the elite Italian team Saeco. This marked the first time an American brand had sponsored a European road team, and the first time such a team had raced on oversized aluminum frames. Any doubts about aluminum's place in the peloton were soon erased, with Saeco's Ivan Gotti winning the Giro d'Italia on a bright red Cannondale, and superstar sprinter Mario Cipollini winning two stages and wearing the race leader's *maillot jaune* (yellow jersey) for four straight days in the 1999 Tour de France.

Following industry trends, Cannondale introduced a carbon frame in 1997, but, true to type, added innovation. The Super-V Raven mountain-bike frame featured an aluminum skeleton surrounded by a carbon-fiber skin. This combination was used in 2004 for the Six13 road bike, which was so light that weights were added to meet UCI regulations, inspiring the "Legalize my Cannondale" campaign. Today, the "Handmade in the USA" tag is gone, but Cannondale continues to thrive.

Grabbing the headlines
Damiano Cunego promotes Cannondale's "illegal" Six13 model at the 2004 Giro d'Italia.

Aerodynamic Time-Trial Bikes

Inspired by the radical machines that had taken track racing by storm in the late 1970s, road Time-Trial bikes began to feature plunging front ends with a cut-down handlebar. By the mid-1980s, low-profile TT bikes were being ridden by amateurs hungry to copy their heroes in races against the clock. Reduced frontal area was soon followed by fairing or disc wheel, and by the end of the decade, bicycles also featured aerodynamic triathlon bars.

Saddle with infill under its "nose" to channel air

Special cage for aerodynamic water bottle

Rear derailleur design
The 1985 Shimano Dura-Ace derailleur set a new standard by combining two inventions from other makers—dual spring-loaded pivots and a slant parallelogram cage.

Ingenious delta wing bar in front of head tube

Frame in the blue and yellow Renault-Elf team colors

◁ **Gitane Delta E 1983**

Origin	France
Frame	Steel
Gears	Single speed
Wheels	28 in (70 cm)

French road time-trial machines with radical designs gained mass exposure thanks to Renault-Elf riders such as Laurent Fignon and Greg LeMond. The flat-tubed Delta featured a low-slung handlebar and a short wheelbase.

Short wheelbase with very tight clearances

Campagnolo seat post with ovalized top section

Campagnolo disc wheels front and rear

Smooth Cinelli aero joints

▷ **Cinelli Laser Track Bike 1984**

Origin	Italy
Frame	Steel
Gears	Single speed
Wheels	Front 26 in (65 cm), Rear 28 in (70 cm)

Italian style and engineering came together in the Laser, one of the prettiest aerodynamic track machines. Designed by Antonio Colombo in response to new rules that outlawed nonstructural aerodynamic aids, its Columbus tubes were shaped to pass through the air with minimum turbulence.

One-piece aero-bars attached to a standard headset

Aero components
It is questionable how much difference this aerodynamic Dia-Compe BC46 brake made to the bicycle's speed, but it was certainly stylish.

◁ **Schwinn Lo-Profile Time Trial 1987**

Origin	US
Frame	Steel
Gears	6-speed
Wheels	28 in (70 cm)

This bike is an example of Schwinn's forays into cutting-edge design. This machine's steel frame had a faired-in section behind the seat tube to allow air to flow around the back wheel. The carbon bars and chainring were also ahead of their time.

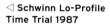

Bullhorn handlebars without tri-bars

Aero versus air-in
Aerodynamics were restricted when a slot was needed to get to the tire valve; the gap could be covered with adhesive tape to restore airflow.

Carbon-fiber rear disc wheel

△ **Bottecchia TT 1989**

Origin	Italy
Frame	Steel
Gears	16-speed
Wheels	Front 26 in (65 cm), Rear 28 in (70 cm)

The Bottecchia frame was built with Columbus air tubing, and featured a steeply angled top tube and steel fork. This machine was similar to one ridden by Greg LeMond in the 1989 Tour de France, although his had Mavic components.

Larger, radially spoked rear wheel

Campagnolo's stylish Croce D'Aune chainset

Rare Campagnolo Delta brakes

◁ **Rossin Time Trial Bicycle 1990s**

Origin	Italy
Frame	Steel
Gears	16-speed
Wheels	Front 26 in (65 cm), Rear 28 in (70 cm)

Founded in 1974, Mario Rossin quickly became known for innovative aerodynamics, and by the end of the 1980s Rossin was building bikes for many professional teams. The TT was a typical lo-pro with aero frame, and was equipped with Campagnolo's Croce d'Aune groupset.

Track-Racing Bikes

Bicycles built to race around banked tracks resist design changes more than any other type of bike. Pared down to the absolute minimum, they have no need for brakes or anything other than one carefully chosen gear. Comfort is irrelevant on smooth wooden boards or concrete, and the wheels can be bolted into place since flat tires are rare. Weight is also not critical because there are no hills to climb. However, though this was largely the case in the early 1980s, advances in technology began to alter how track bikes evolved aerodynamically as the decade progressed.

▷ **10 Speed Spokes Experimental High Speed Bike** *c.* **1980**

Origin	US
Frame	Steel
Gears	Single speed
Wheels	Front 26 in (65 cm), Rear 28 in (70 cm)

A long-wheelbase track machine, the Spokes had a double-reduction gear system that provided an over-sized gear ratio without the need for a large chainring. For high speeds, the bike also had a motorcycle-style fork to resist gravitational forces on bankings. Although an interesting and arresting machine, it never caught on.

Reduction gear requires two chainrings

Large chainring

Triple-triangle seat stay

Chainset with carbon infill

◁ **GT American Olympic Team Pursuit Bike** *c.* **1980**

Origin	US
Frame	Steel
Gears	Single speed
Wheels	Front 24 in (60 cm), Rear 28 in (70 cm)

GT's distinctive triple-triangle frames featured seat stays running almost parallel to the down tube. These Olympic team bikes were also radically designed to place the rider in the most extreme position. This example has been fitted with a non-original riser handlebar unsuitable for track use.

Small front wheel lowered front end even further

Saddle almost over rear wheel

Chromed tubes by Columbus of Italy

▷ **Moser Hour Record Bike 1984**

Origin	Italy
Frame	Steel
Gears	Single speed
Wheels	28 in (70 cm)

In 1984, Italian champion Francesco Moser broke the World Hour Record, completing 31.78 miles (51.15 km) in the hour. This radical-looking bike used disc wheels for the first time in such a record attempt. Under the swooping looks was a conventional steel frame designed to rotate the bike into a streamlined tuck on purpose-made bullhorn bars.

Disc wheels front and rear

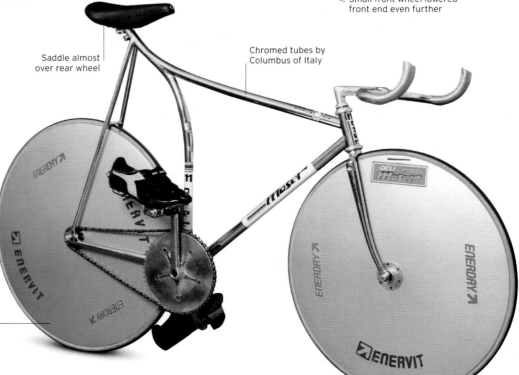

Cut-down bars for single riding position

Steel plates brace frame

▷ **Dave Marsh Motorpace** *c.* **1985**

Origin UK

Frame Steel

Gears Single speed

Wheels Front 26 in (65 cm), Rear 28 in (70 cm)

The high speeds of dernys (motorized bicycles) inspired the Dave Marsh, a highly specialized bike with reversed steel forks. The handlebars were braced to resist high gravitational forces on the banking at speeds well over 40 mph (64 km/h).

Handlebar braced to stiffen front end

Dinner-plate-sized chainring

Fork reversed with smaller front wheel

Raised saddle

▽ **Bianchi Pista** *c.* **1980**

Origin Italy

Frame Steel

Gears Single speed

Wheels 28 in (70 cm)

Handcrafted from Columbus tubing and painted in the Italian maker Bianchi's trademark celeste pastel, this Pista bike stood out with its kinked top and subtly curved seat tubes. Designed for speed, it was ideal for kilometer time trials and pursuit riding.

Seat tube gently curved

Handlebar positioned below saddle height

Large track wheels with tubular tires

Close clearance of front wheel to down tube

Specialized Stumpjumper

Although its fat tires and functional looks won few plaudits for aesthetics, the Specialized Stumpjumper was revolutionary in bringing off-road cycling to the masses. One of the first factory-built mountain bikes in the world, the Stumpjumper was a performance machine that helped pioneer this new form of cycling. Thanks to production in Asia, it was cheaper than the handmade bikes that dominated the new sport that had sprung up in California in the early 1980s.

THE STUMPJUMPER BICYCLE was the product of the business sense and cycling expertise of Mike Sinyard, the founder of Specialized Bicycle Components. Sinyard began importing high-quality road-bicycle components from Europe in 1974 and selling them to consumers, retailers, and manufacturers in the US. After supplying steel tubing to some of the pioneering frame-builders—including Tom Ritchey—who created the first purpose-built mountain bikes, Sinyard saw the potential of this new breed of bicycle. Basing the Stumpjumper around the design of the Ritchey-built MountainBike, he arranged factory production in Japan to achieve a lower retail price and higher volume.

Affectionately known as the "Stumpy" by its fans, the Stumpjumper was popular from the start—the first 125 frames sold out just six days after going on sale in 1981. Although lacking the elegance and refinement of its groupset-equipped road-cycling cousins, and crude in comparison to the lightweight, suspension-assisted machines that mountain bikes have evolved into, the early Stumpjumper was groundbreaking in its opening up of the great outdoors to more two-wheeled, off-road adventurers than ever before.

With components selected for durability and function, the Stumpjumper featured 15 gears for tackling steep, loose climbs and fast descents, while Specialized's own Stumpjumper tires provided traction for a variety of surfaces.

SPECIFICATIONS	
Origin	US
Designer	Tim Neenan/Tom Ritchey
Year	1981
Frame	Steel
Gears	15-speed
Brakes	Cantilever
Wheels	26 in (65 cm)
Weight	Approx. 29 lb (13.2 kg)

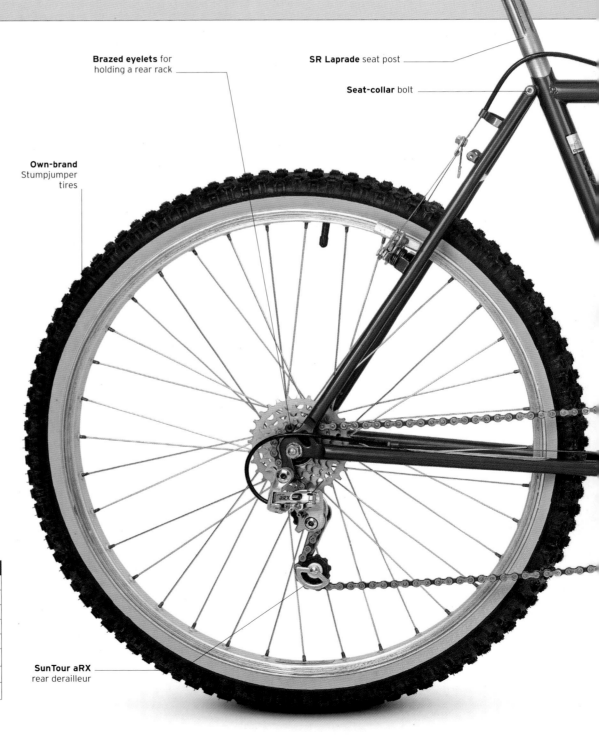

Brazed eyelets for holding a rear rack

SR Laprade seat post

Seat-collar bolt

Own-brand Stumpjumper tires

SunTour aRX rear derailleur

"It's not **just** a bicycle, it's a **whole new sport**."

STUMPJUMPER ADVERTISEMENT, 1982

SunTour Mighty gear levers
mounted on the handlebars

Handlebars and stem modeled
after BMX and motorcycle designs

TIG-welded frame made from
Special Touring Series chromoly

Touring crankset
from French firm TA

BMX pedals for
improved grip

Mafac cantilever brakes—
normally found on tandems—
to accommodate the wider tires

Specialized logo

To give the brand connotations of
the specialized, dedicated frame-
builders in Italy, Mike Sinyard
named his company Specialized.

THE COMPONENTS

The Stumpjumper's ungainly looks were partly due to the lack of purpose-made components for a sport that had not yet been named—mountain bikes were known as "clunkers" in the early 1980s. Parts were supplied by 11 different manufacturers, from French firm Mafac's cantilever brakes and Italian motorcycle company Tommaselli's brake levers to Japanese component specialist SunTour's derailleurs and cogs.

1. BMX-style Specialized stem **2.** Lower head-tube junction with Specialized alloy headset and chromoly-steel, biplane-style fork **3.** Tommaselli Racer motorcycle brake lever and SunTour Mighty gear lever on Specialized IV steel handlebar **4.** Mafac tandem cantilever brake on Araya alloy rim **5.** SunTour aRX front derailleur and TA Cyclotourist crankset **6.** MKS BMX-7 pedal **7.** SunTour aRX rear derailleur and 5-speed cogs, ranging from 14 to 28 teeth

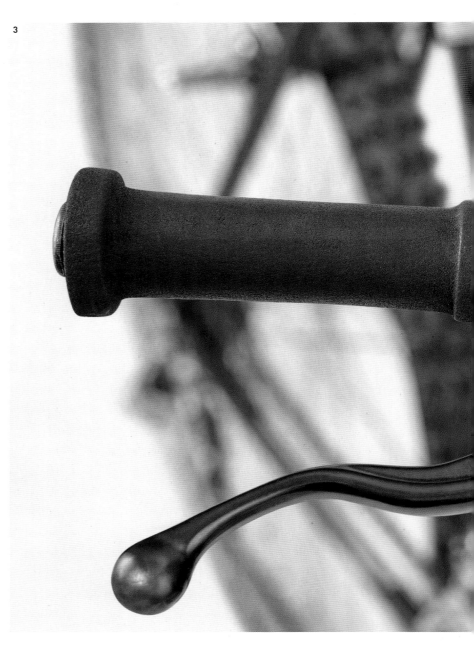

Early Mountain Bikes

In the 1970s, pre-war balloon-tired bikes were modified and ridden around northern California's Marin County. Known as "Klunkers," these led to the design of bikes specifically for off-road use. The first mountain bike, the "Breezer," was created by designer and frame-builder Joe Breeze in 1977. Tom Ritchey followed in 1978, supplying frames to businessman Charlie Kelly and track racer Gary Fisher. Kelly and Fisher assembled their frames with components from cyclo-cross racing bikes and motorcycles and sold them through their company, MountainBikes. In 1981 Mike Sinyard's company, Specialized, had 125 frames—the StumpJumper—manufactured in Japan. Although they were met with reserve and viewed by many as simply an adult's BMX, the bikes nonetheless sold out. Frame-builders of all backgrounds began producing mountain bikes.

Roller cam brakes, designed by Richard Cunningham of WTB in 1982 and licensed to SunTour

Hite-Rite saddle dropper by Joe Breeze and Josh Angell

Two-piece tubular steel cranks and bottom bracket by Bullseye

Rear derailleur

△ **Cannondale SM900 1987**

Origin	US
Frame	Aluminum
Gears	15-speed
Wheels	26 in (65 cm)

Cannondale made its first mountain bike frame in 1984. This SM900 showcased its signature large-diameter aluminum tubes and smooth welds. With a sloping top tube and high bottom bracket for good ground clearance. An agile bike, it used SunTour's first indexed mountain-bike gears—XC 9000.

▽ **Highpath Engineering 1985**

Origin	UK
Frame	Steel
Gears	12-speed
Wheels	25 in (63 cm)

A short, high, steep frame geometry meant the rider's weight was centered—advantageous for all-day use rather than cross-country or downhill racing. The bike features 650B wheels, a wide bottom bracket, and wide hubs, as well as custom-made hub brakes with shoes that self-regulate for pad wear.

Hub brake
Bespoke "Swing Cam" hub brakes with external cooling fins, sealed bearings, and long-action arms, activating brake shoes that self-regulate for pad wear.

Frame-mounted shoulder carrying strap

Nokian Speed Hakkapeliitta 650B tires with tungsten studs

Bottom bracket with custom press-fit bearings and grease injection port

Seat stay-mounted
Shimano U-brake

Reinforcing sleeve
on top of seat tube

12.5-in- (32-cm-) high
bottom bracket for
ground clearance

△ Overbury's Pioneer 1988

Origin	UK
Frame	Steel
Gears	21-speed
Wheels	26 in (65 cm)

Fillet-brazed by frame-builder Andy Powell, this
bike used Reynolds and Columbus steel tubing.
A short, steep, rear triangle, and shallow head
angle provided excellent climbing ability and quick,
stable handling, leading to success in UK races.

▷ TBG Kona Explosif 1988

Origin	Canada
Frame	Steel
Gears	21-speed
Wheels	26 in (65 cm)

Kona started in 1988, using design input from
successful racer Joe Murray and frame-builder
Paul Brodie. The sloping top tube and resulting
smaller frame triangles provided greater stand-
over height and a lighter stiffer frame, and all first-
year models featured the "splatter" paint finish.

FIRST ALL-SUSPENSION MOUNTAIN BIKE

In 1988, Moulton Bicycles, UK, introduced what is arguably
the first production full-suspension mountain bike, the
AM-ATB off-road bicycle. It was based on their steel AM
Space-Frame and featured leading link suspension at the
base of the front forks, and pivoting rear forks at the rear.
While its 20-in (50-cm) wheels were ideal for general
off-road cycling, they were less suitable for rough terrain.

Moulton AM-ATB

Tange Prestige
double-butted,
TIG-welded frame

First-year Kona
Project Two
straight-blade,
non-tapered fork

Grease port on
bottom bracket for
easy maintenance

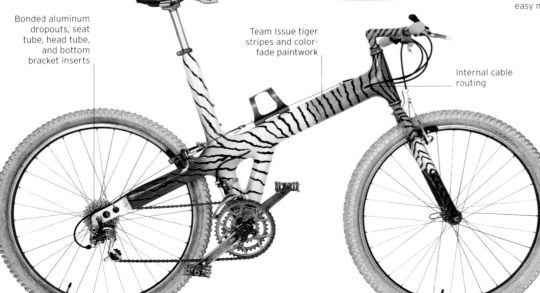

Bonded aluminum
dropouts, seat
tube, head tube,
and bottom
bracket inserts

Team Issue tiger
stripes and color-
fade paintwork

Internal cable
routing

◁ Trimble Inverse-4 1989

Origin	US
Frame	Carbon fiber with aluminum inserts
Gears	21-speed
Wheels	26 in (65 cm)

Constructed from a composite of 30 percent
carbon fiber and 70 percent fiberglass, lighter
parts used six plies, with up to 24 plies for
higher-stress areas. The Trimble's excellent
stand-over height and elevated chainstays
provided flex while also eliminating chain slap
and allowing chain removal without tools.

Bikes for Leisure and Touring

As proof that the traditional European cycling scene did not have a monopoly on innovation, touring bikes from America began to branch out, favoring Japanese components and gears with ultrawide ratios inspired by the burgeoning mountain-biking scene. Steel's versatility and vibration-absorbing properties meant that it remained the material of choice for frames. Manufacturers could tailor their bicycle frames to suit sporty riders with lighter tubes and tighter angles, or add threaded inserts for extra racks and bigger frame clearances to accommodate the fatter tires required by long-distance travelers. For the ultimate handmade touring bike, however, the small specialist frame-builder was still the only choice for the discerning tourist.

▷ **Schwinn Voyageur 11.8 c. 1980**

Origin	US
Frame	Steel
Gears	14-speed
Wheels	28 in (70 cm)

This rare chrome version of the sought-after Voyageur featured a frame handmade in Japan with Cro-Mo steel tubes, elegant lugwork, and a chrome fork with a generous rake. The Shimano gears, Sugino Super Maxy chainset, and SR bars were also Japanese.

Frame suitable for lightweight touring

Japanese components matched European versions

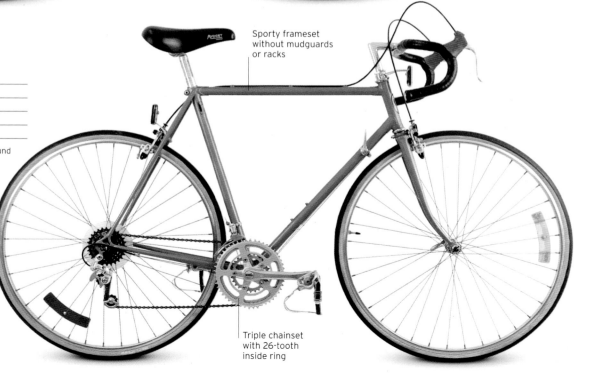

Comfort saddle for long-distance cycling

Rear rack installed without fender

◁ **Raleigh Alyeska 1980s**

Origin	UK
Frame	Steel
Gears	18-speed
Wheels	28 in (70 cm)

This Nottingham-built steel tourer had chromoly main tubes and very relaxed geometry. The Alyeska was a comfortable, stable ride, with more than adequate room to add mudguards and fat tires. A triple chainset with alloy Japanese parts offered plenty of reliably efficient gears.

Sporty frameset without mudguards or racks

▷ **Trek 520 1983**

Origin	US
Frame	Steel
Gears	18-speed
Wheels	28 in (70 cm)

Trek USA's 520 had more of an all-around specification than a dedicated touring bike. It featured a solid Reynolds frame with a triple chainset that could tackle even the steepest hills in its lowest gear, and an Avocet saddle designed for a comfortable ride.

Triple chainset with 26-tooth inside ring

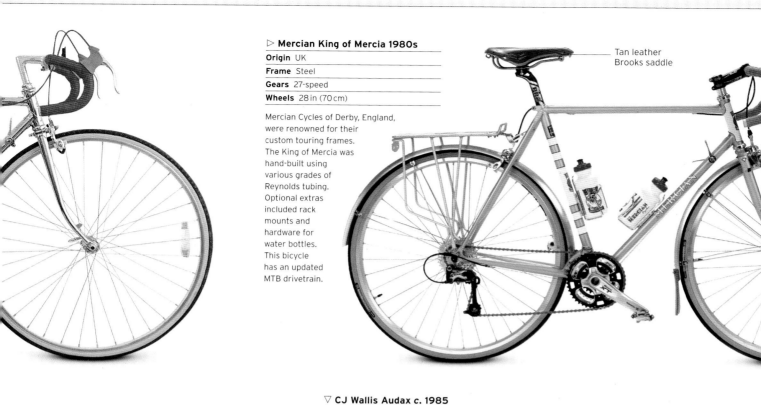

▷ **Mercian King of Mercia 1980s**

Origin	UK
Frame	Steel
Gears	27-speed
Wheels	28 in (70 cm)

Mercian Cycles of Derby, England, were renowned for their custom touring frames. The King of Mercia was hand-built using various grades of Reynolds tubing. Optional extras included rack mounts and hardware for water bottles. This bicycle has an updated MTB drivetrain.

Tan leather Brooks saddle

Ergonomic handlebars for comfort

▽ **CJ Wallis Audax** *c.* **1985**

Origin	UK
Frame	Steel
Gears	21-speed
Wheels	28 in (70 cm)

Long-distance Audax bikes predated sportives and reflected the all-day challenge of combining comfort with performance. The CJ Wallis featured Reynolds tubing with elegant lugs, a triple chainset, cantilever brakes, and mudguards.

Brooks leather saddle— a touring favorite

Peg for top-tube-mounted pump

Long-reach rear derailleur for wide ratios

Experimental Design

Since the earliest days of bicycle production, new designs, materials, and technologies have been used in attempts to improve efficiency. There have been failures along the way, but also discoveries, and bicycles have been built using everything from wood to plastics, aluminum, magnesium, and carbon fiber. Frames have been made with single and multiple tubes and die-cast metals. The rider's energy has been transmitted by chains, driveshafts, and rubber belts. Gearing has developed from single to 21-speed using derailleurs, multiple chainrings, and planetary hub gears.

Wide handlebars for stability

Extra-long seat post

Molded plastic front rack

Short, compact frame

Rear box frame with integrated rack

Folding kickstand

Small front wheel with reflector

▷ **Heinz Kettler Cityhopper Alu Rad 1980**

Origin Germany

Frame Aluminum

Gears Single speed

Wheels Front 10 in (25 cm), Rear 20 in (50 cm)

Intended for short trips in urban areas, this bicycle was made from round- and box-section aluminum tubing, and had front and rear racks. The small wheels relied on large-section tires for comfort.

Experiments with Plastic

Bicycle manufacturers thought plastic bicycles could be produced cheaply and would resist corrosion. However, cycle dealers, fearing difficulties with repairs, largely rejected the use of plastic. Some concept bikes, like the French Speelo plastic racer, were never even put into production for fear of negative reactions from the cycling press.

Built-in rear carrier

Enclosed rear panels to protect rider's clothing

▷ **Winora Rainbow Prototype 1982**

Origin Germany

Frame Steel

Gears 4-speed

Wheels 27 in (68 cm)

Winora cycles were noted for their innovative designs and use of new materials. This prototype featured an enclosed rear section and chaincase.

Twin kickstands

Collapsible, folding handlebars

Light aluminum-alloy beam frame

Central hinge for folding

◁ **Bickerton Folding Bike** *c.* 1970

Origin	UK
Frame	Aluminum
Gears	3-speed
Wheels	Front 14 in (35 cm), Rear 16 in (40 cm)

This folding bicycle had a lightweight aluminum-alloy frame, which folded using a central hinge. The handlebars swung down into the center, making it very compact and easy to carry; the folded bicycle could fit into the trunk of a Mini. Over 600,000 were built.

Head tube and forks combined

One-click release lever for folding

Molded plastic wheels

Rubber drive belt

▷ **Strida** 1987

Origin	UK
Frame	Aluminum
Gears	Single speed
Wheels	16 in (40 cm)

This bicycle was aimed at city riders and commuters. Its simple construction, belt drive, and one-click folding mechanism meant it was simple to store and maintain, as well as light and easy to carry.

Frame folded when saddle was pulled upward

Alloy-tubed frame with plates at stress points

Hinged seat post folded into "packed" frame

Folding rear rack

◁ **Airframe** *c.* 1980

Origin	UK
Frame	Aluminum
Gears	3-speed
Brake	16 in (40 cm)

This bicycle was built in small numbers until 2008. Made using narrow tubing arranged in triangles, it unfolded when the seat was pulled up and the rider's weight forced the wheels apart, bracing the bottom tubes at the axles.

Built-in rear rack

One-piece plastic monocoque frame

▷ **Itera Plastic Bike** 1980-83

Origin	Sweden
Frame	Plastic
Gears	3-speed
Wheels	27 in (68 cm)

The Itera represented a Swedish attempt to shift bicycle-building into injection-molded plastic. The radical design suffered many development problems: it was very heavy, and did not handle well. The project ceased after only three years.

Molded plastic wheels

The craze for bicycle motocross, or BMX , was at its highest during the early 1980s. There was a period when seemingly every child and teen wanted a BMX bike. Riders performed incredible freestyle stunts for large groups of spectators—such as this one in Germany—and entered races. The latter consisted of several riders completing a course (often on bare earth) that comprised dips, ramps, and banked turns. Freestyle BMX, on the other hand, had more in common with skateboarding.

Freestyle BMX Bikes

By the 1980s, BMX had become an established sport with multiple disciplines and national federations. The International BMX Federation was founded in 1981, and in 1982 it hosted the first World Championships in Dayton, OH. BMX boomed along with skateboarding. Freestyle BMX saw riders perform daredevil tricks at every opportunity; they even used empty swimming pools to practice in. Meanwhile, dirt and tarmac tracks for BMX racing popped up on farms and in parks as the popularity of the sport went global.

Mushroom-style rubber grips

Smooth freestyle tyres

Dice-style valve caps

△ **Hutch Trickstar II 1980s**

Origin	US
Frame	Steel
Gears	Single speed
Wheels	20 in (50 cm)

Anodized in red, this was one of the first freestyle stunt bikes to appear on the market. Popular with riders, it had a twin top tube and small chainstay platforms, which gave the rider multiple areas to stand on.

▽ **GT Performer 1985**

Origin	US
Frame	Steel
Gears	Single speed
Wheels	20 in (50 cm)

This 4130 chromoly steel freestyle frame was often sold with Mag three-spoke wheels that looked good, but lacked strength. Most of the components were GT branded. The Performer was produced for 15 years.

Frame strengthening
For extra resilience, the seat tube passed through the top tube. The junction was further reinforced with a gusset.

Tangle-free cabling
The front brake cable fed through the headset, and the rear brake cable through a gyro mounted on the steerer tube so that the rider could perform bar spins without the cables becoming tangled.

Distinctive curved top tube

Stunt pegs

Small plastic saddle

Trick platform for stunts and grabs

Side-pull front brake

◁ Schwinn Predator Freeform Pro 1987

Origin US

Frame Steel

Gears Single speed

Wheels 20 in (50 cm)

The Predator was a high-end freestyle stunt bicycle with features such as chromed standing platforms and dual position pegs. The front brake cable ran within the fork blade so that the cable did not touch the tire. The bicycle had wheels with 48 spokes to make it more robust.

Chromoly steel handlebars with "mushroom" rubber grips

▷ Haro FSX 1987

Origin US

Frame Steel

Gears Single speed

Wheels 20 in (50 cm)

The Haro was built using an affordable trimoly steel frame with an unconventional "two-into-one" top tube that created a standing platform. Bob Haro started out making custom number plates for top BMX racers. Haro's freestyle team dominated the sport for many years.

Wide platform pedals with pins for grip

Large rear pegs for stunts

Brake cables run outside the frame on cheaper model

◁ GT Vertigo 1988

Origin US

Frame Steel

Gears Single speed

Wheels 20 in (50 cm)

The Vertigo was an entry-level bicycle that had a freestyle-design frame with a chromoly steel down tube and fork. It had stunt pegs and a gyro that allowed the handlebars to be spun through 360 degrees without tangling the brake cable. The name "GT" derives from the name of company co-founder Gary Turner.

Leisure Bikes

A new style of bicycle began to creep into the market by the late 1980s—the all-terrain bike. To many new riders, the traditional leisure roadster seemed to be old-fashioned, heavy, and inefficient, and, although cheap, made for a sluggish riding experience. Instead of adding the usual gimmicks, manufacturers turned back to traditional wheel sizes and borrowed design cues from the new-style all-terrain bikes to create what would later be termed a "hybrid." Bikes remained well-equipped for everyday errands and included mounts for racks and mudguards as well as tires suitable for mixed terrain. They offered a relaxed, upright riding position.

Rear rack

One-piece down tube

Hand-finished leather grips with white stitching

Handmade leather head badge

Hinge point with quick-release butterfly nut

△ Schwinn Tri-Wheeler 1980

Origin	US
Frame	Steel
Gears	3-speed
Wheels	Front 20 in (50 cm), Rear 16 in (40 cm)

The Tri-Wheeler was an experiment that did not pay off for Schwinn. It was designed as a shopper with a rack at the rear, but was difficult to steer around tight corners and took up more space in a garage compared to a two-wheeler.

◁ Trussardi 1983

Origin	Italy
Frame	Steel
Gears	3-speed
Wheels	28 in (70 cm)

This was an unusual folding bike designed for World War II soldiers. It was reintroduced in the early 1980s by Italian fashion brand Trussardi, which added saddlebags and leather details.

Alloy rear rack

Curved top tube for easy mount

▷ Raleigh Caprice 1985

Origin	UK
Frame	Steel
Gears	3-speed
Wheels	26 in (65 cm)

Raleigh was the main British bike brand of the 1980s, and their leisure bike catalog had a large range of models that all came equipped with racks, fenders, and kickstands. The Caprice had an added attachment for a basket.

Plastic chainguard

The start of the final time trial
Greg LeMond averaged 34.1mph (54.5 km/h) during the final run from Versailles to the Champs-Elysées. He won by eight seconds and set a time-trial speed record that stood until 2015.

"I was like a **punch-drunk boxer** in a world of **frenzied noise.**"

LAURENT FIGNON, DESCRIBING HOW IT FELT TO LOSE BY ONLY EIGHT SECONDS

The winner of the 1988 Tour, Spanish rider Pedro Delgado, started as favorite for the 1989 event. However, problems in the first two stages cost him time, only some of which he was able to make up. So with Delgado playing catch-up, the battle to win came down to a fight between two men: French rider Laurent Fignon, winner of the 1983 and 1984 Tours, and Greg LeMond.

Fignon had come through a difficult couple of years leading up to the race, but was back at full strength. He had already won the Giro d'Italia—one of cycling's three Grand Tours—in June that year, and his form continued into the Tour de France in July.

LeMond's performance was improving too, and he had a secret weapon. Cyclists had always known that wind resistance was their biggest enemy when trying to ride faster, especially if they were riding alone, but it was a skier who came up with a solution. Boone Lennon, once the coach of the US ski team, designed a device called a "tri-bar," which could be bolted to standard handlebars. It enabled the rider to assume a ski-tuck riding style—a far more aerodynamic position than the standard one racers used in time trials.

TESTING THE NEW DEVICE

Lennon approached LeMond shortly before the 1989 Tour and asked him to test his invention. He did, and it made him faster. LeMond used the tri-bars in the first long time trial of the 1989 Tour, won it, and took the yellow jersey. He then lost the jersey to Fignon in the Pyrénées and retook it in the Alps, only to lose it again. By the start of the final stage of the Tour, LeMond was in second place, only 50 seconds behind Fignon.

Since 1975 the final stage of the Tour has been a road race that finishes with several laps of a circuit that includes the Champs-Elysées, in the center of Paris. In 1989 it was different. France was celebrating its 200th anniversary as a republic, so the organizers decided to mark the occasion by making the final stage a time trial from Versailles on the edge of Paris to the Champs-Elysées, a distance of 15.5 miles (24.5 km).

LeMond used his tri-bars and his new riding position, while Fignon rode a normal time-trial bike in a standard riding position. Fignon struggled with injury, and his bike setup was not as fast as LeMond's. Slowly but surely, LeMond gained time on Fignon: coming into the finishing straight he had clawed back the Frenchman's 50-second lead; gaining a further eight seconds, he won his second Tour de France.

KEY FACTS

RESULTS
First: Greg LeMond, US
Second: Laurent Fignon, France
Third: Pedro Delgado, Spain
Points: Sean Kelly, Ireland
Mountains: Gert-Jan Theunisse, Netherlands

THE COURSE
The 1989 Tour de France had three geographical sections, plus the final time trial. The first section went from hilly Luxembourg through the Ardennes mountains in Belgium. The second section was flat stages from Dinard to Bordeaux. Next up was the Pyrénées, followed by three flat stages across southern France. Then the race went into the Alps before a transfer to Paris for the finale.

76th Tour de France

© Andrei I. Loas 2012

The 1989 race
The sections ridden by the cyclists are marked in dark red, while the light red shows the riders' transfer routes.

1 — 23 July 1989 - **3285.3 km**

Recumbent Bikes

In 1967, British-born engineer, David Gordon Wilson, organized a competition to design a bicycle. The first prize was awarded to a design for a recumbent cycle, which led to a renewed interest in this type of machine, and to Wilson's involvement in the Avatar project. The foundation in 1976 of the US-based International Human Powered Vehicle Association (IHPVA) also stimulated interest in recumbents, especially those with streamlined fairings. The first International Human-Powered Speed Championships had been staged by the IHPVA the previous year. In 1980, interest in Europe was boosted when Wilson took an Avatar to Germany, and in the same year, the Aspro Clear Speed Championships were held in Brighton, England. Both events contributed to developments in recumbent bikes.

"The **laidback** movement, more or less, **prohibits stagnation.**"

MIKE BURROWS, TELEVISION INTERVIEW, 2007

Brake and gear levers
These were both mounted onto the handlebars, beneath the seat.

Rider "sat" in a semi-recumbent position

▷ **FoMac Avatar 2000 1980s**

Origin	US
Frame	Steel
Gears	14-speed
Wheels	Front 16 in (40 cm), Rear 28 in (70 cm)

First launched in the late 1970s, the Avatar was the first commercially available recumbent. The long wheelbase design offered comfort as well as being aerodynamic. David Wilson, Richard Forrestall, and Harold Maciejewski are credited with the design and with rekindling interest in the type. Australian Tim Gartside set a world speed record of 51.9 mph (83.5 km/h) on Avatar Bluebell in the US in 1982.

Rear wheel mounted on suspension

Rear wheel mounted on one side of the main beam

Molded fiberglass seat

Joystick steering control

Designed for Speed

The Brighton Speed Championships of 1980 sparked development of fast recumbents. Mike Burrows built the first Speedy (right) as a training trike, but developed it into a successful racer, which was sometimes equipped with a fairing. The Kingsburys produced several variants of the Bean. British veterinarian, Pat Kinch, broke the Human-Powered Vehicle (HPV) World Hour Record in 1990 riding Bean I.

△ **Burrows Windcheetah SL Mark VI Speedy 1987**

Origin	UK
Frame	Steel
Gears	24-speed
Wheels	Front 20 in (50 cm), Rear 28 in (70 cm)

This is a "tadpole" trike, meaning that it had two front wheels. (A trike with two rear wheels was a "delta.") Mike Burrows, from Norwich, England, produced the first Speedy in 1981. This Mark VI version also had a fiberglass fairing (not shown), which made it noisy but very fast.

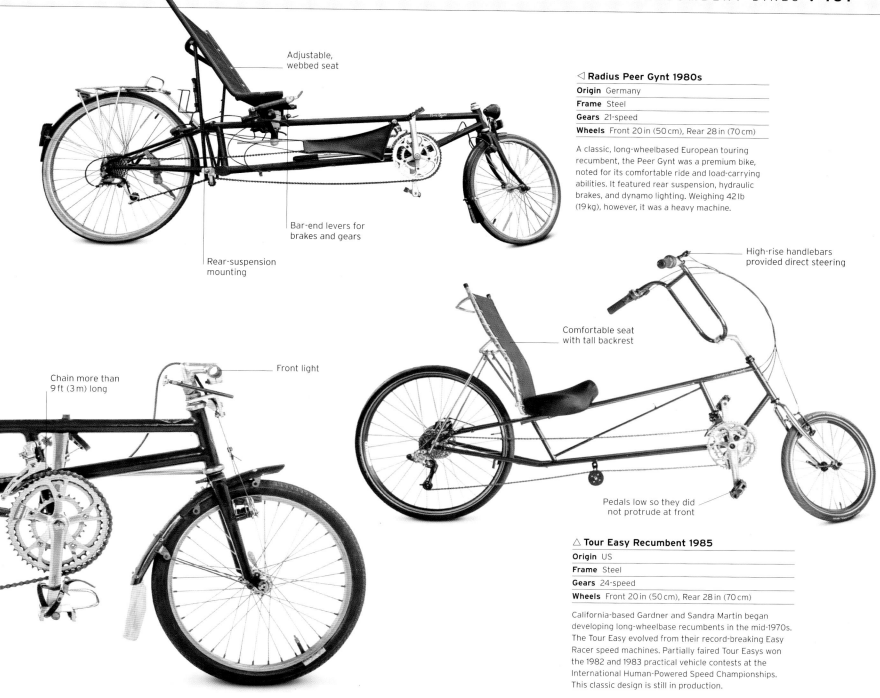

Adjustable,
webbed seat

Bar-end levers for
brakes and gears

Rear-suspension
mounting

◁ Radius Peer Gynt 1980s

Origin	Germany
Frame	Steel
Gears	21-speed
Wheels	Front 20 in (50 cm), Rear 28 in (70 cm)

A classic, long-wheelbased European touring
recumbent, the Peer Gynt was a premium bike,
noted for its comfortable ride and load-carrying
abilities. It featured rear suspension, hydraulic
brakes, and dynamo lighting. Weighing 42 lb
(19 kg), however, it was a heavy machine.

Chain more than
9 ft (3 m) long

Front light

High-rise handlebars
provided direct steering

Comfortable seat
with tall backrest

Pedals low so they did
not protrude at front

△ Tour Easy Recumbent 1985

Origin	US
Frame	Steel
Gears	24-speed
Wheels	Front 20 in (50 cm), Rear 28 in (70 cm)

California-based Gardner and Sandra Martin began
developing long-wheelbase recumbents in the mid-1970s.
The Tour Easy evolved from their record-breaking Easy
Racer speed machines. Partially faired Tour Easys won
the 1982 and 1983 practical vehicle contests at the
International Human-Powered Speed Championships.
This classic design is still in production.

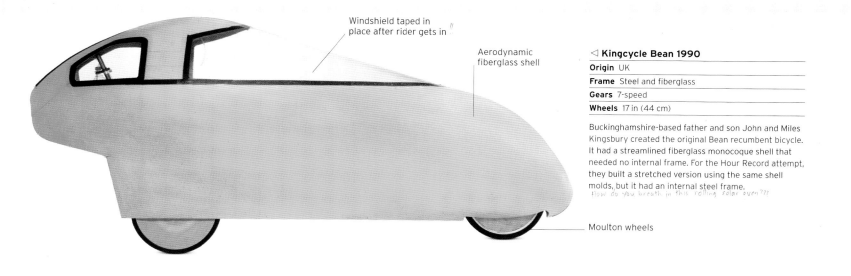

Windshield taped in
place after rider gets in

Aerodynamic
fiberglass shell

◁ Kingcycle Bean 1990

Origin	UK
Frame	Steel and fiberglass
Gears	7-speed
Wheels	17 in (44 cm)

Buckinghamshire-based father and son John and Miles
Kingsbury created the original Bean recumbent bicycle.
It had a streamlined fiberglass monocoque shell that
needed no internal frame. For the Hour Record attempt,
they built a stretched version using the same shell
molds, but it had an internal steel frame.

How do you breath in this rolling solar oven???

Moulton wheels

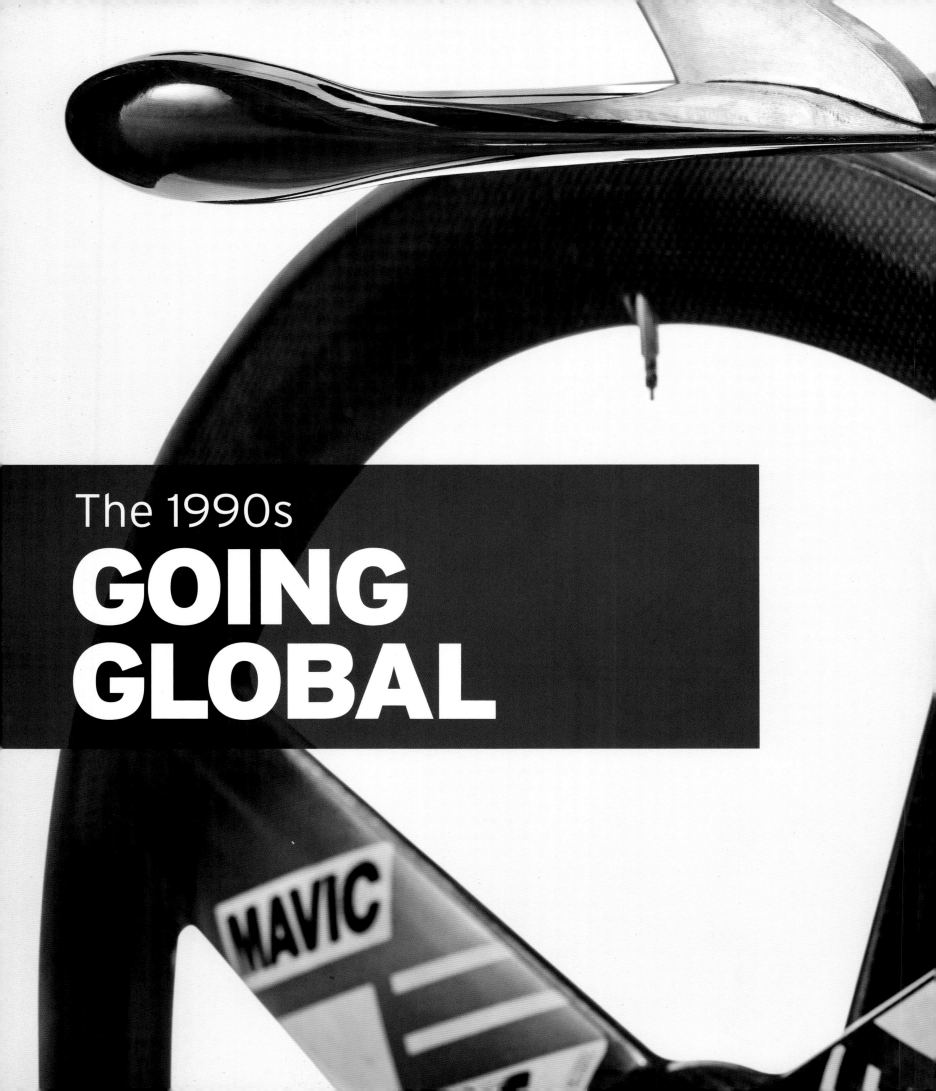

The 1990s
GOING GLOBAL

43 1990

INTER
NATIONALE
FRIEDENS
FAHRT

GOING GLOBAL

The fall of the Berlin Wall in 1989 and the subsequent collapse of the Soviet Union had surprising effects on the world of cycling. Riders from the Eastern Bloc countries had long been at the forefront of amateur racing but had been barred from entry in professional events, such as the Tour de France. Suddenly a rich vein of talent—schooled under a highly organized system of clubs, academies, and training centers run in line with the rigorous Communist approach to competitive sports—flooded the professional ranks, with riders such as Uzbek sprinter Djamolidine Abdoujaparov winning races at the highest level.

Bicycle technology also benefited from the fall of Communism. Stockpiles of titanium—a valuable metal with the same strength but half the weight of steel—reserved by the USSR for military use were released for commercial purposes, with much of this aerospace-grade material finding new life as the frame tubing of high-performance bicycles.

Aerodynamic refinements continued at such a pace that, as the 1990s drew to a close, cycling's governing body, the Union Cycliste Internationale (UCI), placed limits on the advantages that could be gained through equipment and rider position. The trajectory begun by Moser in 1984 culminated in the "Superman" position used by British rivals Graeme Obree and Chris Boardman, in which the arms were extended forward at full length. Both riders set new Hour Records before the UCI halted innovation by requiring the use of a standard drop-handlebar bicycle similar to that ridden by Eddy Merckx in 1972.

△ **Chris Boardman in "Superman" position, 1996**
Boardman set a new Hour Record in 1996 using a modified bicycle, which was subsequently banned. He set a new record in 2000 on a traditional cycle.

> " It was the **ultimate test**—no traffic, one man in a velodrome **against the clock**. I didn't tell myself that I will attempt the record, I said **I would break it**. "

GRAEME OBREE, ON HIS 1993 HOUR RECORD ATTEMPT

Key Events

▷ **1990** Shimano releases the STI, a combined brake and gear lever that allows riders to change gear without removing their hand from the handlebars.

△ **Shimano Total Integration (STI)**
The launch of the Shimano STI combined gear and brake lever is aggressively marketed to competitive racing cyclists.

▷ **1990** The first UCI mountain bike World Championships is held in Durango, CO.

▷ **Early 1990s** Hybrid bicycles, which combine the comfortable position of a mountain bike with the speed and light weight of a road bike, begin to appear.

▷ **1991** Suspension forks—developed for mountain bikes to absorb the bumps of off-road riding—see limited use in cobbled road races.

▷ **1992** Trek releases the OCLV, one of the first mass-produced road bikes with a complete carbon-fiber frame.

▷ **1993** The first UCI BMX World Championships is held in the Netherlands.

▷ **1994** The Sachs PowerDisc, the first mass-produced hydraulic disc brake for bicycles, vastly improves the braking power available to mountain bikes.

▷ **1996** Mountain biking becomes an Olympic sport.

▷ **1996** Chris Boardman sets an Hour Record of 35 miles (56.375 km), the last record to be set before the UCI's rule change.

◁ **The 43rd International Peace Race** was held in Berlin in 1990 to celebrate the fall of the Iron Curtain.

Bikes for leisure

During the 1990s, there was a growing trend for revivalist models that took their design cues from bicycles of the 1930s, 40s, and 50s. Manufacturers moved production to Taiwan and China to create bicycles that were cheaper than ever before. Instead of simple bikes, they could now offer models that had retro appeal and were also affordable. Other cyclists, however, sought more modern designs that suited their lifestyles. That meant models that offered excellent performance and were easy to transport and store.

Synthetic saddle

Busch & Müller Dynamo light

Chrome horn tank

Beige sidewalls styled to look like 1950s balloon tires

Front light with chrome housing

△ Pashley Prospero 1990s

Origin	UK
Frame	Steel
Gears	5-speed
Wheels	28 in (70 cm)

This bicycle's heritage design was inspired by brochures from the British company's archives. The Prospero and its women's counterpart, the Princess, were hand-built with Reynolds 531 steel and had Sturmey-Archer 5-speed gears.

◁ Roadmaster Luxury Liner 1990s

Origin	US
Frame	Steel
Gears	Single speed
Wheels	26 in (65 cm)

The Luxury Liner was a replica of a 1948 model. It featured a chrome horn tank with chrome trim, a headlight, and a "Shockmaster" springer fork and side struts or "bumpers," all of which gave it the look of a café racer motorcycle.

Performance Small-Wheelers

In the 1960s, Moulton small-wheelers were used to break several point-to-point speed records and for many long-distance tours—including England to Australia. By the 1990s, Moulton, Bike Friday, and Airnimal were making performance small-wheelers. Many could be taken apart or folded for transportation by air, rail, or road.

▷ Bike Friday New World Tourist 1996

Origin	US
Frame	Steel
Gears	14-speed
Wheels	20 in (50 cm)

Hanz Scholz built the first Bike Friday in 1991 for his own needs. Tired of compromises, he wanted "a performance bike that could travel with me without hassles." Since 1992, various Bike Fridays have been produced for sport, off-road, commuting, or, in this case, touring.

Synthetic, padded saddle

Angled hinges for easy folding

Front mudguard

Saddle suspension
This bicycle was designed for maximum comfort and featured a classic sprung saddle.

Low gear ratio
The bicycle's oversized wheels meant a small chainring was needed to give a low gear ratio, allowing it to be pedaled from a standing-start.

Upright, chrome handlebars

Curved top tube

Button tread tires

MONSTER CRUISER™

▽ Coker Cycles Monster Cruiser 1998

Origin	US
Frame	Steel
Gears	Single speed
Wheels	39 in (100 cm)

The revival of cruiser bikes in the 1990s hailed the invention of the Monster Cruiser. Its huge wheels and wide 30in (75cm) handlebars gave a comfortable cruising ride. The novelty wheel size proved popular enough for the bike to remain in production today.

Integrated rear rack

Kingpin to allow frame separation

Rear derailleur

◁ Alex Moulton AM7 1997

Origin	UK
Frame	Steel
Gears	7-speed
Wheels	17 in (44 cm)

The Alex Moulton Space-Frame range was launched in 1983 and the AM7 was the original touring model. Its frame, made from Reynolds 531 tubing, was exceptionally rigid and could be split into two parts at a kingpin. The near-identical example shown here is from a 2009 limited edition.

Team Giant-Shimano compete at the 2014 road World Championships

Great Manufacturers
Shimano

A product of Japan's early-20th-century industrialization, Shimano has become the world's largest bicycle component manufacturer. Making everything from gears and brakes to wheels and pedals, Shimano is the biggest supplier of original parts to companies assembling new bicycles, setting the benchmark for functionality and design.

SHIMANO IRON WORKS BEGAN LIFE in Osaka, Japan as a small machine-tooling workshop measuring 430 sq ft (40 sq m), with one borrowed lathe. It was founded in 1921 by Shozaburo Shimano, a 26-year-old engineer with years of experience in bicycle component factories.

Shozaburo Shimano
(1894–1958)

Catering to Japan's growing bicycle industry, Shimano chose to build his company on the production of a single bicycle part—the freewheel. The most complex component on a bicycle at the time, the freewheel had been in existence for some decades, but Shimano identified it as a key component that was ripe for improvement. His Shimano 333 single-speed freewheel, released in 1922, met with immediate success, and by 1930 it was being exported to China, Korea, and Southeast Asia. By 1940 the company had grown to around 300 employees, and in 1945 bicycle hubs were added to the product line. For a

brief period in the 1950s, Shimano produced complete bicycles, but the experiment was short-lived.

The late 1950s was a period of rapid growth: in 1956 the first derailleur was produced, and a year later a 3-speed internal-gear hub was released. Meanwhile, Shimano explored new technology in manufacturing techniques. After learning about cold forging—a method of pressing metal parts at room temperature—at a trade fair in 1957, Shimano immediately saw the potential for low-cost, precision engineering of its metal components. Assisted by industrial scientists and in partnership with a consortium of Japanese companies, Shimano pioneered the processes required. With this in place, Shimano sought to take to the world stage of bicycle manufacturing, and in 1962 the company secured its first contract in the US with Columbia Cycles, the first and oldest name in American cycling. Soon other doors began to open: Schwinn, the most popular brand in the US in the 1960s, placed orders for Shimano's freewheels, and in 1965 Shimano opened a subsidiary in New York.

International growth in the 1960s was assisted by the company's first bestselling product—the Skylark rear derailleur. Released in 1967, the Skylark shared similarities in design with existing derailleurs from rival manufacturers, but was more durable and precise in its gear-shifting.

One-click shifting
The 1984 Dura-Ace groupset was the first to feature Shimano's SIS indexed gear system.

The 1970s dawned with the opening of the Shimonoseki factory in Yamaguchi, Japan. Designed to produce coaster brakes, it was the largest bicycle plant in the world.

Buoyed by strong sales thanks to the strength of the US market, Shimano sought to reach into every sector of cycling. Although children's and utility cycling were served well by Shimano products, touring and road cycling had so far proved elusive. In 1973 Shimano launched the Dura-Ace groupset, aimed at the top level of road racing previously dominated by rival component manufacturers Mavic, Campagnolo, and Huret. Campagnolo had already shown that amateur and recreational bicyclists wanted to ride the same type of equipment as their professional bike-racing heroes. Developing parts for use in tough

Shimano headquarters
The viewing gallery at Sakai Intelligent Plant shows guests the high-tech production facilities.

racing conditions also yielded technological benefits; innovations first tested by professional racers gradually appeared throughout Shimano's range. After seeing the firm's Dura-Ace groupset at a cycle show, Belgian cycling team Flandria took the bold step of using it for the 1973 racing season. Although

SHIMANO

Shimano logo

Shimano's groupset was functionally and cosmetically inferior to rival Campagnolo's Nuovo Record—used by other teams—Flandria still won two stages of the Tour de France, and the team's young star Freddy Maertens came second at the World Championship road race in Barcelona.

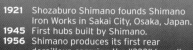

333 freewheel 1922

Skylark rear derailleur 1967

Dura-Ace dual control levers 1990

XTR Di2 rear derailleur 2015

1921 Shozaburo Shimano founds Shimano Iron Works in Sakai City, Osaka, Japan.
1945 First hubs built by Shimano.
1956 Shimano produces its first rear derailleur, carrying the "333" branding.
1957 Internal-gear hubs are added to the Shimano product line.
1960 Cold-forging equipment is installed in Shimano's production plant.
1961 Shimano exhibits its 3-speed internal-gear hub at an international trade fair in New York.

1964 Technical assistance agreement signed with US firm Braun Engineering to perfect cold-forging manufacturing.
1972 Shimano Europe is formed in Dusseldorf, West Germany.
1973 The first Shimano production site outside Japan opens in Singapore.
1973 Shimano becomes the first Asian company to supply components to a team at the Tour de France.
1980s Shimano produces pedals, brakes, and hubs for the growing sport of BMX.

1982 The Deore XT groupset is launched for mountain bikes.
1984 Shimano produces its Shimano Indexing System (SIS) gears, perfecting the technology to move the chain by one gear with a single click of the shifter.
1988 US rider Andy Hampsten wins the Giro d'Italia, the first Grand Tour to be won with Shimano equipment.
1989 The Rapidfire STI for mountain bikes is Shimano's first control unit to combine gears and brakes on the handlebars.

1990 Shimano releases the first STI combined gear and brake unit for road bikes, and the Shimano Pedaling Dynamic (SPD) clipless pedal for mountain bikes.
2000 Shimano adds hydraulic disc brakes to its range of mountain-bike parts.
2002 For the first time, Shimano-equipped riders top the podium in all three Grand Tours.
2008 Di2 electronic gear-shifting system is released.

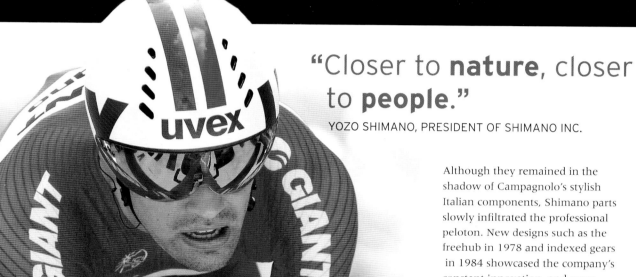

"Closer to **nature**, closer to **people**."

YOZO SHIMANO, PRESIDENT OF SHIMANO INC.

Although they remained in the shadow of Campagnolo's stylish Italian components, Shimano parts slowly infiltrated the professional peloton. New designs such as the freehub in 1978 and indexed gears in 1984 showcased the company's constant innovation, and were successful enough to distance Shimano from rival Japanese manufacturers. In 1989, Shimano permanently changed the nature of bicycle gears with the Shimano Total Integration (STI) concept, featuring a dual control brake and gear lever, combining the brake and gear levers in a single unit on the handlebars for the first time. Riders could now change gear without lifting a hand from the handlebars and could even shift and brake at the same time. This changed the way professional bike riders raced, allowing more spontaneous gear changes and rapid bursts of speed. For recreational riders, the improved safety was an immediate hit, and rival manufacturers scrambled to copy Shimano's revolutionary idea.

Off-road electronics
The XTR Di2 system drives the derailleurs more powerfully than the road version to ensure smooth shifting in rough conditions.

Since the 1990s, Shimano has cemented its position as the world leader in every type of cycling. By investing heavily in research and development, Shimano has created products tailored to every sector, and pushed the technological boundaries with its Digital Integrated Intelligence (Di2) electronic gear-shifting system. Today, nearly half of the world's annual output of new bicycles is equipped with Shimano parts.

High-performance parts
Released in 2008, Dura-Ace 7900 marked a new standard in componentry. The crankset was lighter and stiffer and gave far better shifting than before.

Built for speed
Wearing the colors of the Dutch national champion, Tom Dumoulin uses Shimano gears to power his way through a 2014 time trial.

Carbon-Fiber Racing Bikes

The 1990s were an exciting time for the high-end bike industry. Steel lost ground to aluminum, and the seismic shift toward carbon fiber meant that frames were stronger and lighter than ever before. Traditional diamond frames began to be superseded by the monocoque, allowing far greater freedom in terms of chassis design and looks. The biggest advance was in the creation of aerodynamic framesets with winglike spars and wheel-hugging back ends. Shimano STI and Campagnolo Ergopower combined gear and brake changers, which spelled the end of the traditional down-tube lever.

Seat stays bolted
to the alloy lug

Deep Cinelli
bars and stem

Campagnolo rims
with tubular tires

△ **Greg LeMond TVT 1992**

Origin France

Frame Carbon fiber and alloy

Gears 16-speed

Wheels 28 in (70 cm)

From the mid-1980s onward, TVT produced some of the very first carbon tubes used in the manufacture of bicycle frames. The TVT 1992 featured polished alloy lugs with carbon tubes bonded into them, and a full Campagnolo groupset with Delta brakes.

▽ **Corima Puma track 1990s**

Origin France

Frame Carbon

Gears Single speed

Wheels 28 in (70 cm)

Based in the Drôme region in southern France, Corima first made a name for itself with aerodynamic carbon disc wheels and, later, frames. The Puma all-carbon monocoque track frame was very similar to the one used by the UK's Chris Boardman when he broke the Hour Record in 1993.

Pedal
Clipless pedals use the same technology as ski bindings.

Stiff disc wheel
gave fast
acceleration
on the track

Seat tube and stays
hugged the back wheel

Head tube
shaped to
cleave the air

Aerodynamic,
four-spoke,
carbon front
wheel

Triathlon bar
for solo riding

Pink alloy
lugs hold
black carbon
tubes

◁ **Rossin** *c.* **1990**

Origin	Italy
Frame	Carbon
Gears	18-speed
Wheels	28 in (70 cm)

Founded in 1974, Rossin became known for its finely crafted steel frames. By the end of the 1980s it produced a lugged carbon frame using DuPont carbon-fiber tubes joined by eye-catching lugs.

Single wishbone
tube connected
to the seat lug

Polished
alloy fork
was heavier
than other
models

Unpainted carbon
contrasted with the
silver lugs

▷ **Giant Cadex 980c** *c.* **1995**

Origin	Taiwan
Frame	Carbon
Gears	16-speed
Wheels	28 in (70 cm)

Giant was one of the first bike brands to offer an affordable carbon-fiber road bike. It had eight carbon tubes bonded to aluminum lugs with an alloy fork. Shimano's superb budget 105 groupset kept the price in check.

Traditional diamond
frame made with
high-tech carbon

◁ **Colnago C40**
c. **1998**

Origin	Italy
Frame	Carbon
Gears	18-speed
Wheels	28 in (70 cm)

The now legendary all-carbon C40 was launched in 1993. Exquisitely finished, it was an instant success with the professional peloton. The "C" of its name stands for carbon, while the "40" refers to the number of years Colnago had been in production.

Twin-bolt Look
adjustable stem

Concealed cables
ran inside frame

Colnago's Precisa
straight fork in carbon

▷ **Look KG196** **1990s**

Origin	France
Frame	Carbon
Gears	16-speed
Wheels	28 in (70 cm)

One-piece monocoque carbon frames replaced carbon tubes with lugs in the early 1990s, and Look's futuristic KG196 led the way. An early Shimano Dura-Ace STI was installed on this model.

Mavic Cosmic deep-rim
alloy wheels

Lotus Type 108

Sleek, aggressive, radically aerodynamic—the Lotus Type 108 is as visually stunning today as it was when it burst onto the boards of the Barcelona Olympic velodrome more than two decades ago. Developed in secret by design maverick Mike Burrows and motorsport specialists Lotus Engineering, the Type 108's carbon-fiber monocoque frame and wind-tunnel-tested design were light-years ahead of the competition, and showed what could be achieved by ignoring the accepted conventions of bicycle design.

WHEN CHRIS BOARDMAN ended a 72-year barren spell for Britain's Olympic cyclists, much of the attention was focused on the high-tech "Superbike" that he propelled—through sheer tenacity—to a gold medal in the 4,000-m pursuit.

The Lotus Type 108 evolved from the genius of British engineer Mike Burrows. He saw the full potential of carbon fiber as an incredibly strong, yet lightweight, material that could be molded into any shape, and he developed the Windcheetah Carbon Cantilever track bike in 1986.

When the Union Cycliste Internationale (UCI) relaxed its rules over bicycle design in 1990 to allow monocoque frames—made in a single, shaped form, rather than from multiple joined tubes—Burrows saw an opportunity to prove his design at the highest level: the Olympic Games. Through a chance connection with Lotus Engineering, a motorsport company whose driving ethos of faster, lighter, stronger was a perfect match with the goals of Burrows and British Cycling, the Windcheetah concept was further refined. Molded in an aerofoil shape—similar to an aircraft wing's teardrop profile—the frame's mono-blade front fork was matched by a single rear stay, creating a tiny frontal area that resulted in the most streamlined form possible.

Alloy inserts bonded to the carbon-fiber frame allowed the forks, wheels, cranks, and saddle to be attached

Tubular tires

Carbon-fiber disk wheel

SPECIFICATIONS	
Origin	UK
Designer	Mike Burrows/Lotus Engineering
Year	1992
Frame	Carbon-fiber composite
Gears	Single speed
Brakes	None
Wheels	28 in (70 cm)
Weight	Approx. 20 lb (9 kg)

"It was **like nothing** people had **ever seen** before"

CHRIS BOARDMAN, ON THE TYPE 108

Lotus logo
The Lotus logo features the initials of one of its founders, Anthony Colin Bruce Chapman, who set up the automotive company in London in 1952, with Colin Dare.

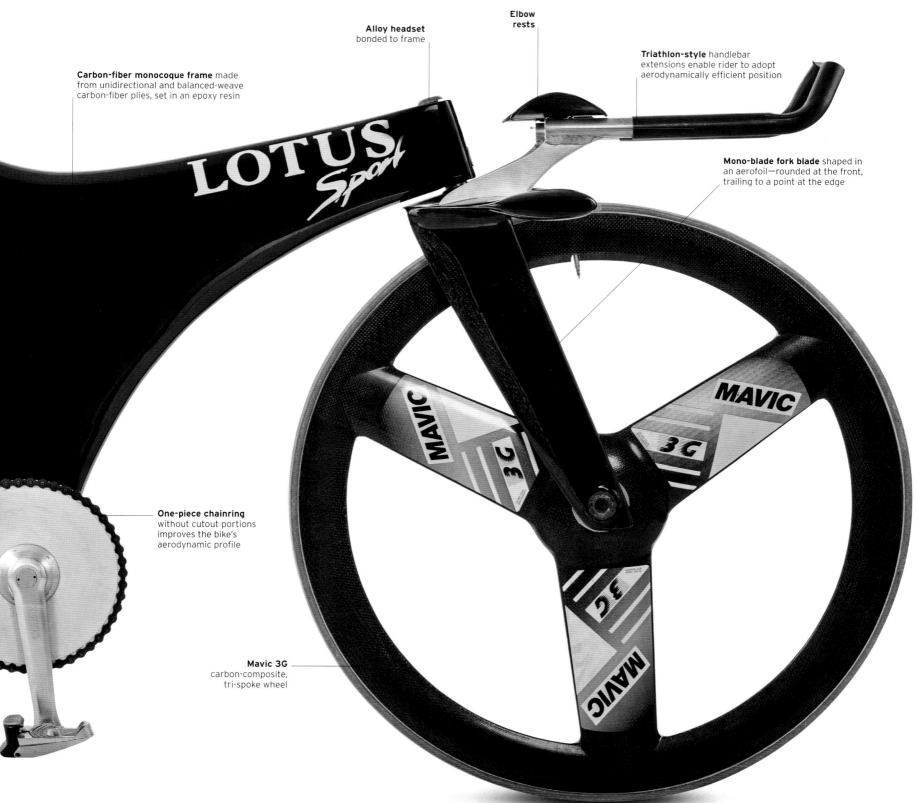

Alloy headset bonded to frame

Elbow rests

Triathlon-style handlebar extensions enable rider to adopt aerodynamically efficient position

Carbon-fiber monocoque frame made from unidirectional and balanced-weave carbon-fiber plies, set in an epoxy resin

Mono-blade fork blade shaped in an aerofoil—rounded at the front, trailing to a point at the edge

One-piece chainring without cutout portions improves the bike's aerodynamic profile

Mavic 3G carbon-composite, tri-spoke wheel

THE COMPONENTS

While the most striking feature of the Type 108 is the frame, each of the parts was selected—and, in some cases, custom-made—with low weight and aerodynamics in mind. In order to fit the Type 108's unique design, French component company Mavic custom-built the hubs to allow the wheels to slide onto the axles, which were bonded to the mono-blade fork and frame.

1. San Marco leather saddle **2.** Rear disc wheel with recess for inner-tube valve **3.** Mavic crank with clipless pedal **4.** Elegantly sweeping carbon-fiber frame **5.** Fixed-gear drivetrain **6.** Mavic tri-spoke front wheel **7.** Profile aero-bar elbow rest **8.** Titanium and carbon-composite aero-bar **9.** Torpedo-shaped handlebar was so small that a three-finger grip was necessary

7

8

6

9

High-Performance Racing Bikes

Exciting advances in technology, led by Japanese component giant Shimano, spelled the end for gear-changing with small levers located on the down tube. By the end of the decade, changing gears using combined brake-and-gear levers became the norm. Where forward-thinking designs for mountain bikes led the way, road bicycles eventually followed. Carbon fiber was yet to take over as the frame material of choice, while hand-built steel frames still faced stiff competition from aluminum and titanium. Aerodynamics was also being taken more seriously, with concealed cables, V-shaped rims, and reduced frontal areas.

Adjustable dropouts for responsive ride

△ Gios Compact Pro 1990s

Origin	Italy
Frame	Steel
Gears	14-speed
Wheels	28 in (70 cm)

The Compact's rear triangle had adjustable dropouts, allowing the back wheel to be moved to within a whisker of the seat post—the aim being to offer a responsive ride. The distinctive blue finish with chrome lugs added a dash of style.

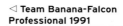

Shimano STI levers

Dura-Ace groupset and gears

◁ Team Banana-Falcon Professional 1991

Origin	UK
Frame	Steel
Gears	16-speed
Wheels	28 in (70 cm)

Team Banana-Falcon bicycles had a steel frame customized with Reynolds 731 tubing, the lightest steel tubeset at the time. The bicycles used Shimano's Dura-Ace groupset with the first version of its revolutionary combined braking-and-gear-change STI levers.

Custom handlebar

Seat tube extends almost to saddle

Wishbone seat stay

▷ Cougar Lo-pro TT 1992

Origin	UK
Frame	Steel
Gears	14-speed
Wheels	28 in (70 cm)

Before the advent of oval tubes and aerofoil carbon spars, frames such as the Cougar's beautifully crafted steel one were the best. Although the lugless Cougar was barely more aerodynamic than a standard frame, it looked fast even when standing still.

Seat post with oval profile

Campagnolo deep-rim wheels

◁ Alan Road Bike c. 1990s

Origin	Italy
Frame	Aluminum
Gears	18-speed
Wheels	28 in (70 cm)

Alan bikes were distinctively assembled with anodized tubes screwed and bonded into chunky aluminum lugs. They had a Campagnolo groupset combined with their deep-rim, early aerodynamic wheels, resulting in a fast, modern bike.

▽ **Colnago Titanio TT** *c.* **1995**

Origin	Italy
Frame	Titanium
Gears	18-speed
Wheels	28 in (70 cm)

Although light, compliant, and impervious to corrosion, titanium was expensive and tricky to weld into a bicycle frame, and it lost out to mass-produced carbon frames in the late 1990s. The Titanio was rare, exotic, and rust-free.

> **"**It is **very easy** for me to make **great bicycles**, it is the **only thing** I do. **"**
>
> ERNEST COLNAGO, ONLINE INTERVIEW, 2007

Triathlon bar for time-trialing

Lightweight saddle

Vivid graphics

Aero, tri-spoke, carbon-fiber wheels

Rear caliper brakes
A high-quality rear brake, the Shimano Dura-Ace was made from anodized, cold-forged aluminum. The dual-pivot design featured coated bushings, reducing friction for smooth braking.

Rear derailleur
The nine-speed rear derailleur made by Shimano housed the jockey wheels in a short cage specifically designed to work with a cassette with small ratios.

Colnago emblem
Traditionally, a brass or alloy head badge was attached to the front of the bike. In an effort to save weight, a light decal of the Colnago clover—one of the most famous emblems—was used instead.

Handlebars
Bicycles used for time trialing had aero-bars. This type of handlebar drew the body forward into a "tuck" position and could save a rider up to 90 seconds in a 25-mile (40-km) time trial.

Lightweight Racing Bikes

Custom frame-builders—for more than a century the main purveyor of high-end bicycles—went into a sad decline as aluminum became the metal of choice. Mass-manufactured, it was lighter and more affordable than steel. TIG-welded aluminum frames were quick to make and production was outsourced to Taiwan and China where the quality was high and wages low. Racing cyclists abandoned steel in favor of lighter, cheaper frames, although steel still appealed to riders who appreciated the ride quality, wide range of sizes, and hint of luxury.

Rearward-mounted drop-out

Early SRAM bar-end gear-shifters

Campagnolo C-Record Delta brakes

△ Cannondale Criterium 1990s

Origin US

Frame Aluminum

Gears 16-speed

Wheels 28 in (70 cm)

Aluminum racing frames from Cannondale were popular in the early 1990s. They were lightweight and had the ability to resist flex. The Criterium model was a short-circuit racer, equipped with French Mavic components and bar-end gear-shifters.

◁ Pinarello Montello Cromovelato 1990

Origin Italy

Frame Steel

Gears 14-speed

Wheels 28 in (70 cm)

This model had a lightweight, steel frame made of Columbus tubing, and high-quality Campagnolo components. The name, Cromovelato, referred to the finish of the frame, where the thin layers of paint allowed the chrome plating to shine through.

Lightweight "Flite" saddle with titanium rails

Campagnolo rims and hubs

▷ Carrera Team Replica 1990s

Origin Italy

Frame Steel

Gears 18-speed

Wheels 28 in (70 cm)

This racing bike had the latest Nivacrom steel tubeset and was still being used in competition in the mid-1990s. It was flawlessly constructed with short-point lugs, shot-in seat stays, and a full chrome fork.

Campagnolo Chorus groupset

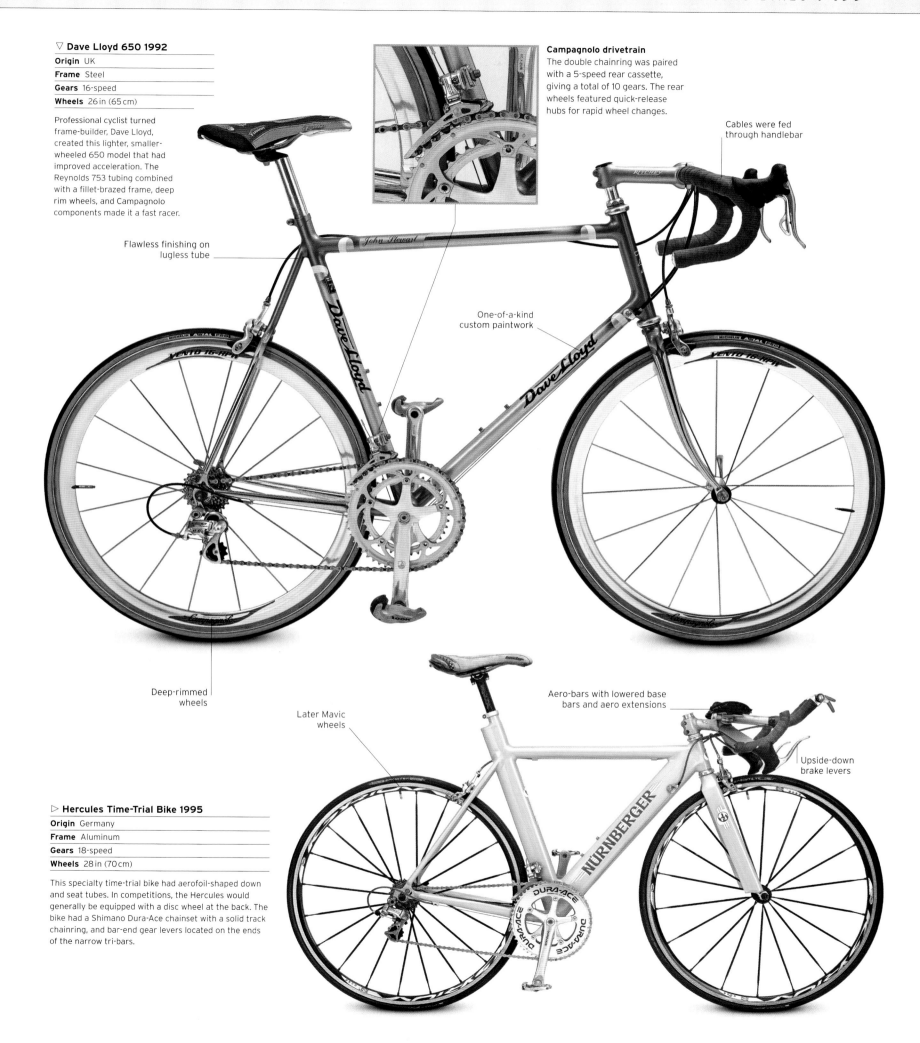

▽ Dave Lloyd 650 1992

Origin	UK
Frame	Steel
Gears	16-speed
Wheels	26 in (65 cm)

Professional cyclist turned frame-builder, Dave Lloyd, created this lighter, smaller-wheeled 650 model that had improved acceleration. The Reynolds 753 tubing combined with a fillet-brazed frame, deep rim wheels, and Campagnolo components made it a fast racer.

Campagnolo drivetrain
The double chainring was paired with a 5-speed rear cassette, giving a total of 10 gears. The rear wheels featured quick-release hubs for rapid wheel changes.

Cables were fed through handlebar

Flawless finishing on lugless tube

One-of-a-kind custom paintwork

Deep-rimmed wheels

Later Mavic wheels

Aero-bars with lowered base bars and aero extensions

Upside-down brake levers

▷ Hercules Time-Trial Bike 1995

Origin	Germany
Frame	Aluminum
Gears	18-speed
Wheels	28 in (70 cm)

This specialty time-trial bike had aerofoil-shaped down and seat tubes. In competitions, the Hercules would generally be equipped with a disc wheel at the back. The bike had a Shimano Dura-Ace chainset with a solid track chainring, and bar-end gear levers located on the ends of the narrow tri-bars.

Touring Bikes

As the notion of taking an annual vacation on a bicycle loaded up with clothing, provisions, and maybe a tent began to lose its formerly widespread appeal among cyclists, the bike industry responded with more versatile machines. Lighter models came without the fenders and racks that were standard on traditional tourers. These items could be retrofitted, but many cyclists looking for a comfortable bike for all-day rides had no need of bad-weather or overnight extras. A wide range of gears, increased considerably with the addition of a triple chainset, remained common to all types of touring bikes.

▷ **Nishiki Prestige 1990**

Origin	Japan
Frame	Steel
Gears	16-speed
Wheels	28 in (70 cm)

Handmade in Japan using Tange Cro-Mo double-butted tubing, the Prestige had the looks of a custom-made bike from a high-quality builder. With fender eyes and enough clearances around the forks and rear stays, the Prestige could also be equipped with fenders for light touring. Gears and chainset were from Shimano.

Tange frame with hand-finished lugs

Shimano chainset

Saddlebag for carrying tools

Front-bar bag for maps and camera

Rear derailleur with long arm for wide ratios

◁ **Cannondale T700 1995**

Origin	US
Frame	Aluminum
Gears	24-speed
Wheels	28 in (70 cm)

Cannondale's touring bikes were widely admired for the quality of their strong and light aluminum frames, with multiple mounting points for racks front and rear, bottle cages, and fenders. Gears were Shimano with a triple chainset and wide-ratio cassette. Shimano V-brakes also provided excellent stopping power when laden.

Shimano brake levers with concealed cables

Avocet saddle for comfortable ride

▷ **Novara Trionfo 1993**

Origin	US
Frame	Steel
Gears	16-speed
Wheels	28 in (70 cm)

Designed in the US and made in Taiwan, the Trionfo was a sign of the times as it became more economical to subcontract frame-building to Asia. Using Tange tubing, it was more of a sports bike than a tourer, but the smooth-riding frame and wheels made all-day rides possible too.

Shimano 600 chainring

▷ **Claude Butler Dalesman mid-1990s**

Origin UK

Frame Steel

Gears 27-speed

Wheels 28 in (70 cm)

A touring-ready, long-distance machine from the famous British marque, the Dalesman came with fenders, rack, and bombproof wheels. Bar-end gear-shifters made changing gear possible with both hands in full control of a load. These were cheaper and more reliable than racing-bike STIs.

Stable and comfortable long wheelbase

Generous rake on front fork

▽ **Bridgestone RBT mid-1990s**

Origin US

Frame Steel

Gears 24-speed

Wheels 28 in (70 cm)

Grant Petersen was the gifted designer behind US company Bridgestone's innovative, high-quality, Japanese-built bikes into the 1990s. The Road Bike Touring (RBT) made touring bikes look classy again with its elegantly relaxed, steel frame and forks.

Cantilever brakes allow for fat tires

Bar-end gear shifters were easy to reach

Triple chainset

The Seattle Police Department set up a bicycle patrol unit in summer 1987 because biking was an easy way to get around in urban areas. Early success meant that, by the following summer, a special squad had been formed. Over time, the bicycle units grew, and in 1995 they were equipped with mountain bikes so that the police could negotiate any area of the city with ease: roads, steps, or narrow passageways. Here, the bike unit is controlling a demonstration.

Great Races
MTB World Championships 1990

The very first official Mountain Bike & Trials World Championships took place in 1990 in Durango, CO, organized by the Union Cycliste Internationale (UCI). The first competition consisted of only downhill and cross-country events.

Olympic recognition
The 1996 Atlanta Olympics was the first to include a mountain-bike race.

BEFORE 1990, A COUPLE OF EVENTS were billed unofficially as world championships, one of which was held in Durango, CO. So it was no surprise when the UCI chose this as the venue for the first official World Championships in 1990.

The first championships consisted of two cross-country races (one for men and one for women) and two separate men's and women's downhill races. There was also an unofficial uphill event, but it never became part of the world championship program.

There was little specialization in the early days of mountain biking. Most competitors took part in both cross-country and downhill events and used the same bike for both. For example, British racer David Baker rode the downhill on his cross-country bike, which had no suspension; he just pumped the tires a little harder and wore leggings instead of shorts in an attempt to protect his legs if he crashed. The downhill course was one that had been used in a long-standing race known as the Kamikaze. It was a natural downhill route, with nothing altered to increase difficulty or make it safer. It even included a 33-ft (30-m) uphill stretch, which does not feature as part of the race now.

The first men's downhill ended in an American clean sweep. Greg Herbold won on a bike equipped with the revolutionary RockShox RS-1 suspension forks, followed by Mike Kloser and Paul Thomasberg. Fourth-place John Tomac, another American, rode a bike with suspension forks, but it had drop handlebars. Tomac was an experienced

The founding fathers of US mountain biking
Charlie Kelly, Gary Fisher, and Joe Breeze (center) invented a race called "Repack" in October 1976. This was a downhill event that took place on a fire road in Fairfax, CA. They rode adapted cruiser bikes with drum brakes, which got so hot they had to be repacked with grease after each descent.

The start of the first men's cross-country
The eventual winner of the Durango championships, Ned Overend (in red, white, and blue), led right from the beginning, and was closely followed by riders from Switzerland, Germany, and Belgium.

mountain biker, but he was trying to break into European road racing at the time. He found that if he used drop handlebars on his mountain bike, he did not have to switch riding positions when swapping between road- and mountain-bike racing.

Canada took first and second in the women's downhill race, with Cindy Devine and Elladee Brown, while Penny Davidson took the bronze

The first men's mountain bike world champion
Not only did Ned Overend win in Durango, he also won a world title at Xterra, an off-road triathlon with a wild-water swim. In 2012, at the age of 57, he won the world cyclo-cross title for the 55 to 59 masters category, and he is still competing now.

medal for the United States. The unofficial uphill race, called the Ezakimak ("Kamikaze" backward), was won by Britain's Tim Gould.

Gould also finished third in the men's cross-country, behind Ned Overend of the US and Switzerland's Thomas Frischknecht. Overend was a mountain-bike specialist, while Frischknecht and Gould were cyclo-cross riders. Frischknecht had been junior cyclo-cross world champion in 1988. He became cross-country mountain-bike world champion in 1996, winning the mountain-bike marathon title in 2003.

The women's cross-country saw another clean sweep of the medals by Americans: Juli Furtado was first, Sarah Ballantyne came second, and Ruthie Matthes arrived third. Furtado had been a member of the US women's ski team, but had to abandon her ski career because of injury.

MORE DISCIPLINES

The competition soon developed. The second event was held in Barga, Italy, in 1991. A trials title was added to the World Championships in 1992, a team relay in 1999, then the dual slalom in 2000, which was replaced by the 4X (four-cross) in 2002. The 2003 championships in Lugano, Switzerland, also added a marathon cross-country event, but that is now held at a separate venue each year.

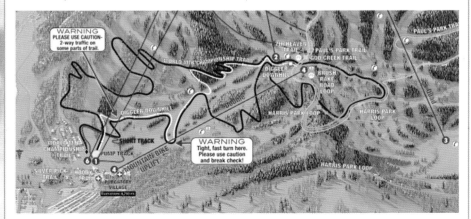

4X competitors
This discipline was added to the world title program in 2002. Heats of four riders race on prepared downhill BMX tracks, and progress from heats to semifinals and a four-up final.

The World Championships are organized by nationality, not by commercial teams. Races are usually held toward the end of the season in different venues around the world. Championship winners are presented with a gold medal and are entitled to wear the rainbow jersey for a year in events of the same discipline. The sport's profile was raised further when cross-country racing was recognized as an Olympic sport and was included in the 1996 games in Atlanta, GA.

"It was in my **hometown** ... everyone was calling me the **favorite** ... I wanted to **win**."

NED OVEREND, RACE WINNER, 1990

KEY FACTS

RESULTS
MEN'S CROSS-COUNTRY
First: Ned Overend, US
WOMEN'S CROSS-COUNTRY
First: Juli Furtado, US
MEN'S DOWNHILL
First: Greg Herbold, US
WOMEN'S DOWNHILL
First: Cindy Devine, Canada

THE COURSES
This map shows the cross-country (black) and downhill (white) courses used for the world championships in Durango, CO. Lifts, marked in red, took the riders from the resort village, at the base of the mountain, to the top of the downhill course. Loops marked in other colors are mountain-bike trails that now form part of the resort.

A center for mountain and trial bikers
Purgatory Village in Durango is a thriving mountain-bike venue with many trails through the forest.

Hardtail Mountain Bikes

Mountain biking (MTB) boomed worldwide in the 1990s. Product designers, machinists, promoters—even aeronautical engineers—all introduced developments to this new form of cycling sport. Riders wanted the latest and best equipment, especially expensive "boutique" components. The availability of front or full suspension, new frame materials, and MTB-specific groupsets made this possible. Bicycles were extravagantly machined and finished in an array of exotic colors, and each one had its own "race-proven" merits. New bicycle standards were adopted, dropped, then reinvented. Sponsorship and marketing played a key role—the more exposure achieved by a bike or component, the better, and the first "million dollar" sponsored rider arrived.

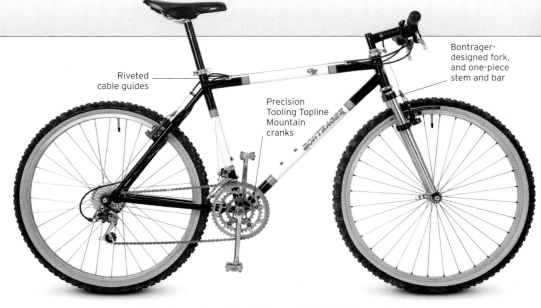

Riveted cable guides

Precision Tooling Topline Mountain cranks

Bontrager-designed fork, and one-piece stem and bar

△ Bontrager RaceLite 1992

Origin	US
Frame	Steel
Gears	24-speed
Wheels	26 in (65 cm)

Handmade from small-section, True Temper 4130 tubing, this bicycle had a frame that was both strong and light. Wishbone seat stays, reinforcing gussets, and toughened steel plate dropouts provided extra strength.

Rear derailleur
Mountain bikes popularized wide-ratio derailleur gearing with triple chainwheels.

▽ Specialized Epic 1991

Origin	US
Frame	Steel
Gears	21-speed
Wheels	26 in (65 cm)

Ned Overend won the first UCI MTB World Championship on an Epic. These bicycles were hand-assembled at a rate of two per day, and were very expensive. The wound carbon tubes were made from nine layers of fibre, and externally tapered lugs reduced weight.

Flat handlebars
This style became popular on mountain bikes as the sport's popularity grew. Brake levers and gear-shifters on the bars were the norm.

Snowflake laced wheel spokes

Ringlé "Trail Stem"

Specialized "Ground Control" tires

Lightweight Tioga
Carbo handlebars

◁ Kestrel CSX 1992

Origin	US
Frame	Carbon fiber
Gears	24-speed
Wheels	26 in (65 cm)

Bevil Hogg and Tom French started Kestrel in 1986, and, with Brent Trimble, created the first monocoque, carbon-fiber frames. The CSX was its second production MTB; its geometry was perfected by Keith Bontrager.

Tioga Revolver
tubular chromoly cranks

Wheel made from
tensioned Kevlar
cord covered with
alloy mesh

Brake and gear cables
routed through the frame

Finished with several
coats of enamel paint

Horizontal, rear-
facing dropouts

▷ Klein Attitude 1993

Origin	US
Frame	Aluminum
Gears	24-speed
Wheels	26 in (65 cm)

Gary Klein's bikes were among the most expensive MTBs. The Attitude's frame, Mission Control fork, and one-piece stem and bar were all made from thin-wall, 6061-T6 aluminium tubing.

Transitional-formed
chainstays

Pace suspension forks with
reverse-mounted brakes

◁ Pace RC200 F3 1994

Origin	UK
Frame	Aluminum
Gears	24-speed
Wheels	26 in (65 cm)

Pace's "Load Dedicated" approach to frame design used varying tube sections (square, rectangular, and round), plus a round head tube with vertical webs. Depth of external butting varied according to stress forces.

Frame mountings for
"Crud Catcher" fender

Iconic tricolor paint
scheme

Multicolor anodized
Mavic Sunset
wheel rims

▷ Rhygin Custom 1994

Origin	US
Frame	Steel
Gears	21-speed
Wheels	26 in (65 cm)

Rhygin built durable, lightweight frames from Reynolds, Tange, and True Temper steel, depending on the rider's weight and riding style. It made the first Columbus Metax stainless-steel frame.

Suspension Mountain Bikes

Initially met with skepticism, full suspension eventually changed the way mountain bikes were ridden. The 1988 "Nitro" concept from Kestrel featured early Rock Shox suspension forks with an air/oil rear shock. The 1990 Offroad Pro-Flex, the first production mountain bike with full suspension, had an elastomer rear shock, and hinged front "Flexstem" bumpers. Mountain Cycles' 1991 San Andreas had twin disc brakes and a radical, seam-welded, sheet-aluminum frame. From 1992, all manufacturers introduced full-suspension bicycles into their ranges, and it soon became a prerequisite for the growing sport of downhill racing.

Campagnolo Centaur MTB groupset

Campagnolo Centaur MTB groupset

Lightweight Sugino XP crankset

SPD M737— Shimano's first clipless pedal

The rear hub was custom-made by Campagnolo for Fisher

△ Gary Fisher RS-1 1991

Origin	US
Frame	Aluminum
Gears	21-speed
Wheels	26 in (65 cm)

This bicycle had a four-bar-linkage rear suspension with virtual pivot points and elastomer shocks behind the seat tube. It featured Mountain Cycle "Pro-Stop" mechanical disc brakes on moving mounting plates.

▷ Boulder Defiant 1992

Origin	US
Frame	Steel
Gears	24-speed
Wheels	26 in (65 cm)

This bicycle's elegant design has a rear suspension unit concealed within the top tube for increased rigidity. The rear swing arm is joined to the main triangle using two links of motorcycle chain. The frame was available in steel, aluminum, or titanium.

Boulder-designed aftermarket "Brake Tamer" brace

Color-matched Rock Shox Mag20 fork with magnesium legs

Shimano's first XTR racing groupset, the M900

Manitou-specific
large-diameter
seat post

Long weld areas on diagonal
joints provide strength

▷ Answer Manitou FS 1993

Origin US	
Frame Aluminum	
Gears 24-speed	
Wheels 26 in (65 cm)	

Answer's Manitou had full suspension with
elastomer shocks, the rear of the bicycle
featuring a shortened version of the front-
suspension fork. The lightweight frame was
constructed from large-diameter aluminum
tubing and machined connections. The bike
had minimal suspension travel of around
2 in (5 cm) both ends.

Low bottom-bracket pivot
point so suspension is
always active

SunTour XC Pro front- and rear-
mechs and thumb-shifters

Coil-sprung,
oil-damped AMP
Research F3 XC fork

◁ AMP Research B4 1995

Origin US	
Frame Aluminum	
Gears 24-speed	
Wheels 26 in (65 cm)	

The lightweight, all-aluminum AMP Research
set new standards for full suspension
efficiency. The disc brakes, a four-bar
articulating fork, and a Horst link pivot
on the chainstays— directly ahead of the
rear axle—allowed the axle to be attached
to the seat stay and isolated braking forces
from suspension.

CODA Magic Motorcycle
cranks, rings, and
external bearings

Rocker-tuned
suspension
mounted behind
bottom bracket

Spin tri-spoke,
carbon-fiber wheels

▷ GT RTS-1 1995

Origin US	
Frame Aluminum	
Gears 24-speed	
Wheels 26 in (65 cm)	

This design had a shock that was activated by a
"rocker" fixed to a subframe, which pivoted on
the main frame. The design resisted lateral flex
and was unaffected by chain tension. The bike
was as good uphill as downhill, and riders won
multiple cross-country and downhill World
Championships on this model.

Noleen-built
custom shock

AFTER 2000
BICYCLES FOR ALL

STAGE

197 KILOMETERS

5

TOUR DE FRANCE 2012

ORCHIES
BOULOGNE-SUR-MER

TUESDAY 3 JULY

BICYCLES FOR ALL

The 21st century has seen a consolidation in bicycle manufacture and use, with progress occurring in gradual refinements rather than sudden bursts. The sheer variety in types of cycling has led to a cross-fertilization of technology, with advances made in one field filtering gradually into others. Hydraulic disc brakes—first developed for mountain bikes—now appear on top-of-the-line road cycles. Carbon fiber has become the frame material of choice, wireless electronic gear-shifting is commonly seen, and carbon belt-drives and electronic motors threaten the monopoly of the humble metal-link chain.

While the bicycle has evolved into a machine of endless possibilities, it also offers empowerment around the world. Development charity World Bicycle Relief designs cycles for use in Africa, providing schoolchildren, healthcare workers, and entrepreneurs with the Buffalo Bike—a robust, low-cost, single-speed machine that can be locally built and maintained. A similar project enables craftsmen in developing countries to build the Bamboosero, a bicycle with a treated bamboo frame that can be sold locally or shipped to Western countries.

Gradually, and in spite of the dangers of sharing the same roads as motorized vehicles, the bicycle's promise as a low-carbon, health-promoting transportation solution has begun to be realized. Bike-sharing programs—such as the Vélib bicycle stations of Paris—have spread to cities on five continents, while major businesses such as UPS and IKEA deliver goods via cargo bikes. As the reasons to cycle are more numerous, and with a growing variety of bikes and bicycling, the bicycle has the potential to be truly for all people and purposes.

△ **Bamboosero City Bike**
City frames, perfect for all-weather urban commutes, are agile in traffic, but also handle dirt roads well.

"It may be the **simplest bike** I've ever ridden, but the humble **World Bicycle Relief** bike is also the most **important** ... It helps people **move out of poverty**."

WARREN ROSSITER, *CYCLING PLUS* MAGAZINE, 2011

◁ **The 2012 Tour de France** was won for the first time by a British cyclist—three-time Olympic track champion Bradley Wiggins

Key Events

▷ **2000** Mountain bikes continue to be refined, with the "29er" wheel—a diameter used on road bikes—offering smoother rolling on off-road terrain than a standard 26-in (66-cm) wheel.

▷ **2005** Nonprofit organization World Bicycle Relief is founded in response to the 2004 Sri Lankan tsunami.

▷ **2007** The Gates Carbon Drive, the first production belt-drive, is released.

▷ **2008** BMX racing becomes an Olympic sport.

▷ **2008** Craftsmen in Ghana become the first local tradesmen to be trained in the construction of Bamboosero bamboo-framed bicycles.

▷ **2012** The Olympic Games include triathlon for the first time.

▷ **2012** Professional cycling is sullied by the revelation that the Tour de France's most prolific champion, American Lance Armstrong, doped during each of his seven victories (1999–2005).

▷ **2014** The Union Cycliste Internationale revises the Hour Record rules, allowing up-to-date technology to be used.

▷ **2014** Dutch racer Marianne Vos—nicknamed "The Cannibal" after Eddy Merckx—becomes cyclo-cross world champion for the sixth successive year, taking her world championship titles across all disciplines to 12; she also has two Olympic gold medals.

△ **Victory for Marianne Vos**
The Dutch racer becomes cyclo-cross world champion for the sixth time in 2014.

Carbon-Fiber Racing Bikes

As interest in the Tour de France grew rapidly, led largely by the success of Lance Armstrong's US-led teams, the bicycle industry responded in kind. Bicycle manufacturers began developing carbon-fiber frames, which soon became the standard for performance machines. Aluminum frames, although light, were also fragile and stiff. Carbon fiber had the high-tech allure of the aerospace industry and the glamour of Formula 1 racing. Componentry also advanced with the introduction of 10- and 11-speed cassettes, electronic gears, and hydraulic brakes.

Bontrager Race rims

Bonded carbon fiber frame

Compact FACT 7r carbon frame

△ **Trek OCLV Limited Edition 2005**

Origin	US
Frame	Carbon fiber
Gears	20-speed
Wheels	28 in (70 cm)

Trek used the process of Optimized Compaction Low Void (OCLV) to create ultralight carbon frames. Made famous by Lance Armstrong in the Tour de France, this Discovery Channel model was produced in the team colors used for the Texan's seventh (now disallowed) Tour win.

Special-edition San Marco carbon saddle

Fulcrum Racing Speed CF7 aero wheels

Ferrari-inspired, carbon frameset

△ **Specialized Roubaix 2009**

Origin	US
Frame	Carbon fiber
Gears	20-speed
Wheels	28 in (70 cm)

Inspired by the Paris–Roubaix race over a cobbled track in northern France, this bike came with a carbon frame that had bump-absorbing Zertz dampers in the seat stays and fork. A higher front end meant an upright riding position, which made long rides more comfortable.

Rear derailleur

After a break of 20 years, a new, ultralight version of Campagnolo's Super Record was launched in 2008 and is featured on the CF7. It has an 11-speed cassette.

▷ **Colnago CF7 2008**

Origin	Italy
Frame	Carbon fiber
Gears	22-speed
Wheels	28 in (70 cm)

Only 99 Ferrari special-edition versions of the CF7 were produced, and few people could afford the $17,500 price tag. The bikes came with Campagnolo's ultralight Super Record groupset and deep-section carbon wheels. The bicycle had a high-modulus carbon frameset, which was based on Colnago's expanded polystyrene (EPS) model.

All-carbon frame and fork laid up by hand

Tri handlebars
This style of handlebar is designed to allow riders to lower their position to create the most aerodynamic profile. The rider is effectively over the front wheel, as opposed to behind it, as on conventional bikes.

△ **Giant Trinity Advanced 2010**

Origin	Taiwan
Frame	Carbon fiber
Gears	20-speed
Wheels	28 in (70 cm)

Introduced in 2009, this time-trial bicycle's radical looks and wind tunnel-honed, aerofoil-shaped spars were Union Cycliste Internationale (UCI) legal. Its racing abilities were proven in prototype form by professional riders.

Electronic gears operated by buttons on handlebar

3T Aduro aero handlebar

Campagnolo Ergopower combined brake and gear levers

△ **Cervélo P5 TT** *c.* **2012**

Origin	Canada
Frame	Carbon fiber
Gears	22-speed
Wheels	28 in (70 cm)

Time-trial bikes resembling stealth jet fighters were the norm in 2012, when the Canadian high-performance bike brand, Cervélo, introduced its P5 aero missile. It had brakes hidden behind cowlings on the front fork and under the bottom bracket.

Integrated handlebar and stem
The robust, threadless headset on this bicycle has a handlebar stem that is clamped directly to the head tube, and is an extension of the handlebar itself. Patented in 1992, the design is a crossover from mountain biking.

Carbon wheels
Fulcrum of Vicenza, a company founded in 2004 by three aerospace engineers, designed the wheels of this all-Italian bicycle. They are made of carbon fiber and have deep aerodynamic rims.

Racing Bikes For All

Carbon-fiber bicycles were used to win the Tour de France in 1986, but it would be another 15 years before carbon became the default choice for top-end racing bicycles. As the new century dawned, mass-produced carbon frames put high-performance cycling within the reach of many new cyclists inspired by the technology and growing popularity of the Tour de France. At the same time, interest grew in traditional materials such as steel, and advances in aluminum frames came close to the performance of carbon-fiber frames. Women's bicycles, with adapted geometry and special-sized parts, also complemented a growth in women's cycling.

Monocoque carbon main triangle

Seat post painted to match frame

Deep-rim, alloy wheels

△ Isaac Force c. 2006

Origin	Netherlands
Frame	Carbon and aluminum
Gears	20-speed
Wheels	28 in (70 cm)

The Isaac Force is a light, smooth riding bicycle that features a monocoque carbon main triangle, and chainstays with tubed aluminium seat stays. Isaac are proud of the care that goes into its frames, which are built by hand.

◁ Colnago Master 55 2008

Origin	Italy
Frame	Steel
Gears	22-speed
Wheels	28 in (70 cm)

Produced to celebrate 55 years of hand-crafted frame-building, the Master 55 has fabulously polished lugs joining the distinctively fluted top and down tubes. The first straight-bladed fork, Colnago's Precisa, was now universally adopted.

▷ Trek Lexa Women's 2012

Origin	US
Frame	Aluminum
Gears	18-speed
Wheels	28 in (70 cm)

The growth in women's cycling led Trek to produce a female-friendly range of bicycles with its Lexa models. Aluminum frames combine women-specific geometry with Bontrager and Shimano components to give fitness cyclists an affordable ride.

Rear stays with mountings for a rack

Triple crankset callout points to rear wheel

Aluminum frame

◁ Specialized Dolce 2014

Origin	US
Frame	Aluminum and carbon
Gears	24-speed
Wheels	28 in (70 cm)

An elegant and versatile women's sports bicycle, the Dolce has female-specific components, an aluminium frame, and a carbon fork with a Zertz damper to absorb vibration from the road. A wide-ratio, eight-speed cassette with triple crankset arms the rider with a gear for every occasion.

▽ **Renovo R4-56 2012**

Origin	US
Frame	Wood
Gears	20-speed
Wheels	28 in (70 cm)

Sustainable, strong, and capable of absorbing vibration, Renovo's wooden frame weighs only marginally more than the best carbon-fiber frames, while riding just as well. Portland, OR-based Renovo has equipped the bike with internal cabling with Shimano gears and a radially spoked front wheel.

Wooden frame
The complex frame joints are bonded using special epoxy resins that are incredibly strong, and resistant to moisture and high temperatures. Aluminum sleeves are used to join the head tube, bottom bracket, and seat tube.

Ergonomic bars shaped for comfort

Inlaid wood frame with tough finish

Rear dropouts made from alloy

Contemporary, chromoly-steel frame

Lightweight but comfortable seat

◁ **Genesis Equilibrium 2015**

Origin	UK
Frame	Steel
Gears	20-speed
Wheels	28 in (70 cm)

In order to appeal to the many new cyclists in the UK, Genesis designed the Equilibrium as an all-arounder. Reynolds double-butted tubes, with neat welds and a carbon fork, ensure a stable and comfortable ride suitable for sporting, touring, or commuting in style.

Giant rider John Degenkolb wins the 2015 Milan-San Remo

Great Manufacturers
Giant

A success story of Asian manufacturing, Giant is an innovative, far-reaching global cycling brand offering a huge variety of bicycles and accessories. The largest bicycle company in the world by revenue, Giant achieved its enviable position not by going head-to-head with its rivals, but—in many cases—by building bikes for them.

GIANT STARTED OUT as a builder of low-cost bikes for major US brands and has since become a pioneering company that designs and makes its own high-quality machines. It was founded in Taiwan in 1972, at a time when the bicycle industry was dominated by a stable of established US and European names trading on their decades-long heritage. Steel was the only material for bicycle frames, and the finest bikes were handcrafted by artisan frame-builders in small workshops producing a few hundred bikes a year.

Giant's founder, King Liu, was a 36-year-old Taiwanese engineer-turned-entrepreneur with a string of creative business ventures to his name. When a typhoon destroyed his eel farm in 1971, he and ten friends formed a bicycle company, naming it after the leading Taiwanese baseball team—the Giants. They wanted to capitalize on Taiwan's status as a leading export base to take advantage of the boom in 10-speed racing cycles sweeping the US. Liu assembled the necessary machinery and skills to

Inspirational leader
Giant's founder King Liu fostered an ethos of continual innovation and challenging conventions. Although a late convert to cycling, Liu completed a ride around Taiwan in his 70s and again in 2014 at age 80.

mass-produce bikes to order, adhering to the stringent Japanese Industry Standard of manufacturing. He urged Taiwan's other bicycle companies to unify their component specifications, to enable greater cooperation.

The early years were a steep learning curve. Some companies accused them of being a mere testing lab that was short on output, while rivals in Taiwan and Japan shipped large orders—many of questionable quality—for overseas firms. But Liu's attention to detail and hunger for quality eventually bore fruit. In 1976 chief executive Tony Lo won a major client: Schwinn cycles, founded in 1895 and still at the very heart of the US bicycle industry. After inspecting the quality and finish of one of King Liu's steel frames, Schwinn signed a contract that made Giant an Original Equipment Manufacturer (OEM). Lo later revealed that without Schwinn's

Carbon-frame technology
Giant's successful development and research program led to a market-leading position in carbon-fiber frame production.

business, Giant would not have survived. Schwinn not only invested financially in its new Taiwanese partner, but also sent experts to train Giant's staff in its frame-building, finishing, and quality-control processes, and supplied the factory molds and tooling needed to create bicycles. Schwinn's patronage lent prestige to this as-yet small, unknown company. The relationship blossomed, and grew even closer in 1980, when a strike at Schwinn's Chicago factory sent more business to Taiwan.

By the mid-1980s, Giant was producing more than two-thirds of Schwinn's bicycles. But Schwinn floundered, its finances in disarray, as Giant went from strength to strength. The two companies parted when Schwinn moved production to the China Bicycle Company in 1985.

Giant was left reeling by the sudden hole in its order book, but Liu and Lo took the unprecedented step of transforming their company into a self-standing bicycle brand. Giant had been producing small numbers of own-brand bicycles for the Taiwanese market since 1981, and

the loss of Schwinn spurred the company into new areas. Joining forces with Taiwan's government-funded Industry Technology Research Institute, Giant began work on a project to

High flier
Giant is a pioneer of mountain biking technology, especially in downhill racing.

develop carbon-fiber technology. Within two years the company had its first carbon-fiber bicycle: the Giant Cadex 980C road bike, with carbon tubes bonded to aluminum lugs.

In 1986 Giant founded its first European headquarters, based in the Netherlands, and over the next five years, outposts were created in the US, Japan, Canada, Australia, and China. At first consumers were wary of the Giant name, associating its "Made in Taiwan" tag with inferior,

> "Our **mission** is to make more and more people **love** and **enjoy** riding **bicycles**."
>
> KING LIU, FOUNDER AND CHAIRMAN OF GIANT

Cadex 980C 1987

TCR road bike 1997

ATX1 DH mountain bike 2000

Twist Esprit e-bike 2011

1972 The Giant Manufacturing Company is founded in Taichung, Taiwan.
1974 Production reaches 3,800 bikes, but orders remain slow.
1976 Giant signs a contract with Schwinn.
1980 Giant produces 1 million bicycles for Schwinn owing to a strike at the latter's Chicago factory.
1981 Wary of overreliance on Schwinn, Giant sells own-brand bikes in Taiwan.
1986 Giant strikes out on its own, as the majority of Schwinn's business is lost.

1987 "Affordable carbon" arrives with the launch of Cadex 980C.
1988 Giant's sponsorship of professional cyclists now includes road, mountain, and track cycling disciplines.
1991 US sales reach 300,000 bicycles, just over half as many as Schwinn, which files for bankruptcy the following year.
1995 US bank Goldman-Sachs invests $12.5 million in Giant for a nine percent stake, lending international credibility to the company.

1996 Giant opens factory in the Netherlands.
1997 The TCR bicycle is released.
1997 Giant launches the MCR1 carbon-composite road bike. Its single-piece molded "monocoque" frame is later deemed illegal for racing by the UCI.
2004 The Maestro full-suspension mountain bike is launched, designed to improve braking and pedaling efficiency.
2007 Giant's production tops 5 million bicycles.

2009 Russian road cyclist Denis Menchov wins the Giro d'Italia on a Giant bike.
2010 Giant starts to use its global reach to champion cycling advocacy, and funds bicycle-friendly transportation routes.
2011 The company launches a new e-bike, the Twist Esprit, and continues to develop hybrid technology.
2011 Giant sponsors the Rabo-Liv women's team. Its leader, Marianne Vos, wins the cyclo-cross World Championships and Giro d'Italia Femminile.

Taking center stage
Giant's TCR compact-frame road bike, ridden here by ONCE's Laurent Jalabert in 2000, stood out from the crowd in the pro peloton.

Company logo

mass-produced goods. But they were soon won over by the high quality of Giant bicycles, not to mention the lower cost.

As an own-brand manufacturer, Giant put its energies into new forms of cycling. It acquired the technology and expertise to tap into mountain biking and BMX, and developed the machinery and processes to mass-produce aluminum frames. The company stepped up its sponsorship of professional cycling, from the Giant-Manitou mountain-bike team in 1995 to the Spanish road cycling team ONCE in 1998. While still overshadowed by more established bicycle brands in public, in private Giant's expertise was highly sought after by its rivals.

In 1997 Giant released a landmark bike that challenged conventional thinking on what a road bicycle should look like. In keeping with the company's approach to efficiency in materials and manufacturing, the Total Compact Road (TCR) frame was compact, with an angular, sloping profile when viewed from the side. The shorter frame tubes—the most dramatic of which was the diagonally sloped top tube—were the masterstroke of British designer

Mike Burrows, and were already a feature on Giant's mountain bikes.

While its innovative road- and mountain-bike designs caught the headlines, Giant's steady push into the hybrid, women's, children's, and e-bike sectors made it a dominant force in the 2000s. In 2008 Giant opened its first women-only bike shop in Taiwan's capital, and in 2011 the company introduced a female-only brand, Liv. With seven factories in China and one each in the Netherlands and Taiwan, together producing around six million bicycles per year, Giant employs around 15,000 people around the world. Giant continues to shape not just the cycling industry itself, but also the bicycles that the world rides.

Wind-tunnel tested
The carbon-fiber Trinity Advanced Pro TT was Giant's most aerodynamic time-trial frame yet.

Hardtail Mountain Bikes

Suspension was first achieved in mountain bicycles (known as MTBs) simply by substituting a sprung front fork for a rigid one. As the sport developed, however, different types of fully suspended MTBs were created for specific purposes with varying configurations. But the simplicity of a hardtail—a rigid-frame MTB with a front-suspension fork—had much to recommend it, and these machines still have a big following. Hardtails are generally considered to be more efficient for climbing hills, since they are typically lighter, and there are no energy losses on the rear suspension. They are also good all-around machines for cross-country rides that have lower levels of technical difficulty.

▷ **Trek 4300 2014**

Origin	US
Frame	Aluminum
Gears	27-speed
Wheels	26 in (65 cm)

Based in Wisconsin, Trek was founded in 1975 and is one of the world's biggest bike manufacturers. The 4300 first appeared in 2000 and, after a few years' break, was reintroduced. It has an exceptionally good aluminum frame for a relatively modest price.

Shimano hydraulic disc brakes

Maxxis Aspen tires front and rear

Long-travel suspension fork

Disc brakes

◁ **Charge Cooker 2014**

Origin	UK
Frame	Aluminum
Gears	18-speed
Wheels	29 in (74 cm)

Founded in 2005, Charge is a small specialty MTB-maker. Its Cooker range includes steel- and aluminum-frame bikes at different price levels. This model has 29-in (74-cm) wheels; later ones had wide-section 27.5-in (70-cm) rims, to accommodate fatter tires.

NON-SUSPENSION BIKES

Hardtail and fully rigid mountain bikes have several advantages over fully sprung models. The suspension fork of a hardtail is easily replaced, but the sprung frame required for rear suspension is a different matter. An unsprung frame will be lighter and mechanically simpler, which means less time spent on maintenance. And because the frame is cheaper to build, the maker has more budget to devote to components like gears, brakes, and wheels.

Surly Pugsley 2005 Surly was first established in Bloomington, MN in the late 1990s. The Pugsley model was introduced in 2005. It is described as a "fat bike" because it has extra-wide tires, which makes it suitable for use on soft surfaces such as snow and sand.

▽ **Cannondale Trail 1 2016**

Origin	US
Frame	Aluminum
Gears	30-speed
Wheels	28 in (70 cm)

Cannondale's Trail bicycles are built to bring riders into the world of performance mountain biking. The Trail 1 is a sport hardtail rather than a true trail bike. For 2016, the Trail range has introduced 28-in (70-cm) wheels on all bicycles.

Ultrawide ratio, 10-speed cassette

Shimano M506 hydraulic disc brakes

Compact triple chainring

▷ **Scapin Nope 2000s**

Origin	Italy
Frame	Steel
Gears	24-speed
Wheels	26 in (65 cm)

An Italian bicycle-maker, Scapin, started producing road bicycles in the mid-1950s. The Nope is a hand-built MTB designed to achieve high speeds. While this model has an all-steel frame, in later versions the seat tube and head-tube liner were made from carbon fiber.

SunTour suspension fork with 4 in (10 cm) travel

Suspension fork with 3 in (7 cm) travel

Stylish curved seat stays

Radial-spoked front wheel

▽ **Rocky Mountain Vertex SC Team 2000s**

Origin	US
Frame	Aluminum
Gears	27-speed
Wheels	26 in (65 cm)

Rocky Mountain Bicycles has been a specialty MTB manufacturer since the early 1980s. Its Vertex is a light, high-end hardtail MTB with a TIG-welded, Easton SC7000 scandium aluminum frame with air-sprung, front-suspension forks.

Easton seat post

RockShox SID fork gives 3 in (7 cm) of travel

Full-Suspension Mountain Bikes

In recent decades, mountain bike manufacturers have become obsessed with offering both front and rear suspension, even if many of their customers rarely ride the sort of trails that require it. Cheap, full-suspension systems have trickled down to models at the bottom of the market, and many brands, such as the ones featured here, have sunk enormous amounts of money and research time into creating excellent forks and rear suspension systems. Technology has advanced exponentially, and today there is a multitude of full-suspension systems, ranging from single pivot, split pivot, or Horst link to soft tail or unified rear triangle.

Coil-spring rear suspension

Tektro alloy V-brakes
Despite the increasing use of disc brakes, direct-pull cantilever brakes, such as these Tektros, remain popular. They are often called V-brakes, which is a Shimano trademark.

Avid Juicy 3 brakes

RockShox Tora 302 front forks with 4-in (10-cm) travel

Scott Genius LC-R shock absorption

△ **Diamondback S20 2000s**

Origin	US
Frame	Aluminum
Gears	24-speed
Wheels	26 in (65 cm)

Originally a BMX manufacturer from the 1970s, Diamondback built mountain bikes in the 1980s. The S20 was an entry-level bike in the full-suspension market but holds its own with its four-bar-linkage suspension system.

△ **Scott Reflex FX-25 2007**

Origin	Switzerland
Frame	Aluminum
Gears	27-speed
Wheels	26 in (65 cm)

With its Reflex FX-25, Scott solved the problem of varying terrain by including a Genius LC-R shock-absorption system that can be switched from all-travel mode to lock-out mode at the flick of a lever.

Ritchey Comp OS top tube

Cane Creek 40 headset

▷ **Boardman Team FS 2012**

Origin	UK
Frame	Aluminum
Gears	27-speed
Wheels	26 in (65 cm)

This full-suspension bike, with its RockShox forks and rear suspension, is aimed at both cross-county and enduro riders. It is manufactured to the specifications of former British Olympic road cyclist, Chris Boardman.

Truvativ Firex 3.2 GXP chainset

Front suspension
Japan-based SR SunTour makes a huge range of suspension forks to suit every budget. The original equipment used on this bike was an inexpensive coil-sprung XCC fork.

Wheels and tires
The wheels of this entry-level bike have basic alloy rims and quick-release hubs. The tires are suitable for a mix of urban and off-road use.

ALUXX SL-grade aluminum frame

RockShox BoXXer World Cup front suspension fork

SRAM XO 1x10-speed drivetrain

RockShox Vivid R2C rear shock

▷ **Giant Glory 0 2014**

Origin	Taiwan
Frame	Aluminum
Gears	10-speed
Wheels	26 in (65 cm)

This machine was designed specifically for downhill mountain-bike racing and has components that are built to take a beating. The Maestro suspension system features 8 in (20 cm) of travel.

Roval Control SL 29 carbon-fibre wheels

Syntace F109 stem with 6-degree rise

◁ **Specialized S-Works Epic 2015**

Origin	USA
Frame	Carbon fibre
Gears	33-speed
Wheels	29 in (74 cm)

Specialized are very proud of what they call "Brain Technology" in the front and rear suspension on the S-Works Epic. In practice this means that the suspension adapts as the rider moves from flat to bumpy terrain.

Shimano XTR Di2 11-speed chainset

Recumbent Bikes and Trikes

Although balance and maneuverability can be a problem in recumbent bicycles—
especially for first-time riders—they are still more comfortable than upright bikes.
Recumbents also offer more efficient braking because of their lower center of gravity.
Additionally, these bicycles are faster on flat ground than their upright counterparts
because of their aerodynamic riding position, and riders of recumbents regularly set
new world speed cycling records. There are several variants available on the classic
model, including low-racers (where the very low seat makes for better aerodynamics),
high-racers (with larger wheels), tandem recumbents, recumbent tricycles (a delta with
two rear wheels, and a tadpole with two front wheels), and recumbent mountain bikes.

DESIGN EVOLUTION

Manufactured in Germany, the HP Velotechnik Gekko fx is a recumbent tricycle
that incorporates many cutting-edge features, including advanced front and rear
suspension. The most notable, however, is the optional electrical motor that can
be built into the rear wheel, giving assistance up hills and over long distances.

Recumbents are larger than conventional bikes. However, this model can be
folded up in a matter of seconds, for easy transportation and storage.

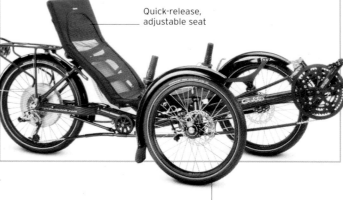

Quick-release,
adjustable seat

▽ **Hase Pino Allround 2008**

Origin	Germany
Frame	Aluminum
Gears	27-speed
Wheels	Front 20 in (50 cm), Rear 26 in (65 cm)

Unlike most bicycles for two, this
part-recumbent, part-upright tandem
places the captain upright at the
rear and the stoker in the front.
It can be dismantled in just 10
minutes and fitted into the back
of an average hatchback car.

Racktime Addit rack

Robust, lightweight
aluminum frame

Handlebar-mounted
gear-shifters

Wider, flatter
tricycle tire

Front pedals

Steering
joint

Rear brake
Mechanical disc brakes offer greater
stopping power and predictable braking,
even in the wet. The steel disc at the
wheel's center is unaffected by water
buildup, unlike a traditional rim brake.

Rear crank and pedal
Made from aluminum, the crank is
attached to a tapered bottom bracket.
A Shimano clipless pedal is installed and
the rider has to wear specific shoes with
cleats to engage with the pedals.

Front seat
The weather-resistant, bucket-style seat
is constructed from synthetic fabrics
and mesh. The fabrics are quick-drying
to ensure that sweat does not build up
and make the rider uncomfortable.

Front tire
Made by German manufacturer Schwalbe,
the partly-treaded front tire is suitable
for any terrain. Inside the tire is a rubber
belt that gave protection against
sharp stones and glass.

Euro Mesh seat

FS Gossamer crankset

Bacchetta dual-pivot road brake

◁ **Bacchetta Corsa 650c 2004**

Origin	US
Frame	Aluminum
Gears	27-speed
Wheels	26 in (65 cm)

The Corsa was designed by one of Bacchetta's founders, Mark Colliton. This bicycle is built for speed, with a light aluminum frame and performance parts. The one concession to luxury is the inclusion of a soft EuroMesh seat.

▷ **Bike Friday SatRDay 2006**

Origin	US
Frame	Steel
Gears	27-speed
Wheels	16 in (40 cm) or 20 in (50 cm)

This bike looks rather bulky with its high seat and handlebars, boom, and folding rear rack. However, it can be folded up small enough to fit into an accompanying travel bag or Samsonite suitcase.

High-clearance fenders

DualDrive hub

Seat incorporated into frame

Optional Streamer canopy

◁ **HP Velotechnik Scorpion fs 2007**

Origin	Germany
Frame	Aluminum
Gears	27-speed
Wheels	20 in (50 cm)

Designed for speed and long-distance touring, this recumbent tricycle has a lightweight aluminum frame and a long wheelbase. The front and rear suspension is fully adjustable and is designed so that it is not affected by the rider's pedaling action.

Chain tube

Aluminum U6 front fork

Hydraulic rear suspension

▷ **Challenge Hurricane 2009**

Origin	Netherlands
Frame	Aluminum
Gears	14-speed
Wheels	20 in (50 cm)

This mid-racer has an unusual rear-suspension design with the central shock absorber below the frame. The pass-through link to the seat spine and swing-arm pivot keeps power delivery high and the ride smooth.

Performance Tandems

No other bike turns heads like a tandem. First invented in the 1890s, like other types of bicycle, their design—and the materials used—have steadily evolved. While most current models are designed for touring, and are constructed from steel, carbon fiber racing tandems and off-road two-seaters are also available. One drawback of early tandems was their size. In order to retain strength and rigidity, the frames were short, giving an uncomfortable riding position. The use of modern materials means that the frames can be longer without reducing their integrity, so giving a more enjoyable riding experience. Being longer means that modern tandems are even trickier to store and transport than older machines. Recognizing this, some manufacturers, such as Orbit and Santana, produce cleverly engineered "demountable" frames that can be split in a matter of minutes.

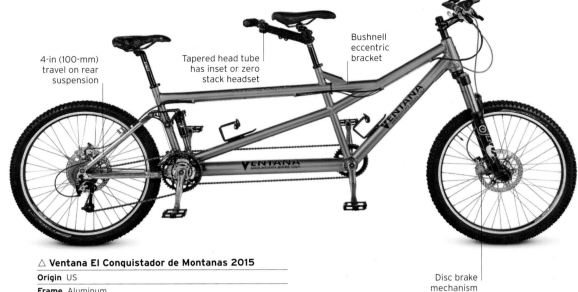

4-in (100-mm) travel on rear suspension

Tapered head tube has inset or zero stack headset

Bushnell eccentric bracket

Disc brake mechanism

△ Ventana El Conquistador de Montanas 2015

Origin	US
Frame	Aluminum
Gears	27-speed
Wheels	26 in (65 cm), 27 in (68 cm), or 29 in (73 cm)

With suspension in the front and rear, fairly aggressive frame geometry, and a shorter wheelbase for tighter turning, this tandem is designed to soak up anything the trails might throw at it. Ventana's owner, Sherwood Gibson, is a former BMX rider.

Tubus cargo rack

Padded seat for long-distance comfort

Tange Techno stainless-steel, cartridge-bearing headset

S&S torque couplings

Front derailleur on rear chainring

△ Orbit Summit 2015

Origin	UK
Frame	Steel
Gears	30-speed
Wheels	26 in (65 cm) or 28 in (70 cm)

Orbit has manufactured tandems in Yorkshire since the 1950s, and in 2015 produced 18 different models. The Summit, its Reynolds 631 frame built to order by Bob Jackson of Leeds, comes in three models, all with Orbit full chromoly steel forks and S&S couplings.

Schwalbe Racing, Ralph Performance tires

Cannondale Fatty Tandem 29, OPI, steerer forks

Demountable frame
Because of their length, tandems can be difficult to transport and store. To overcome this, some models, such as this Santana, have specialized joints in the frames so they can be taken apart easily.

Magura MT5 hydraulic disc brakes

△ Cannondale Tandem 29er 2015

Origin	US
Frame	Aluminum
Gears	10-speed
Wheels	29 in (73 cm)

The aluminum frame on this tandem, coupled with its 1.5-in (4-cm) steerer fork, makes for great handling, even on bumpy off-road trails. The wheel size also ensures that riders could take on roots and rocks without the fear of being thrown off.

Avid V Single Digit (SD) 7 third brake

Spinergy hubs front and rear

Bengal caliper rear brake with Santana 10-in (25-cm) rotor

△ Santana Team Titanium 2015

Origin	US
Frame	Titanium
Gears	30-speed
Wheels	28 in (70 cm)

Tandems are rarely light because of the extra frame and components. Yet with this titanium model, Santana keeps the frame weight below 7 lb (3.17 kg). Santana claims it is the only bike-builder to use seamless, custom-drawn, tandem-specific tubing.

▽ Cyfac Le Duo Carbone 2015

Origin	France
Frame	Carbon fiber
Gears	30-speed
Wheels	Variable

French manufacturer Cyfac produces this road tandem in a variety of build options and customized specifications. The T800H IM carbon frame with Kevlar reinforcement ensures that the bike remains incredibly light and fast.

Carbon tapered forks

Shimano Ultegra derailleurs

Gates carbon drive timing belt

Urban Bikes

After 2000, manufacturers rebranded hybrid bicycles as urban bikes, aiming to appeal to young, upwardly mobile adults and commuters. These bicycles, like the hybrids of the late 1990s, have elements of mountain and touring models but vary greatly in specification. Some have 28-in (70-cm) wheels and slick tires designed for road-only use, while others use 26-in (65-cm) wheels with some tread, making them ideal for light terrain. Frames have mounts for fenders and a rack or basket. Urban bikes are inexpensive, built from lightweight aluminum and their manufacturing outsourced.

Suspension fork absorbs shocks

Polished alloy seat post

Plastic fender

△ Carrera Crossfire 2005

Origin	UK
Frame	Aluminum
Gears	8-speed
Wheels	28 in (70 cm)

A manufacturer for the budget-conscious, Carrera generally makes heavy bikes produced in Asia and equipped with entry-level components. The front-suspension fork is intended to absorb shocks but in reality slows the handling.

◁ Mustang Aztekker Plus 2005

Origin	Netherlands
Frame	Aluminum
Gears	8-speed
Wheels	28 in (70 cm)

Typical of the modern utility bikes commonly found across Europe, the Mustang Aztekker Plus is low-tech, affordable, and bombproof. A plastic chainguard keeps the rider's clothes away from the chain and kept maintenance to a minimum.

Triple-butted, aluminum top tube

▷ Cannondale Bad Boy 2005

Origin	US
Frame	Aluminum
Gears	8-speed
Wheels	26 in (65 cm)

Relatively expensive compared to other urban bicycles, the Bad Boy was the first to harness all the qualities of a mountain bike and adapt them to urban commuting. Its lightweight aluminum frame and disc brakes make it popular.

Steel spokes add durability

Lightweight saddle with foam padding and CrMo rails

Plastic water-bottle cage

Front brake cable with outer housing

◁ Specialized CrossTrail 2005

Origin	US
Frame	Aluminum
Gears	8-speed
Wheels	28 in (70 cm)

This lightweight, fast-rolling bike features a carbon fork with Zerts rubber inserts that are designed to absorb frame vibration. With its upright position, the CrossTrail is popular with commuting cyclists.

▽ Trek Navigator 2012

Origin	US
Frame	Aluminum
Gears	22-speed
Wheels	26 in (65 cm)

The Trek Navigator, with its plush tires, suspension forks, and adjustable handlebar stem, is a ride designed for practicality and comfort. Its alloy frame and large tires mean the bike can go anywhere, and its low cost makes it popular with weekend fitness riders.

All-terrain gears
This model was designed to be used off-road, as well as in the city, and features a large number of gears to suit all cycling environments.

Rubber grips with palm support

Foam-padded saddle with synthetic cover

Alloy rear rack

Durable aluminum frame

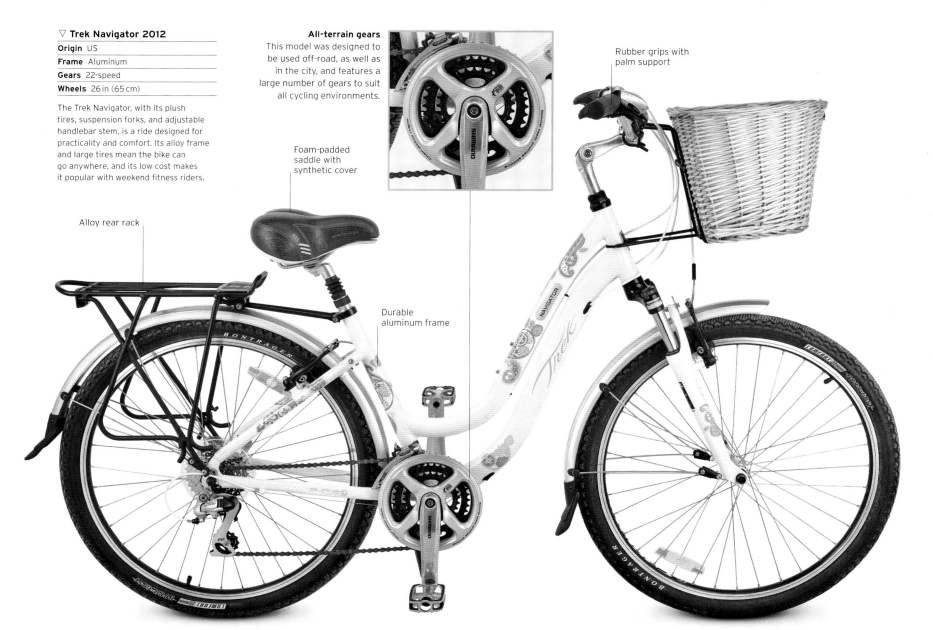

▷ Pashley Sonnet Bliss 2013

Origin	UK
Frame	Steel
Gears	5-speed
Wheels	28 in (70 cm)

The Sonnet married traditional elegance with modern manufacturing techniques to bring together the best of both worlds. British company, Pashley, uses chromoly steel, and the vintage looks hide the fact that the bike is lighter than early-20th-century originals.

Brooks Flyer leather saddle

Wicker basket

Durable tires with reflective print for additional visibility

CYCLING IN CITIES

In many countries before World War II, commuting by bicycle was the norm. As the automobile took over, traffic discouraged cyclists. To tempt cyclists back to the inner cities, town planners created more bike lanes and paths, and manufacturers now promote bikes suitable for city use.

Safer urban cycling The increase in urban cycling has been such that many cities around the world are now creating segregated routes for cyclists.

The bicycle is the only reliable, cheap form of transportation for families and workers in many poor and less accessible parts of the world, especially in war-torn places such as Kabul, Afghanistan. This Afghan man is riding his bicycle—heavily laden with watering cans for his market stand—past the ruins of the Darul Aman Palace, west of Kabul. This area was the scene of some of heaviest fighting between opposing warlords and the Taliban in the 1990s.

Cargo and Passenger Bikes

First invented for tradesmen to use on deliveries, these solid workhorses were extremely popular during the early part of the 20th century. After World War II, however, they became less common as vans and trucks were used for deliveries. Cargo bicycles enjoyed something of a revival in the 1980s when businesses became more ecologically-minded. They later developed into high-tech machines capable of transporting heavy loads, camping gear, or even children, as families sought alternative, greener ways to travel. The front wheels are normally smaller than the rear wheels to make room for the load containers and improve stability by reducing the center of gravity at the same time. Some models feature two wheels at the front for extra stability.

Stiff, straight-blade no-taper forks

Schwalbe Big Ben puncture-resistant tires

Heavy-duty, twin-leg bicycle stand

△ Xtracycle Edgerunner 2015

Origin	US
Frame	Chromoly steel
Gears	24-speed Shimano Acera
Wheels	Front 26 in (65 cm), Rear 20 in (50 cm)

The rugged-looking Edgerunner is a dedicated and adaptable load-lugger. The smaller rear wheel lowers the center of gravity, while the extended wheelbase makes the bike more stable, even when carrying a heavy load. A child seat, carry bags, or a sidecar can also be added.

▽ Nihola 4.0

Origin	Denmark
Frame	Aluminum
Gears	8-speed
Wheels	Front 17 in (44 cm), Rear 22 in (55 cm)

This sturdy machine, with a load capacity of 265 lb (120 kg), has room for four small children in its enormous cabin at the front. Safety is never compromised thanks to the cabin's double-tube frame welded together with steel sections.

Magura parking brake

Waterproof rain hood

Aluminum seat post

Schwalbe Marathon Plus tires

Seat belts and rain cover for the cargo box

◁ Babboe Curve 2015

Origin Netherlands

Frame Steel

Gears 7-speed Shimano Nexus

Wheels Front 20 in (50 cm), Rear 26 in (65 cm)

Ideal for carrying young children, these bikes are a common sight in many Dutch cities during the school run. They have a load capacity of 220 lb (100 kg), and passengers and cargo can be kept dry by fitting an optional cover.

Beechwood cargo box

Enclosed chaincase

SRAM DB1 hydraulic brakes

Fender with mudflaps

Kenda Kwest tires fatter than on standard models

▷ Omnium Mini-Variant 2015

Origin Denmark

Frame Chromoly steel

Gears 3-speed

Wheels Front 16 in (40 cm), Rear 28 in (70 cm)

The load-bearing capacity of this bike was not huge, but what it lacked in strength it more than made up for in maneuverability. Extra-fat tires, a step-through frame, and an upright riding position added to all-around rider comfort.

Saddle provides comfortable upright position

Large carrying capacity

Jumbo 80 twin-leg kickstand

◁ Pedalpower 2015

Origin Germany

Frame Aluminum

Gears 24-speed

Wheels Front 20 in (50 cm), Rear 26 in (65 cm)

At 104 in (266 cm) in total length, this cargo bike from Pedalpower can transport almost anything. Low to the ground, it is also surprisingly stable. Its NuVinci N360 drivetrain is the first continuously variable bike transmission commercially available.

Hydraulic disc brakes

Waterproof plywood box

▷ Christiania Classic 2015

Origin Denmark

Frame Steel

Gears 8-speed

Wheels 20 in (50 cm)

Christiania's galvanized steel tricycle bike features disc brakes on the front wheels, which greatly shortens the stopping distance. The hand brake has a parking function, which adds to safety.

Disc brakes on front wheels

Aluminum front hub with deep-groove ball bearings

Commuter Bikes

After the first mountain bike was introduced in 1981, it became a popular option for commuters: with its sturdy frame and load-carrying ability, it could be used as both a utility bike and a sports bike. In 1988, a new type of bike, the hybrid, was introduced to address the growing needs of the urban cyclist. Hybrid bicycles combine features of the mountain bike, road bike, and touring bike. Hybrids designed for commuting have flat bars and wide tires designed for comfort, load-carrying capacity, and versatility over a wide range of road surfaces. Small-wheeled, folding cycles are another popular option for commuters, and are most frequently used for traveling to work via mass transit.

▷ Montague Swissbike XC90 2007

Origin	US
Frame	Aluminum
Gears	30-speed
Wheels	26 in (65 cm)

The Montague was a high-spec, off-road, folding mountain bike. Unusually for a folder, it had full-size 26-in (65-cm) wheels. The frame was based on a rectangular center section with the rear triangle swiveling through 180 degrees at the bottom bracket, making a compact package when folded.

Unique folding and swivelling frame design

Front and rear disc brakes

Frame can be folded in seconds

Single-tube frame design

Built-in rear rack and transporter wheels

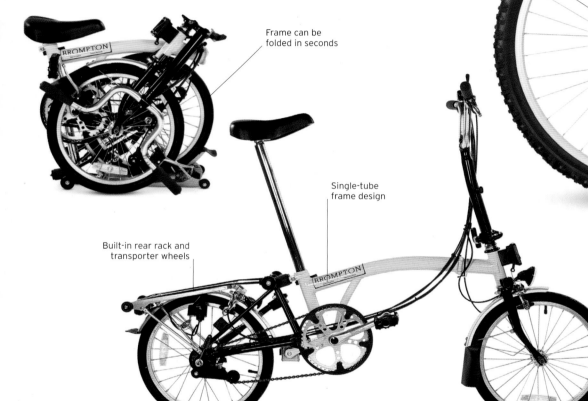

◁ Brompton Folding Bike 1975

Origin	UK
Frame	Steel
Gears	5-speed
Wheels	16 in (40 cm)

The unique design enabled the Brompton to be folded down into a portable, compact package so that it could be carried in car trunks and on mass transit. When ridden, it was agile and stable and its small wheels helped maneuverability in traffic.

Hybrid Bikes

The hybrid bike is a derivative of the mountain bike. Raleigh pioneered the style in 1988, closely followed by Bianchi. The aim was to keep the good braking, wide-ratio gearing, and upright riding position of the mountain bike, but with the lighter frame and slimmer tires seen on road bikes. There are different types of hybrids, and most can be used for both urban and recreational riding.

▷ Mongoose Oxford c. 2010

Origin	US
Frame	Steel
Gears	21-speed
Wheels	28 in (70 cm)

The double-butted steel frame and front-fork suspension of this bicycle made for a comfortable ride over rough terrain. Its low seating position provided a rear weight bias, aiding stability and grip off-road.

Low seat position

Cable-operated, v-brakes brakes

Slim tires for speed

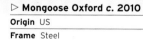

Cable-operated
V-brakes

Double-walled wheel
rims for strength

Large-section
aluminum
down tube

△ **Indigo Folding Bike 2013**

Origin	UK
Frame	Aluminum
Gears	3-speed
Wheels	16 in (40 cm)

The Indigo's stepover frame design
was based on a large-section,
aluminum, down-tube frame that
offered rigidity and lightness. The
height-adjustable handlebars and seat
stems made the bicycle easy to fold.

Full-size, heavy-
duty wheels

Slimline
sports saddle

Foldable
main tube

▷ **Dahon Vigor P9 2014**

Origin	China
Frame	Aluminum
Gears	9-speed
Wheels	20 in (50 cm)

The Dahon's thick wheels gave
this bicycle stability and excellent
handling. Its aluminum frame,
forks, and wheels reduced weight
and the bicycle could be easily
folded into a small package.

Double-
walled
wheel rims
for strength

Front and rear
disc brakes

Strong, compact
frame design

◁ **Marin Fairfax 2014**

Origin	US
Frame	Aluminum
Gears	27-speed
Wheels	28 in (70 cm)

Built for multipurpose urban use,
the Marin Fairfax had a wide range
of gears, powerful disc brakes,
handlebars and an aluminum
frame. It also had rack and fender
mounts so it could double as a
touring bike.

Triple-ratio
crankset

Cutting-Edge Designs

After more than a century and a half of near-continuous evolution, bicycle design and technology are increasingly characterized by a single trait—specialization. From speed-hungry race bikes with a set of components "integrated" with the frame to optimize aerodynamics, to bombproof, go-anywhere "fat bikes" with oversized tires for traveling on snow or sand, bicycles are available in any shape, size, and specification to suit any taste. While advanced technologists, from Formula One specialists to world-beating bicycle brands, redefine the capabilities of cutting-edge materials, such as carbon fiber, there is still space for artisans to hand-build esoteric creations from the purist's favorite—steel.

▷ **Pegoretti Marcelo 2012**

Origin	Italy
Frame	Steel
Gears	To order
Wheels	28 in (70 cm)

Every frame built by Dario Pegoretti is unique, whether in its paint finish, geometry, or the signature detailing added at will by the enigmatic Italian craftsman. The Marcelo features Pegoretti's TIG-welded steel tubes, which are larger in diameter than most steel frames for improved ride quality.

Bicycle sold as frameset only

Conn Rust textured paint finish

Components added by customer

TIG-welded, triple-butted steel frame

Frame clearance for tires up to 4 in (10 cm) wide

Disc-brake as frame lacks hardware for rim brakes

◁ **Ritchey Commando 2015**

Origin	US
Frame	Steel
Gears	To order
Wheels	26 in (65 cm)

Built by mountain-bike pioneer Tom Ritchey, the Commando is available as a frameset-only. It is a classically styled take on "Fat Bikes"—off-road bicycles with ultra-wide tires for riding on loose surfaces, from sand and mud to ice and deep snow.

Custom carbon stem with integrated Garmin GPS mount

Top tube flows into "Duo Blade" seat stays

▷ **Caterham Duo Cali Limited EPS 2015**

Origin	UK/Germany
Frame	Carbon fiber
Gears	22-speed
Wheels	28 in (70 cm)

Designed by Caterham Cars, this model was released in a limited run of 73, marking the inaugural year of the British sports car brand. Priced at approximately $25,000, the exclusive machine features a unique "Duo Blade" frame that channels air flow around the bicycle.

Electronic Campagnolo Super Record EPS gears

Pegoretti Falz ("scythe"), carbon-fiber fork

▽ Santa Cruz V10 CC 2016

Origin	US
Frame	Carbon fiber
Gears	7-speed
Wheels	27.5 in (70 cm)

With more elite-level Downhill race wins to its name than any other mountain bike, the V10 is one of the most sophisticated, full-suspension bikes around. Its carbon-fiber frame is strong enough for downhill racing.

Suspension system for constant damping during travel

Large-diameter disc-brake rotor

Seven gears for downhill purist

▽ Trek Madone 9 Series RSL 2016

Origin	US
Frame	Carbon fiber
Gears	22-speed
Wheels	28 in (70 cm)

The Race Shop Limited (RSL) is a replica of the bike used by the Trek Factory Racing top-tier professional team. Every component has been selected or customized to produce a fully integrated, aerodynamic racing bike built for pure speed.

One-piece, aerodynamic handlebars and stem

Brake and gear cables hidden inside frame

IsoSpeed seat tube for improved comfort

Custom Trek center-pull brakes

Kammtail aerofoil-section tubes for improved aerodynamics

Aerodynamic, deep-section, carbon-fiber rims

Great Races
Women's Olympic Road Race 2012

This women's road race, one of the cycling events at London's 2012 Olympic Games, took place on July 29. The course started and ended in front of Buckingham Palace, running through central London and then out into the English countryside.

THE RIDERS SET OFF IN POURING RAIN, with Nicole Cooke of Great Britain, who won gold at the Beijing Olympics (also in the rain), the defending champion. The women's road race followed the same route as the men's, although they rode fewer laps of the Surrey Hills section (see opposite). Their ride was a total distance of 87.2 miles (140.3 km).

In usual road-race style, there were several early breakaway moves, but all the favorites remained in the peloton, keeping an eye on each other. Later, teams at the front of the peloton started sending riders off in attacks to try to draw the strength from their rivals. While this was going on, there was almost as much action at the back of the peloton. The heavy rain had washed sharp grit onto the roads, causing several riders to have flat tires. The difficult conditions also led to a number

Crossing the finish line
Marianne Vos was overjoyed at winning her second Olympic title after a closely fought battle in very wet conditions.

The London Olympics in 2012 was the first time in history that women had event parity in cycling with men.

of crashes. All of these incidents meant that some riders lost valuable time.

The first serious attacks came before the first ascent of Box Hill, with Great Britain's Emma Pooley, the USA's Kristin Armstrong, and a Dutch rider, Ellen Van Dijk, being the most active. The attacks continued throughout the famous climb, and increased in intensity afterward. Pooley mounted a tremendous attack that another Dutch rider—Marianne Vos—had to chase. This meant that Pooley's teammate Lizzie Armitstead could follow her wheels and save a bit of energy. Eventually, with 31 miles (50 km) still to race, the attacks saw a select group of 30 riders go ahead. These riders stayed together until Vos, Armitstead, Russia's Olga Zabelinskaya, and the USA's Shelley Olds

The start of the women's road race
As they roar off down the Mall, the race only minutes old, the Dutch team, in orange, are already close to the front. Lizzie Armitstead (in white and blue, center) and Emma Pooley (second from left) are also there for Great Britain.

Winners of the 2012 Olympic women's time trial
The individual time trial was the other big road event of the
Olympics. The USA's Kristin Armstrong (center) won gold,
silver went to Germany's Judith Arndt (left), and bronze (for
this and the road race) to Olga Zabelinskaya of Russia (right).

pulled clear. With 15.5 miles (25 km) to go, Olds
had a flat tire, which meant the front group was
now down to three, although Zabelinskaya was
struggling. However, the chasers, led by the
German team, were not making any impression on
the trio's lead. The three riders stayed together until
they reached the Mall again. The battle for gold
came down to a sprint duel between Armitstead
and Vos over the last 656 ft (200 m). In the end, Vos
outsprinted Armitstead and won gold by the length
of a bicycle. Zabelinskaya took bronze. Nicole
Cooke managed only 31st place.

In 2013, Vos achieved her third world road-race
title and became road-race world champion, while
also being the cyclo-cross world champion. To date,
she has won seven cyclo-cross world titles, two
track world titles, and two Olympic gold medals.

KEY FACTS

RESULTS
Gold: Marianne Vos, Netherlands
Silver: Lizzie Armitstead, Great Britain
Bronze: Olga Zabelinskaya, Russia

THE ROUTE
The women's road race was 87.2 miles (140.3 km) long, with
the starting line on the Mall, in front of Buckingham Palace.
The outbound route went through central London, then
southwest toward Richmond, Surrey, meeting the inbound
route briefly at Hampton Court Palace. The route then went
via Weybridge toward the Surrey Hills. It continued south to
Gomshall, then east to Dorking, where it turned north for a
short section to the start of the steep Box Hill climb. After
two laps of a grueling circuit up and down Box Hill, the riders
headed back toward London via Leatherhead, Esher, and
Kingston-upon-Thames. They rejoined the outbound route
at Richmond Park and retraced it back to the Mall again. Vos
completed the race in 3 hours, 35 minutes, 29 seconds. In
all, 66 riders started out, but seven failed to finish.

Map of the London Olympic road race
The men's and women's road race followed the
same route. The women had to complete two
laps of the famous, steep Box Hill section (bottom
right); the men had to ride it nine times.

"**What does it mean?** It means four years of hard work has **paid off**."
LIZZIE ARMITSTEAD IN A POST-MEDAL CEREMONY INTERVIEW

Competitive or professional road cycling demands incredible fitness levels in cyclists, who pedal their way through amazing scenery, encouraged by hundreds of spectators. The prestigious Grand Tour events—the Tour de France, the Giro d'Italia, and the Vuelta a España—cover several thousand miles over the course of three weeks. Here, the UK's Chris Froome (bottom left, leading the field) is riding for Team Sky on one of the arduous mountain stages of the 2013 Tour de France.

BICYCLE
COMPONENTS

Anatomy of a Bicycle

When running smoothly and efficiently, the array of components that makes up a bicycle is barely perceptible. It is only when the rider stops to inspect a skipping gear or rubbing brake pad that the sophistication of the interrelated parts becomes apparent. The frame is the skeleton of the bicycle, while the key contact points—saddle, pedals, and handlebars—form a tactile interface between rider and bike. Brake and gear systems allow control of acceleration and deceleration, the two main forces of cycling, while the wheels transmit those efforts to the ground.

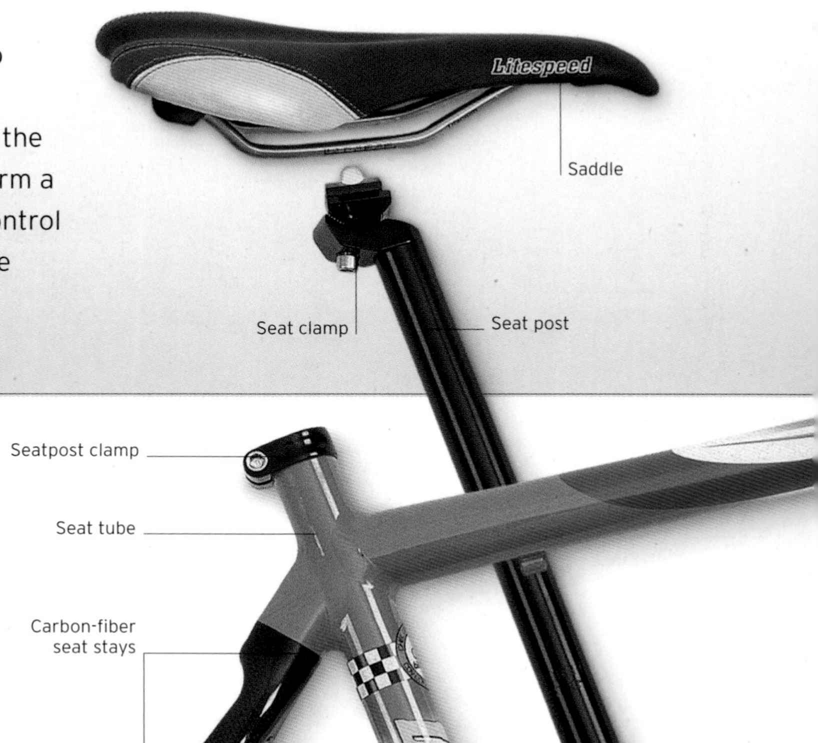

Saddle

Seat clamp

Seat post

FRAME DESIGN

The frame is the core of the bicycle, since everything else—potential use, ride quality, and component options—is dependent on it. Bike frames can be built from a variety of materials, ranging from the commonly used steel, aluminum, and carbon fiber to the less widespread titanium, wood, and bamboo. Regardless of the chosen material, a frame must be stiff enough to support the rider and any extra equipment, and to allow efficient power transfer from the cranks to the rear wheel, while being "compliant" or forgiving enough to offer some comfort to the rider. Consisting of the main "triangle"—formed by the seat tube, top tube, and down tube, plus the head tube—and rear triangle, which comprises the chainstays and seat stays, most bicycle frames are still built to the basic diamond-frame pattern first seen in the 1890s.

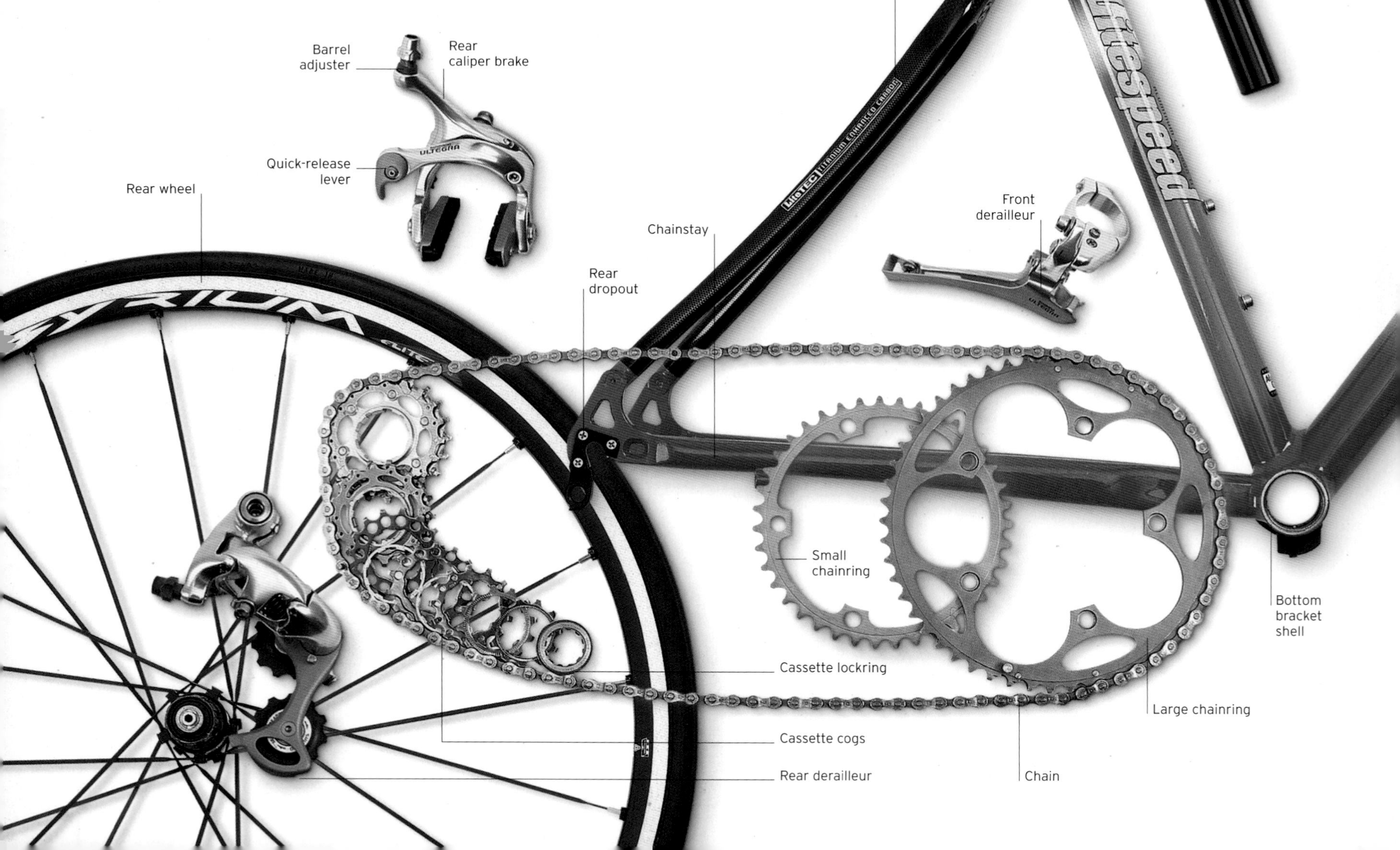

Seatpost clamp

Seat tube

Carbon-fiber
seat stays

Barrel
adjuster

Rear
caliper brake

Quick-release
lever

Front
derailleur

Rear wheel

Chainstay

Rear
dropout

Small
chainring

Bottom
bracket
shell

Cassette lockring

Large chainring

Cassette cogs

Rear derailleur

Chain

Brake cable inner

Brake lever

Gear cable inner

Gear-shifter

Handlebars

Stem

Top tube

Head tube

Down tube

Headset cap

Barrel adjuster

Brake shoe

Replaceable brake pad

Bearing cover

Shim washer

Steerer tube

Compression ring

Upper bearing

Lower bearing

Crown race

Crank spider

Cartridge bottom bracket

Crank arm

Clipless pedal

Spoke

Hub

Rim

Inner tube

Tire

FRAME MATERIALS

Each material has its own characteristics. Steel is known for its forgiving ride and ease of working and repair, while aluminium delivers a stiff ride but has been supplanted by carbon fiber as the material of choice. Titanium does not rust or corrode and is strong and light, but is expensive.

Steel frames are usually built with lugs—preformed sleeves into which the tubes are brazed—or TIG-welded, a process by which tubes are joined with an electrical charge. Fillet-brazing is another method, in which tubes are mitered and butted against each other before being brazed with brass or bronze solder.

SCAPIN NOPE 2000

Titanium frames require meticulous welding to join the tubes together, making them very expensive compared to steel and aluminum. Tubes can be bonded— a rarer method that is useful for joining to another material, such as carbon-fiber seat stays—using an adhesive.

SCHWINN PARAMOUNT TITANIUM 1970s

Carbon-fiber frames can be built as a monocoque (a continuous molded piece) or formed from ready-made tubes glued together with internal or external lugs. Carbon fiber offers myriad customization options.

SPECIALIZED ROUBAIX 2009

Brakes and Gears

Braking and shifting gears are two of the key skills that every bicycle rider learns once the fundamentals of balance and pedaling have been achieved. But the simplicity of stopping and of changing gears belies the complexity of the mechanical parts that perform these functions, not to mention the huge variety of different braking and gear-shifting technologies—from cable-activated rim brakes to hydraulic disc brakes and electronic gears—that have evolved over the years.

Brakes are essential for safe riding on any bicycle, and must be well adjusted and regularly inspected to make sure they function effectively. Brake-pad wear can be an issue on rim brakes because of the erosive effect of water and grit on the wheel rim, while hub and disc brakes tend to be more effective in wet and dirty conditions. As for gears, the drivetrain can consist of a single fixed gear or up to 30 derailleur gears, but at either extreme, accurate adjustment and chain lubrication are important.

TYPES OF BRAKES

Braking is the most essential feature of the bicycle—without the means to stop, the earliest boneshakers would never have caught on. Modern bicycle brakes come in three main varieties according to their location on the wheel: rim brakes, hub brakes, and disc brakes. Activated by a lever located on the handlebar, rim brakes and disc brakes can be operated with either a metal cable or a hydraulic line, while hub brakes are almost always operated with a cable.

RIM BRAKES

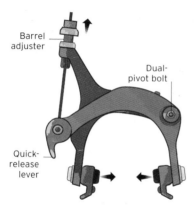

Dual-pivot calliper brake
Side-pull caliper brakes have two arms that squeeze two rubber brake blocks onto the wheel rim, creating resistance. The dual-pivot variety is widely used on road bikes.

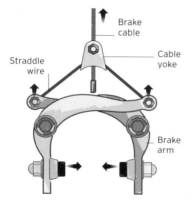

Center-pull caliper brake
A popular 1960s and 1970s design, center-pull brakes feature two symmetrical arms connected to the brake cable via a "yoke," distributing the pull evenly across both arms.

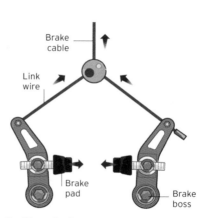

Cantilever brake
Popular on cyclo-cross bikes because of good mud clearance, cantilever brakes consist of two arms (cantilevers) that pivot around bosses attached to the frame or fork.

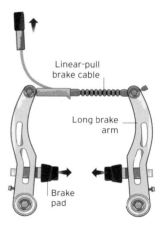

V-Brake
A type of cantilever brake, V-brakes have longer arms for greater leverage and more powerful braking. They are popular on hybrid, children's, and low-range mountain bikes.

DRUM BRAKES

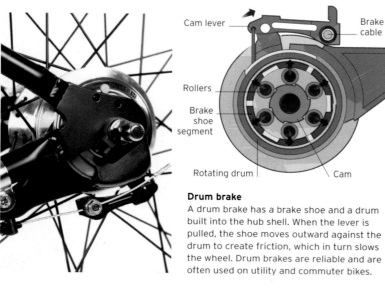

Drum brake
A drum brake has a brake shoe and a drum built into the hub shell. When the lever is pulled, the shoe moves outward against the drum to create friction, which in turn slows the wheel. Drum brakes are reliable and are often used on utility and commuter bikes.

DISC BRAKES

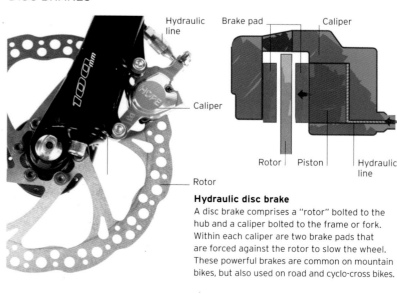

Hydraulic disc brake
A disc brake comprises a "rotor" bolted to the hub and a caliper bolted to the frame or fork. Within each caliper are two brake pads that are forced against the rotor to slow the wheel. These powerful brakes are common on mountain bikes, but also used on road and cyclo-cross bikes.

DRIVETRAIN CONFIGURATIONS

The drivetrain is the collection of components that transfers the up-and-down movement of the rider's pedal strokes into the forward motion of the rear wheel. The chain connects the chainset with the cassette, two components that together determine the gear ratios of the drivetrain, and therefore how fast the bicycle will go in relation to the terrain and the power of the rider. Light and comparatively cheap, front and rear derailleurs are used on most bicycles, while internal hub gears are more durable but heavier and more expensive.

Crankset and cassette

The crankset comprises two arms—to which the pedals are attached—and the chainrings, on which the chain runs. The cassette consists of different-sized sprockets that take the drive from the chain and transfer it to the rear wheel.

ANATOMY OF A CHAIN

The fundamental component of any drivetrain, the chain links the chainset— and hence the rider's power output—with the cassette and rear wheel. It must be strong and flexible enough to wrap around the chainrings and sprockets, and to withstand being pushed from one cog to the next by the derailleurs.

Inner plate — *Pin* — *Barrel* — *Outer plate*

Gear cable
Cassette
Cable clamp
Rear derailleur
Jockey wheel cage
Front derailleur
Chainring
Chainset

Rear derailleur

A parallelogram in form, the rear derailleur swings left and right to "derail" the chain from one sprocket to another. It also holds the chain under tension to prevent it from sagging when a smaller sprocket or chainring is engaged. The rear derailleur is usually controlled by a handlebar-mounted lever or switch, allowing the rider to change gear quickly.

Pivot point — *Derailleur plate* — *Jockey wheel*

Pivot point — *Derailleur cage*

Front derailleur

Like the rear derailleur, the front derailleur also features a parallelogram design to swing left and right, "derailing" the chain from one chainring to another. Both derailleurs are most commonly controlled via a cable held under tension that connects the derailleur and the gear-shift unit. Growing in popularity are electronic gears, in which a switch on the handlebar activates a small motor in the derailleur.

Internal hub gear

With a complex gear-shifting mechanism encased inside the hub, internal hub gears are reliable, long-lasting, and virtually impervious to rain and dirt. An external sprocket driven by the chain is connected to a system of internal cogs and rings that interact to determine the selected gear.

Combined control lever

Most modern bicycles feature combined control levers that house both the brake and gear levers in a single unit, enabling the rider to brake and change gears at the same time.

Contact Points

While the frame is key in defining the handling and ride characteristics of a bicycle, the points of contact with both the rider and the ground are equally important to the overall "feel" of the bike. The chosen types of handlebars, saddle, and pedals affect how the rider interacts with the bicycle, while wheel construction and tire choice also have a part to play in determining the bike's responsiveness and level of comfort while pedaling, braking, descending, climbing, or cornering.

Suspension can have a dramatic effect on the rider's experience in the saddle. The most sophisticated suspension systems are found on mountain bikes, where shock absorbers can deliver 8 in (20 cm) or more of wheel "travel" for riding over rough terrain. Some utility and hybrid bikes have suspension to improve comfort, while carbon frames can be tuned through their layup to provide vertical flex for comfort.

SADDLE DESIGNS

Perhaps the most important link between rider and bike, the saddle supports the majority of the rider's weight. Most saddles feature parallel rails that are fixed to the seat post, allowing a certain amount of front and rear adjustment in order to achieve the optimum riding position.

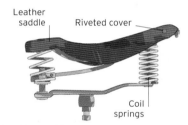

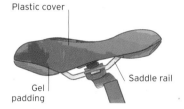

Leather saddle
Traditionally, saddles were made from one piece of leather stretched over a coil-sprung steel frame. Over time, the leather would deform and mold to the unique shape of the rider to provide the ultimate in comfort.

Leisure saddle
Modern saddles consist of a layer of padding, such as silicone gel or foam, sandwiched between a preformed base—typically semi-flexible plastic—and a plastic or leather cover. Leisure saddles usually feature extra padding.

Performance saddle
Saddles for performance use tend to be narrow and sparsely padded to optimize support for the rider. Light weight and strength may be achieved with a carbon-fiber base and titanium rails.

PEDALS

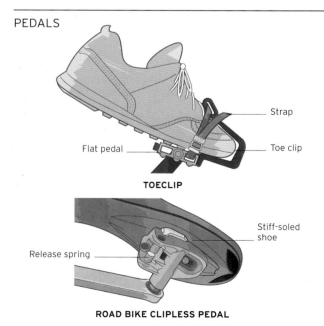

TOECLIP

ROAD BIKE CLIPLESS PEDAL

Most bikes have flat pedals, sometimes equipped with toe clips and straps to hold the shoe on the pedal. Performance bikes use clipless pedals with a mechanism that attaches to a dedicated shoe. For road-bike use, clipless pedals tend to be lighter and wider for improved power transfer, while mountain-bike versions are more robust and have the ability to shed mud.

TYPES OF HANDLEBARS

Handlebars are the rider's primary means of holding on to the bicycle, and must offer sufficient hand positions for the chosen type of riding. Commonly used on road bikes, dropped handlebars provide multiple hand positions to alleviate the stresses and strains of long days in the saddle. The flat or riser bar, used on mountain bikes, allows fewer hand positions but gives a firm and secure platform for the rider to hold onto on rough trails. Covering the bar with a rubber grip or padded tape is essential to cushion the hands from vibration, bumps, and trail shock.

RISER HANDLEBARS

DROP HANDLEBARS

The wheel's spokes or other supporting structure have a crucial job to do in transferring power and withstanding the forces generated by cornering and braking.

SUSPENSION TECHNOLOGY

Many types of front- and rear-wheel suspension have been developed over time, but the main thrust came in the 1990s as mountain-bike designers borrowed from motorcycle technology. While off-road riding is the main application for suspension, some city bikes also feature shock absorbers.

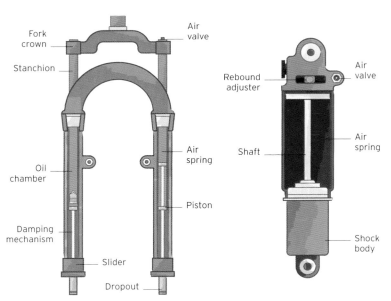

Fork crown

Stanchion

Oil chamber

Damping mechanism

Slider

Dropout

Air valve

Air spring

Piston

Rebound adjuster

Shaft

Air valve

Air spring

Shock body

Front suspension

The most popular type of front suspension is the telescopic fork. A spring (air, metal coil, or rubber) and a damper (usually oil) sit between sliders and stanchions. The spring absorbs the shock from the trail while the damper controls the rate at which the fork recoils from impact.

Rear suspension

Some bicycles with front suspension also have rear suspension to further cushion the rider from shocks and impacts. Rear suspension requires a bicycle frame with a pivoting rear triangle and a shock unit with a spring and a damper to control the up-and-down movement.

WHEEL CONSTRUCTION

A bicycle wheel is composed of a hub and rim connected by a set of spokes or another support system, such as a carbon-fiber disc. Wheels must be strong yet light to keep the effort required to turn them to a minimum.

Hub

The hub is usually clamped into the frame with a quick-release mechanism. Loose or sealed bearings inside the hub allow the wheel to rotate smoothly.

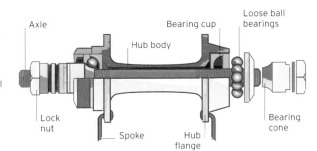

Axle

Bearing cup

Loose ball bearings

Hub body

Lock nut

Spoke

Hub flange

Bearing cone

Rim

The rim supports the tire and, on bikes with rim brakes, also offers a braking surface. Tubeless rims allow low-pressure tires; clinchers are the standard type; and tubulars are used in competitive racing.

Sealed spoke bed

Rim

Tire

No inner tube

Spoke

Inner tube

Tire

Aerodynamic rim

Tire glued to rim

No inner tube

TUBELESS RIM

CLINCHER RIM

DEEP-SECTION TUBULAR RIM

Index

Acknowledgments

The publisher would like to thank the following for their kind permission to reproduce their photographs:

(Key: a-above; b-below/bottom; c-center; f-far; l-left; r-right; t-top)

12 TopFoto.co.uk: Roger-Viollet (bl). **13 Alamy Images:** Uber Bilder (clb). **Lesseps:** (cra). **16 Alamy Images:** Universal Art Archive (tl). **Nationaal Fietsmuseum Velorama, the Netherlands:** (b). **17 Archives du Calvados:** Collection de Sanderval (cr, c). **Sterba-Bike:** (ftl, tr). **RMN:** René -Gabriel Ojeda (ftr). **The Art Archive:** Collection Grob / Kharbine-Tapabor (cra). **24 TopFoto.co.uk:** Roger-Viollet (cl). **Michael Valenti:** (tr). **24-25 Rex Shutterstock:** Roger Viollet. **25 A.S.O:** GEOATLAS.com (tr). **Rex Shutterstock:** John Pierce Owner PhotoSport Int (tl). **31 Colnago:** (br). **36 The Bicycle Museum of America. 40 Alamy Images:** Universal Art Archive. **41 The Art Archive:** Collection IM / Kharbine-Tapabor (tl, b). **46 Courtesy of Campagnolo:** (tl, b). **47 Cannondale Bicycle Corporation:** (ftr). **Gerard Brown:** (br). **Courtesy of Campagnolo:** (ftl, tl, tr, cra, clb). **Chuck Schmidt / velo-retro.com:** (cla). **56-57 Getty Images:** Keystone-France. **60 Alamy Images:** The Art Archive (tr); Universal Art Archive (ftr). **Offside Sports Photography Ltd:** Archivi Farabola (cla). **60-61 AF Fotografie:** (b). **61 Marco Ferreri:** (br). **Rex Shutterstock:** Olycom SPA (tr). **64 Copake Auction Inc,:** (tr). **68 Alamy Images:** Universal Art Archive. **69 Gerrit Does:** (crb). **Offside Sports Photography Ltd:** L'Equipe (ca). **72 Alamy Images:** Vintage Archives (bc); Universal Art Archive (bl). **Getty Images:** Frank Pocklington (tl). **Raleigh UK Ltd:** (cr, cla, fbl). **73 Alamy Images:** Universal Art Archive (cra). **Raleigh UK Ltd:** (fcra). **74 Copake Auction Inc,:** (cl). **77 Bianchi, Cycleurope Group:** (tr). **84-85 Magnum Photos:** Henri Cartier-Bresson. **88-89 Offside Sports Photography Ltd:** L'Equipe (c). **88 Alamy Images:** Universal Art Archive (tr). **Offside Sports Photography Ltd:** L'Equipe (cl). **89 Corbis:** Tim de Waele (tr). **Geographicus Rare Antique Maps:** (br). **94 Alamy Images:** Keystone Pictures USA. **95 AF Fotografie:** (cla). **Getty Images:** Archives / AFP (br). **96 Copake Auction Inc,:** (tr). **97 Copake Auction Inc,:** (cl, tr). **Budget Bicycle Center:** (br). **98 AF Fotografie:** (tl, cl). **Peugeot Cycles:** (bl, r). **99 akg-images:** Alfons Rath (cla). **Alamy Images:** Universal Art Archive (cra); Penrodas Collection (b). **Speed Bicycles:** (tr). **Peugeot Cycles:** (ftl, tl, fcrb). **Peter Kohl:** (ftr). **Roland Smithies / luped.com:** (clb). **101 The Bike Place:** (br). **102-103 Mary Evans Picture Library:** Roger Mayne. **104 Rex Shutterstock:** Colorsport (cl). **105 Speed Bicycles:** (cl). **MH Srl / www.mhsrl.it:** (br, br/1). **110 Copake Auction Inc,:** (b). **110 Copake Auction Inc,:** (cl). **Bukowskis:** (bl). **Steve Lee:** (t). **111 Budget Bicycle Center:** (bc). **112 Bertin Classic Cycles:** (br). **Tim Keith:** (tr). **114 Action Plus:** Imago (c). **Corbis:** Tim De Waele (bl). **Chuck Schmidt / velo-retro.com:** (ftr). **Neil**

Stevens : (tr). **114-115 Offside Sports Photography Ltd:** L' Equipe. **115 www.rvv.be:** (br). **116 Copake Auction Inc,:** (tr). **117 Copake Auction Inc,:** (cr, tl).**118-119 Getty Images. 120 Science & Society Picture Library:** (tr). **121 Copake Auction Inc,:** (bl). **Budget Bicycle Center:** (tl). **124 Chisholm Larsson.125 Joe Breeze:** (cl). **Rex Shutterstock:** Sipa Press (cr). **127 Danny Hellevig, Galaxy Bikes, galaxybikes.com:** (clb). **128 Speed Bicycles:** (br). **129 Getty Images:** John Burke (br). **130 Colnago:** (tl, bl, cla). **131 Speed Bicycles:** (ftl, tl, tc). **TopFoto.co.uk:** ulls282203 (bl). **133 Budget Bicycle Center:** (tl, cr). **John Watson:** (bl). **138-139 Rolling Dinosaur Archive:** Wende Cragg. **140 Budget Bicycle Center:** (tr). **Kelly Schall:** (b). **141 Collection of Chuck DeCroix:** Raymond Klass (bc). **Kelly Schall:** (tl, cr). **142 Getty Images:** Marco Garcia / Stringer (ftr, tr); Peter Read Miller / Sports Illustrated (b). **143 Corbis:** Elizabeth Kreutz (tr); Patrick Mcfeeley / National Geographic Creative (bl). **World Triathlon Corporation:** All Rights Reserved. IRONMAN® / matkindesign.com (br). **147 Budget Bicycle Center:** (cra). **150 Roland Smithies / luped.com:** Bicycle Posters & Prints. **151 Moulton Bicycle Company:** (br). **Press Association Images:** AP (cl). **156 Cannondale Bicycle Corporation:** (tl, bl, cr). **156-157 Cannondale Bicycle Corporation:** (b). **157 Velo Aficionado:** (tr). **Cannondale Bicycle Corporation:** (ftl, ftr, cra). **Corbis:** Stefano Rellandini / Reuters (br). **158 The Bike Place:** (br). **Musée des arts et métiers-CNAM, Paris:** Pascal Faligot (cl). **159 The Bike Place:** (bl). **Olii Erkkila:** (cr). **160 Andy Nesbit:** (cl). **Cor Vos:** (bc). **168 Budget Bicycle Center:** (bc). **Brad Farlow:** (cl). **168-169 Budget Bicycle Center:** (t). **169 Mercian Cycles Ltd:** (tr). **172-173 akg-images:** Manfred Prüfer. **174 Kelly Schall:** (tr). **175 Tim / electrongeek:** (cr). **176 Trussardi:** (cl). **177 Condor Cycles Ltd:** (br). **178 Début Art:** Vince McIndoe (tr). **Offside Sports Photography Ltd:** Offside - L'Equipe (b). **179 Andre I. Loas:**(br). **Rex Shutterstock:** John Pierce (tr). **181 Easy Racers, Inc.:** (cr). **Fred H. H. Heitmann:** flickr.com (tl). **184 Chisholm Larsson. 185 Getty Images:** Gary M. Prior / Staff (c). **Shimano Inc:** (cra). **187 Moulton Bicycle Company:** (bc). **188 Corbis:** Tim de Waele (tl). **Shimano Inc:** (cla, cra, bl, br). **189 Corbis:** BAS CZERWINSKI / epa (bl); Felix Kästle / dpa (cra). **Shimano Inc:** (ftl, tl, tr, ftr, br). **190 Leigh West:** (tr). **191 Giant, www.giant-bicycles.com:** (cra). **Bill Vetter:**(br). **196 Ray Stone:** (tr). **198 Speed Bicycles:** (br). **The Bike Place:** (cl). **200 Budget Bicycle Center:** (bc). **Thomas Baumann:** (l). **200-201 Peter Chu:** (t).**202-203 Alamy Images:** Kim Karpeles. **204-205 Corbis:** Ales Fevzer (b). **204 Jerry E Riboli:** (cla). **IOC/Olympic Museum Collections:** (tr). **205 Getty Images:** Nathan Bilow / Allsport (cr); Doug Pensinger (tr). **www.DurangoMountainSport.com:** (br). **210-211 Gerard Brown. 212 Neil Stevens . 213 Bamboosero:** (clb).

Rex Shutterstock: Photosport Int (br). **217 Evans Cycles. Evans Cycles:** (bl). **218 Corbis:** Imaginechina (ca). **Getty Images:** Bryn Lennon (tl). **Giant, www.giant-bicycles.com:** (bl, crb). **219 Giant, www.giant-bicycles.com:** (ftl, tl, tr, br, bl, ftr). **220-221 Evans Cycles. Evans Cycles:** (t).**220 Evans Cycles. Evans Cycles:** (cl, br). **Surly Bikes Intergalactic:** (bl). **223 Giant, www.giant-bicycles.com:** (cr). **Specialized:** (bl). **224 HP Velotechnik OHG:** (tr). **225 Bacchetta Bicycles:** (tl). **Challenge:** ELAN Recumbents (br). **HP Velotechnik OHG:** (bl). **229 Alamy Images:** Alex Segre (br). **230-231 Getty Images:** AFP PHOTO / SHAH Marai. **234-235 Montague Corporation:** (t). **235 Evans Cycles. Evans Cycles:** (cr). **236 Caterham Cycling:** (bl). **Ritchey Design Inc. :** (cl). **236-237 Gita Sporting Goods Ltd.:** Julian Andretta (t). **237 Santa Cruz Bicycles:** (tr). **Trek Bicycle:** (br). **238 Corbis:** Tim De Waele (fcla).**Jordan Trofan:** (tr). **238-239 Corbis:** Cathal McNaughton / Reuters (b). **239 Action Plus:** Christian Charisius (tl). **Collins Bartholomew Ltd :** © Crown Copyright and database right 2012. All rights reserved. Ordnance Survey Licence number 100046062. (tr). **240-241 Gerard Brown. 242-243 Gerard Brown**

All other images © Dorling Kindersley
For further information see:
www.dkimages.com

Dorling Kindersley would like to thank Richard Gilbert and Chris Sidwells for their support throughout the making of this book.

In addition, Dorling Kindersley would like to extend thanks to the following people for their help with making the book: Lauren Andrich, Public Relations Manager, Cannondale USA; Joe Breeze, Curator, Marin Museum of Bicycling, USA; Irene Chen, Giant INC USA; Lara Clarke-Wardle, Raleigh UK Ltd; Ben Hillsdon, PR Officer, Shimano Europe, Netherlands; Elliot Lambour, Communication Manager, Peugeot Biycles, France; Violet Liu, Marketing Manager, GIANT Europe B.V.; Joshua Riddle, Press Manager, Campagnolo, Italy; James Thompson, Copake Auction INC, USA; Alessandro Turci, Marketing Director, Colnago Bicycles, Italy.

The publisher would like to thank the following people for their help with making the book: Steve Crozier at Butterfly Creative Solutions, Priyaneet Singh for editorial assistance at DK India; Rajesh Singh and Ashok Kumar at DK India for assistance with image reproduction; Joanna Chisholm for proofreading; Vanessa Bird for the index; and the staff at Warwickspace Ltd, Warwickshire (www.warwickspace.org.uk) for the use of their facilities.

The publisher would also like to thank the following museums, companies, and individuals for their generosity in allowing Dorling Kindersley access to their bicycles for photography:

Bicycle Museum of America
7 W. Monroe Street
New Bremen, OH 45869
www.bicyclemuseum.com
Becky Macwhinney, Head Curator
Jim Elking, Museum Assistant
John Boeke, Museum Assistant

Brick Lane Bikes
118–119 Bethnal Green Road, London
www.bricklanebikes.co.uk
Maciek Wrotek

Deutsches Fahrradmuseum
Heinrich-von-Bibra Strabe 24,
97769 Bad Bruckenau, Germany
www.deutsches-fahrradmuseum.de
Mona Buchmann and Ivan Sojc

J.D Tandems
Unit 1 Cawood House,
Asquith Industrial Estate, Gargrave,
North Yorkshire
www.info@tandems.co.uk
Ruth and John Hargreaves

Iconoclassic 2015
Market Square,
Warwick Town Centre, Warwickshire
www.iconoclassic.org
Tom Price-Jones, Steve Brown, Dan Chambers, Justin Rixon, Nick Taylor, Nick Williams, Craig Smith, Caspar Lee

London Green Cycles
Chester Court, Albany Street, London,
www.londongreencycles.co.uk
Roman Magula

Murray Maclean (Private Collection)
The Nursery, Collins Farm,
Abingdon, Oxfordshire

National Cycle Museum
The Automobile Place,
Temple Street, Llandrindod Wells, Powys
www.cyclemuseum.org.uk
John Gill, Trustee

Pedal Pedlar
106 Balls Pond Road, London
www.pedalpedlar.co.uk
Wayne Blenkin

Retrospective Cycles
1–6 Crescent Mews, Wood Green,
London, UK
www.retrospectivecycles.com
Niall McCart

Stuart Bikes
The Nursery, Cote, Oxford, OX18 2EG
www.info@oxfordbicycles.co.uk
Stuart Ranson with assistance from
Tim Bartlett

Universal Cycle Centre
122 Manor Road, Maltby, South Yorkshire
www.universalcyclecentre.co.uk
Dave Marsh

Victory Show 2015
Foxlands Farm, Cosby,
Leicestershire, LE9 1SG
www.thevictoryshow.co.uk
G Bouckley, Russell Pitt, Mark Taylor